# Preserving Capital

# Preserving Capital
## and Making it Grow

## by John Train

*Clarkson N. Potter, Inc., Publishers/New York*
DISTRIBUTED BY CROWN PUBLISHERS

Published by Clarkson N. Potter, Inc., One Park Avenue, New York, New York 10016, and simultaneously in Canada by General Publishing Company Limited

A substantial portion of the material in this book has been previously published in a book entitled *The Dance of the Money Bees*. This edition has been expanded and updated throughout.

Manufactured in the United States of America

Library of Congress Cataloging in Publication Data

Train, John.
  Preserving capital and making it grow.

  Includes index.
  1. Investments—Handbooks, manuals, etc.  2. Finance, Public—Handbooks, manuals, etc.   I. Title.
  HG4527.T7  1983     332.6′78     82-19046
  ISBN: 0-517-54766X

Design by Levavi & Levavi

10  9  8  7  6  5  4  3  2  1

First Edition

Grateful acknowledgment is given to the following publications for permission to reprint figures and tables in this book:

**Figure 1,** page 10: Courtesy of Capital International S.A. Geneva Switzerland. **Figure 2,** page 14, and **Figure 6,** page 27: From *Long-Term Technical Trends* published by Stone & Mead, Inc., Boston, Mass. **Figure 3,** page 18, and **Figure 4,** page 20: Courtesy of BCA Publications Ltd., 3463 Peel Street, Montreal, Canada H3A 1W7. **Figure 5,** page 22: Courtesy of Merrill Lynch Research. **Figure 7,** page 28, and **Figures 9–9e,** page 101 ff.: Courtesy of Securities Research Company, 208 Newbury Street, Boston, MA 02116. **Figure 8,** page 74: Courtesy Investor's Intelligence, Larchmont, NY 10583. **Figure 10,** page 122: Courtesy of Indicator Digest, Palisades Park, NJ 07650. **Figure 11,** page 133: Courtesy of Schabacker Investment Management. **Table 1,** page 100: Reprinted by permission of *Forbes* magazine, August 30, 1982, copyright © 1982 by Forbes, Inc. **Table 4,** page 181: Courtesy Managed Account Reports. **Table,** page 215: Reprinted by permission of *Harvard* magazine, copyright © 1983 by *Harvard* magazine.

*For Francie*

# Contents

# Foreword

I get the credit for this book.

John Train is my investment adviser.

He has done most handsomely by me for many years, following the particular philosophy that he describes here.

He insists that a client understand what he is doing, and some years ago began writing out some of his concepts and principles and sending them to me: "oligopoly," the "double play," "Gresham's Law stock," "swarming," and the "up escalator."

They were so illuminating and amusing that after a while a brisk bootleg or *samizdat* circulation sprang up around my office and among my friends.

Scenting a good thing, I urged John to make them into a book . . . this book.

Cass Canfield

# Introduction

Few people succeed in preserving capital (that is, maintaining the value of their savings in real terms for future use), and even fewer will succeed in the future. Social trends are against them.

One of the Rothschilds is said to have observed that if he could be sure of transmitting a quarter of his capital he would settle for that. Alas, he probably didn't make it. (By a curious turn of fate the Rothschilds' business interests are no longer significant on a world scale, but what have remained are their frivolities—the art collections, the racing stables, the wine châteaux.)

There are so many great families whose former grandeur survives only as an echo—in the names of museums, converted mansions, streets, and towns. Their descendants don't have it anymore. Taxes, inflation, expropriation, and changing times have pulled them down. If they, armed with the cleverest advisers, bankers, and lawyers couldn't keep their money, can it be easy?

Survival is a competition. What you have, including your savings, others want, and will struggle to get. The push to take it back from you is as relentless as that of the sea to overcome the dikes that contain it or the jungle to enfold a

1

patch of cleared ground. The whole order of nature pushes to reclaim its own. Governments bow to that kind of pressure. Pieces of paper are a weak defense.

Only through deep understanding and superior tactics can the investor hope to preserve even part of what he has saved, and the job gets harder every year.

In many countries it is virtually impossible, and almost everybody eventually becomes a ward of the state, whose pretensions thus become irresistible. The barons being impoverished, King John is supreme.

Property means a degree of economic freedom, without which the other freedoms are eggshell-thin. But think what has happened to familiar forms of investment property in recent years. Bondholders, including government bondholders, pensioners, and insurance beneficiaries have been slaughtered with a smile, what with the depreciation of the currency and taxes on income. The investors, often of modest means, who put their savings into New York rental buildings have been largely wiped out by rent control. The Dow Jones Industrials, adjusted for inflation, are lower than they were sixty years ago, and the long-term holder of U.S. Steel or General Motors has lost nine-tenths of his former buying power.

It's not easy!

In preserving capital the right attitude is indispensable. You must be passive in deciding to buy, but aggressive in searching out the values and in digging all the way down to the rock of reality: the yin and yang of the job.

In buying, Talleyrand's *Surtout pas trop de zèle* is even more important than in statecraft. It usually pays to wait patiently for the rare bargain in first-class assets, rather than keep swinging for the fences with a succession of exciting speculations.

Enthusiastic hyperactivity is in fact the hallmark of the losing investor. The world is not transformed from one day to the next, and the average investor makes less money with his brain than what in chess is called his *Sitzfleisch,* or patient rear end.

The safe time to invest is when people are discouraged or desperate, and the safe thing to buy is what isn't wanted.

The dangerous time to invest is when the market is all atwitter like a tree full of birds, and when it's standing room only at the brokers'. The dangerous purchase is what the crowd is queuing up to buy regardless of price, having been told that "Truly first-class works of art (or IBM, or land, or diamonds) can only go up." Remember those words. They are the early warning signal of much lower prices.

The active side of investing—ferreting out the values—is no easy matter for the layman, but he can get it done for him by a professional at a reasonable price if he knows what he wants. This book, then, is intended to tell the investor what he should be looking for, where to find it, and how to test what he gets in order to make sure it is authentic.

## The Investor's Apocalypse

In recent times four new challenges to invested savings have become of cardinal importance: taxes, inflation, union labor monopolies, and disguised expropriation.

Taxes have skyrocketed in this century, and now take a huge proportion of all one's earnings. Suppose you earn a salary, pay tax on it, and after living costs have something left over to save. If you put those savings into a common stock, the company whose stock you buy pays a corporate tax of about 50 percent, and then your dividend is taxed all over again by federal, state, and municipal authorities. You will have left to spend only one-quarter or so of what has gone in taxes, or one-eighth if you include the tax you paid on your original salary.* And capital gains taxes and estate taxes come on top of that!

Clearly, a cardinal point of anyone's investment policy

---

*In periods of rapid inflation the tax bite is even worse than this, since the permissible depreciation is inadequate to finance plant and inventory replacement. Thus, corporate taxes for many companies take 70 percent of true earnings, not 50 percent.

has to be to keep down the tax bite. This means that for an individual any investment approach that depends on taxable income or on trading is much less efficient than one that doesn't.

A widow will often work herself into the "income illusion" pickle. She has $800,000 and needs $60,000 after tax to live on. So she invests in bonds and utility stocks for "income," pays the tax, and lives on what's left over. But her principal is shrinking in real terms by the amount of inflation—10 percent a year, let's say. After fifteen years she's a pauper. Differently put, after twenty years of 10 percent inflation you need *five times* your previous income *after tax* to stay even!

Inflation, of course, puts you into higher and higher tax brackets even though your real income doesn't change: "bracket creep." In addition, it increases not only your own living costs but also the costs of whatever companies you own stock in.

Inflation is one of the most extraordinary phenomena of our times, one whose causes might be described as bafflingly simple. I believe it reflects the moral soundness and realism of a society. Eventually prices are determined by how much demand is bidding up how much supply, and if people's demands increase faster than their output (discussed later as the "grasshopper syndrome" and also called the revolution of rising expectations), you will have inflation.

Inflation seems to be part of the price of democratic government.* It always seems politically easier to give way to inflationary wage and welfare demands and then rescue the economy by deficit spending, meaning more inflation.

Also, of course, in the lifetimes of many of its present inhabitants, the world's population will have tripled, from 2 billion to 6 billion. Since a child only pays its own way after many years, a country is always borrowing to finance infrastructure, an inflationary process.

---

*Professor C. Northcote Parkinson once proposed to me the sinister formula: Democracy Equals Inflation.

Any kind of monopoly puts prices up, and the creation of a union labor monopoly armed with the strike weapon not only fuels inflation but also undermines the claims of capital. I am all for unions—to which, indeed, I have spent quite a lot of time as a financial consultant—but everything has its limits. Anyway, the investor must face the fact that if an enterprise enjoys only moderate sales growth and the workers are in a position to demand rapid pay advances, then the owners won't do well. That describes most companies these days.

Disguised (or overt) expropriation happens constantly abroad, and often enough here. Price controls, including rent control, are a form of expropriation, as are many other kinds of regulation, along with confiscatory taxes. If debasement of the currency strips away the benefits of your pension or your life insurance policy, is that not a form of expropriation?

To sum up, for a substantial investor only a program that explicitly takes account of taxes, inflation, labor pressure, and quasi-expropriation is realistic. That rules out most of the stocks and indeed investment strategies that used to be attractive.

Still, don't despair. There are solutions.

This book takes the reader through many of the subjects I discuss with new clients, in much the same way I like to present them. Investing is an interesting but complicated subject, full of surprises. You need to understand how the whole thing really works in order to achieve good results, whether on your own or with whatever professional you engage to help you.

# I.

# The Nature of Markets

# The Dance of the Bees,
## or How the Market Swarms Up and Down

When Von Frisch studied how a honeybee tells his mates the location of a treasure of blossoms, he discovered that the news is transmitted through a dance. The returning Columbus lines himself up at an angle in the hive corresponding to the angle that the path to his discovery bears to the sun, and goes into his honey dance. If he has made a rich find, he does a particularly agitated dance; if the find is minor, he dances more sedately. Depending on the activity of the dancer, more or fewer bees join in. Thus the right number are mobilized and briefed to zoom out from the hive on the "beeline." If the dancer's navigation is faulty, they all tear off in the wrong direction.

Most animals that live in groups transmit emotion to the rest of the group through signals: greed (as in this case) or alarm or indeed panic.

Part of the herd instinct must be a deep compulsion to do what these signals say. My part of the country is graced by numbers of white-tailed deer, which I like to creep up on and observe. When the sentinel finally picks me up, though, and snorts and throws up his tail, even the tiniest fawn bursts into flight. I doubt he could hold himself back however much he wanted to.

CAPITAL INTERNATIONAL INDEX                    HONG KONG

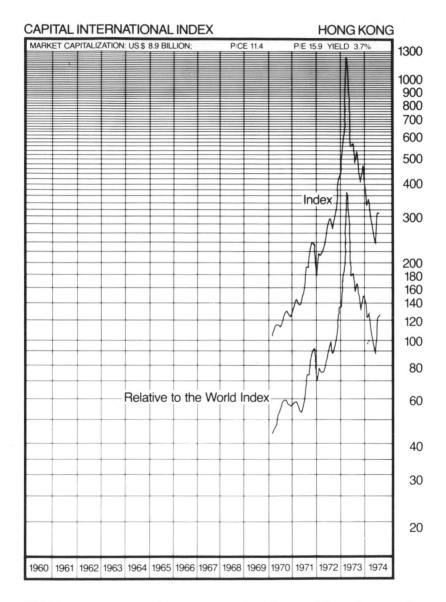

SWARMING  The Chinese are excited by gambling the way the Indians are by firewater. Here the Hong Kong market leaps 1000 percent in three years and collapses in the fourth.

**Figure 1**

My point is that this susceptibility to the contagion of mass emotion, whether based on fact or not, is one of our strongest traits, and one brought deeply into play during major speculative moments. Who is not affected by the fear of losing everything he has? Or the lust to have it double or triple?

The stock market is an index of how investors feel about the future, not the present. In other words, it is a barometer, not a thermometer.

In a ship, the worse the storm and the sicker the passengers, the sooner things will improve and the barometer start rising. (The greatest rise in stock market history was in 1932, in the midst of a financial hurricane, when the Dow Jones Average doubled in less than three months.) Similarly, once the weather is perfect, the next change in the barometer will probably be down.

The market rolls along in an endless series of psychological cycles, which are easy enough to understand—although measuring them is not so easy. The ebb and flow of mass emotion is fairly regular: panic being followed by relief, and relief by optimism; then enthusiasm, then euphoria; sliding off again into concern, desperation, and finally a new panic.

In human affairs excesses provoke corrections, and the momentum of the correction carries on to provoke a new and different excess. So it is with politics, so with religion, so with art, and so with tides of opinion generally, including the stock market.

The typical emotional cycle is roughly four years from peak to peak or valley to valley, although there are plenty of exceptions. The easiest way to measure it is probably not just stock prices, since higher company earnings may hold the market up even though the emotional cycle is fading; rather, one should probably measure it by the rise and fall of price-earnings ratios. If one plots them quarter by quarter, the result is usually a parabola: turning up steeply, flattening, rolling over, and then falling faster and faster.

Let us go through a complete cycle in a few minutes' reading, like a Disney movie that in a short time shows the growth, blossoming, and fading of a flower.

# The Washout: "All Is Lost!"

A convenient place to begin our circular tour is bobbing around in the pool at the base of the waterfall: in the depths of despair in a bear market—1957, 1962, 1966, 1970, 1974, 1978 or 1982. Stocks have just declined 35 percent, say, sliding several percent a week for months on end. Near the end of the slide many famous issues have been cut in half with terrifying speed.

At a major bottom, current business news is usually (but not always) bad. Many authorities feel the situation is likely to get a lot worse. Several spectacular bankruptcies of international importance are usual. Unemployment is usually up. Some major unresolved national problem—the missiles in Cuba in 1962, Vietnam in 1966, the Penn Central and brokerage-house bankruptcies in 1970, Watergate and the Arab oil embargo in 1973–74, the interest rate surge in 1981, and the fear of an international banking crisis in 1982—helps set the tone. The brokerage business itself is likely to be in the dumps. Wall Street's own gloom reinforces the syndrome.

There is a story of a visitor to a western village who is having his hair cut in the local barbershop, which is run by an incurable practical joker. After a while crowds of people start streaming down the street, all heading out of town toward a nearby hill. When the visitor asks what is going on, the barber chuckles and says that he himself as a little joke had started a rumor earlier in the day that there would be a flood. The visitor is amused. As the town empties, however, the barber gets more and more nervous, and finally takes off his apron, puts down his scissors, and says, "I think I'd better get going myself. Don't bother to pay." The customer expresses astonishment. The barber says, "It may be true!"

When a really good panic sets in (or indeed the opposite, a bull-market blowoff), very few people can resist the trend. If they do, they feel acutely uneasy. The herd instinct seems to be the strongest human emotion, one that the race is constantly breeding for as the mavericks are liquidated. Happiness is running with the crowd.

Anyway, in a market collapse everything finally caves in, during a few catastrophic days and weeks. There is an almost audible flushing effect. Stocks are hurled onto the market, regardless of value, for fear they will fall to nothing.

About this time, if you go to a cocktail party you will meet that irritating figure Smugton Loud, who smoothly assures you that he hasn't owned a share for six months. A social broker you occasionally run into, Frank Fishstory, claims that he has gone short in all his accounts.

Eventually a point is reached where everybody who can be scared into selling has been.

The professionals, who have been hovering overhead, so to speak, and the institutions, who always have several billion dollars to spend, accelerate their buying, and finally an equilibrium is reached between the buyers and the sellers. (Figure 2 shows how institutional cash is highest at market bottoms.) Usually the final battle occurs on extremely high volume (a selling climax), but not always. At this point the ordinary investor, who has gone over the waterfall, is groggy, bruised, and sick, his ears ringing. He does not want to hear about stocks, never again. The few professionals and institutions have the field pretty much to themselves. What they buy goes up, since there are almost no sellers left.

Often, some weeks later, the old lows are quietly tested on modest volume, but it doesn't attract much attention. Experienced investors are confident that better weather lies ahead. (For an example of this feeling, see Appendix I, p. 239.)

Now the really big money shows its hand. Exxon buys a string of oil companies for two times cash flow, and a London property syndicate takes over Madison Avenue for a sum

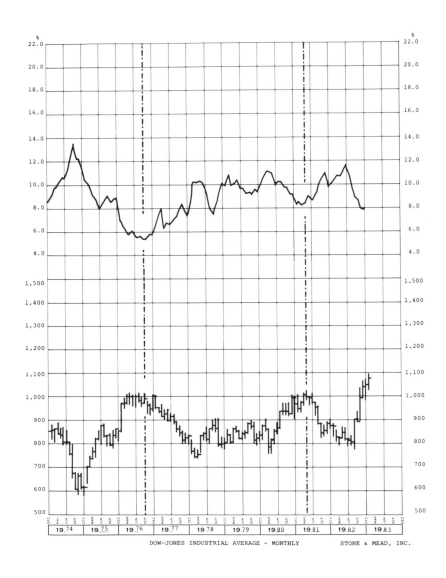

DOW-JONES INDUSTRIAL AVERAGE - MONTHLY          STONE & MEAD, INC.

## MUTUAL FUND CASH POSITION
### Ratio of Mutual Funds' Cash To Total Assets
### S&P 400 Prices, 1969–1981

### Figure 2

equal to the money in the till. Some Japanese banks buy and merge Santa Barbara and San Diego.

## The Early Surge: A Few Buyers, No Sellers

We are at the beginning of the dynamic phase of the bull market. The optimum buying "window" will last for only a few months, but it is prudent to wait until the market has clearly turned, and is full and by on the new course. The professional investor does not mind paying 25 percent more for a stock that has been cut by two-thirds, to be pretty certain that it is not going to go down another 40 percent.

As the months go by, prices rise briskly. The misery of the recent past is quickly forgotten, like a thorn extracted from one's foot. A few mutual funds will have been started during the bottom area, and articles in the financial press begin pointing out that the Hercules Fund has grown 75 percent in six months, or whatever. One starts hearing extraordinary stories of people who bought calls on Intertronics warrants and thus turned $100,000 into $400,000. The institutional issues, such as the Dow Stocks and the big rails, make important moves. Volume, however, usually continues low. The consensus of the advisory services remains cautious. The odd-lotters after a while begin selling on balance again, although the odd-lot short selling has dried up.

The banks recommend staying in short-term bonds "until the situation has clarified," and brokers urge the attractiveness of high-income issues.

## The Surge Continues: Important Buying, Widespread Skepticism

More months pass, and the market can now be seen to have established a rising channel for itself, like a marble rolling from side to side along a gutter. The Dow oscillates from one side of the channel to the other, but continues in the same broad upward path.

Frank Fishstory is quoted in a Wall Street newspaper as expecting one last major down-leg, which will be the time to buy.

There will normally be few significant reactions during this phase of the new bull market.

The rising prices of the principal stocks attract more buying from the professionals and from institutions who have been waiting on the sidelines; this additional buying puts prices still higher. The higher prices, in turn, give confidence to more buyers, who enter the market, putting prices higher still.

The whole system continues to feed upon itself, to rise and build like a prairie twister.

The general public, during this phase, moves from feeling that it's too early to buy to feeling that it's too late to buy.

## The Second Stage of the Rocket

Time passes. Perhaps a year or a year and a half after the beginning, the public, which has been apathetically watching from the sidelines, starts to become interested, like the hive responding to the dance.

Over a period of months there is a pronounced and unmistakable rise in volume, which then falls off again. Later in the cycle one can usually look back and see that this volume bulge appeared approximately two-thirds of the way up the whole eventual slope. (In about one bull market in four, the volume peak at this point does not occur.) The fervor and the tempo of the dance continue to mount. The music plays louder and louder. More and more spectators join in.

Leverage becomes popular. Since everything is going up, why not make twice as much? Margin accounts, hedge funds, options, and investment trusts that borrow money are in the news. This is what the professionals consider to be "weak" buying.

# The Distribution Phase— Not a Cloud in the Sky

More months go by, and the public is hooked. Business news is excellent. The "standard forecast" of the economic outlook is optimistic.

Some particular market area (the major industrials in 1961, the over-the-counter speculations and hedge funds in 1966, the conglomerates in 1969, the sacred-cow growth issues in 1972, the energy group in 1980) emerges as the center of attention and the focus of a self-confirming myth as the brokers and professionals bid up these "talisman" stocks to irrational heights.

# The Blowoff

"Hot" managers become famous. Young, glib, flamboyantly dressed, impatient of conventional wisdom, they collect huge sums from trustful investors who hope for miracles. In some cycles the volume of "hot manager" trading becomes a significant part of the whole market. When that happens, it becomes profitable to jump aboard a trend instantly, before the hot managers get hold of it and run it up. This further undermines the quality of the buying. Brokers specializing in froth can sell any stock by letting it be known that they expect a few big operators to get behind it. Speculations, illiquid securities, "collectibles," commodities, and ventures are palmed off as "investments." Securities firms specializing in issues of glamour companies have long waiting lists for each underwriting.

The taxi driver turns and asks his fare if he knows a stock called Federated Fido, which his nephew had him buy

**SECONDARY STOCK OFFERINGS VERSUS
THE DOW JONES INDUSTRIAL AVERAGE**

**Figure 3**

two weeks ago at 3 and which has gone to 4; the fare thinks
he has heard about it, but asks the taxi driver about Consolidated Canine, which he says he bought yesterday and which
today is up 15 percent.

Most new issues, even of companies without a history or
reliable management, go up. (See Figure 3.)

At cocktail parties people talk excitedly about the latest
prodigy. Smugton Loud's wife explains they are buying a
small house in Antibes with the profits of his last six months'
trading. Frank Fishstory, the social broker, has kept his customers out of the market up to this point, but now jumps in
with both feet, buying them low-quality volatile "story" stocks
on margin and signing them up for as many new issues as he
can get his hands on.

In 1980–82 the dollar volume in soybeans alone, as well
as trading in options, sometimes exceeded the volume on the
New York Stock Exchange.

# Hesitation

As the months wear on, however, the mass of stocks become hesitant; finally they start slowing their upward pace, and only the leaders (whichever have been collectively so designated) go on making new highs. The market analyst detects this situation by the loss of "breadth." For instance, the ratio of advances to declines usually starts falling at this point, even though the Dow stocks are still rising. Speculative volume falls off. (See Figure 4.)

There are also inherent restraining features in a business boom.

- Inventories eventually reach the point of glut. (In the early stages of a business pickup the entire pipeline, from the mine through the mill and metalworking plant, all the way to the warehouse and hardware store, has to be replenished.)
- The price of raw materials is bid up as production increases.
- Money costs go up. (In slack times there are few borrowers, so rates are low. In a boom the manufacturer needs more working capital and wants to finance plant expansion, so interest rates rise.)
- Labor costs soar as full employment is reached, and the unions, profiting by manpower scarcity, increase their demands and get more overtime.
- Efficiency drops as older facilities are brought back into production and high profits mask operating sloppiness.

Beyond a certain level, more business does not mean higher profits; and at this point in the stock market cycle, that economic fact starts to be noticed.

A few enthusiasts still claim that things this time are different. They argue that the government has mastered the business cycle, so that there need not be another downturn, or that there is an absolute shortage of stocks because of the institutional or foreign appetite for them, which will support

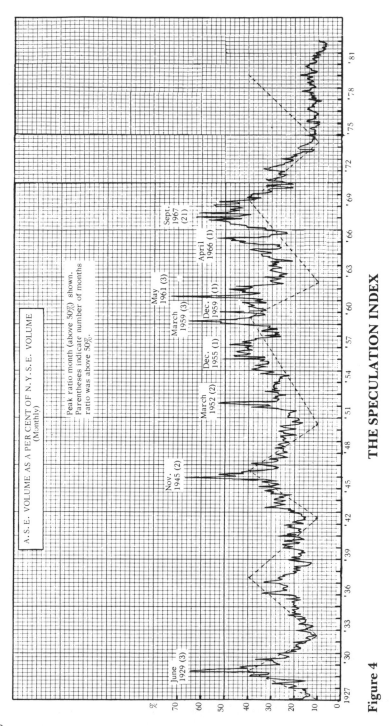

A.S.E. VOLUME AS A PER CENT OF N.Y.S.E. VOLUME
(Monthly)

Peak ratio month (above 50%) shown.
Parentheses indicate number of months
ratio was above 50%.

June
1929 (3)

Nov.
1945 (2)

March
1952 (2)

Dec.
1955 (1)

March
1959 (3)

May
1961 (3)

Dec.
1959 (1)

April
1966 (1)

Sept.
1967
(21)

**THE SPECULATION INDEX**

**Figure 4**

prices at permanently higher levels, or that stocks are the only refuge from inflation. The 1981 theory was that a tax cut had to cause a bull market.

A limiting factor in any bull market, nevertheless, is that enough securities can be "manufactured" to satisfy the desire to invest, however strong it may be. (See Figure 5.) In the 1960s, for instance, advertising agencies and stock exchange firms began selling their shares to the public. This really amounts to the executives of these firms capitalizing their future salaries: collecting them from the investing public ten or fifteen years in advance. Another example is the inflated securities of the conglomerates, billions of dollars of which were floated during the same period. And real estate securities can be brought to the stock market in a massive way, as in England, and mortgages as well; there are enough available to satisfy a virtually infinite investment demand—far more than the value of all the stocks now publicly held.

Figure 4. In the mid 1950s I spent quite a lot of time on technical market analysis, and discovered a useful indicator of future stock market prices: the ratio of American Stock Exchange (previously, Curb Exchange) volume to New York Stock Exchange volume. The rule I developed is that if the ratio of American Stock Exchange volume gets up to 50 percent of New York Stock Exchange volume from its usual level of, say 15 percent to 25 percent, and then collapses, the stock market will fall abruptly quite soon thereafter.

The theory is that institutions rarely trade heavily in over-the-counter or American Stock Exchange securities. So, great activity in them means frenzied public speculation. After the "second stage of the rocket"—the surge of popular buying—has run its course, the market is, as it were, floating in the stratosphere without support. When, therefore, the speculative surge in those issues runs its course, then (goes my theory) the end is very near.

I calculated this indicator, now often called the Speculation Index, back to the 1920s. It has never given a false signal, although it does not call every turn. When it does signal a major top, one should always take it very seriously. Of course, option trading is taking the place of American Stock Exchange speculation and in time will make possible an option-based Speculation Index.

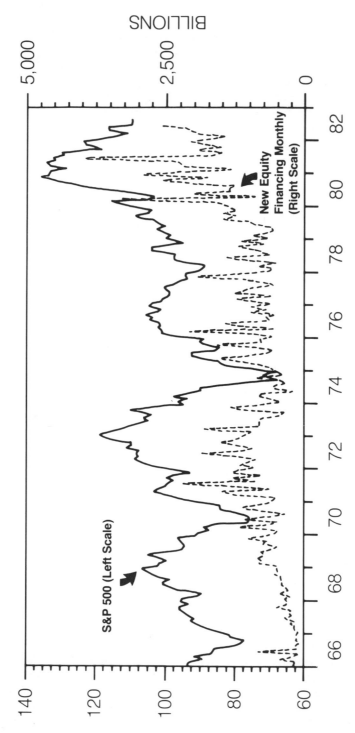

BILLIONS

5,000

2,500

0

New Equity
Financing Monthly
(Right Scale)

S&P 500 (Left Scale)

140

120

100

80

60

66   68   70   72   74   76   78   80   82

NEW EQUITY FINANCING

**Figure 5**

# Topping Out

At last the government, concerned about economic "over-heating" and stock market speculation, starts "leaning against the wind." The Federal Reserve raises bank reserve requirements; the discount rate goes up a notch; margin requirements may be tightened. In time, this process always breaks a bull market.*

The insiders, suspicious of stock price levels, step up the sale of their holdings ("secondary issues").

Another few months pass, and we start to recognize the typical top formation. A series of vicious reactions, or "chops," begins, probably for the first time since the cycle started.

First, over a six-week period or so the market falls rapidly, perhaps 10 percent. Then the arrival of belated "second chance" buyers halts the decline and puts the list up to new highs.

Some time later there is a second vicious chop, which usually bottoms at a higher level than the previous one. The recovery again carries to a new high. Those who sold out at the bottom of either chop feel foolish. Those who jumped in, seeking the second chance, are jubilant.

Frank Fishstory, the social broker, says that the Dow is going up another 30 percent, "although selectivity remains important." The probabilities are if you sell out at about this point you will not regret it. To push the operation to its limit, however, you abandon ship only when the successive chops no longer progress to higher levels, but rather start into a downward pattern, with each peak stopping lower than the last one and each drop continuing below the last one.

The secondary stocks, the ones not in the leading averages, have been sluggish for months.

This is the beginning of the end, a very dangerous moment.

*Since World War II a repulsive custom has arisen: the President pumping vast excess liquidity into the economy at election time. After the election, the winner (sometimes the same man) wrings it all out again, producing a bear market.

# Over the Hill

The public is by this time (for instance, late 1980) heavily in the market, and the professional investors are edging out. They have known for some time that the leading issues are too high, and are waiting to sell as soon as they conclude that the game really is over and there is nowhere to go but down.

It is like the ogre's dinner party, at which the last guests to leave are eaten themselves. When chairs begin to be pushed back and napkins placed on the table, the wise diner prepares to dash for the exit as soon as there is any excuse to do it. This crush at the door is why the market goes down much faster than it goes up.

The lower-quality stocks start declining significantly.

# The Slide

A few more months pass, and a number of issues, although not yet the leaders, have fallen appreciably from their highs, perhaps 25 percent. The mass of the market, as measured by a 1500-stock index, or for instance, as indicated by the advance-decline ratio, has been going down for a considerable period.

Business news is now felt to be not too good. Doubts are expressed as to the economic outlook: Perhaps there will be a recession next year?

The market, like a desperately tired horse that no longer feels the whip, fails to respond to good news, often governmental measures and announcements by well-known figures. The House of Morgan bids 10,000 U.S. Steel above the market. "My son and I have for some days been purchasing sound common stocks," says Mr. Rockefeller. Merrill Lynch is bullish on America. (It has to be, since it, like companies in other industries, will have expanded its facilities, and thus lifted its break-even point, in the preceding boom.)

After a while we may see a severe decline, with perhaps 25 percent marked off the prices of the more volatile issues.

There is often a deceptive recovery, which one might call the "trap rally." It can last a number of weeks and produce a significant bounce-back in the battered leaders.

The usual sequence is that the lowest-quality stocks collapse first, while the top-quality issues struggle forward; then the general market starts giving ground; finally the institutional growth stocks let go, and everything starts slipping faster and faster.

New and secondary public issues dry up, and indeed many old issues are so far down that the companies solicit tenders for their own shares, sometimes amounting to hundreds of millions of dollars in a month.

Smugton Loud quietly sells his Riviera establishment. He lets it be known that he has taken a few losses, but that things have come down so far "there's no point in giving up now . . . it's too late to sell."

# The Cascade

Now the river sweeps over the brink, carrying all with it.

A cardinal point of market strategy is to get out before this cascade, even if one has already lost 15 or 20 percent.

Business news is bad, and the "standard forecast" is for stormy weather ahead.

The hot fund managers have to meet redemptions, but find out that illiquid securities can't be sold, and depart in disgrace.

As for the margin operators and leveraged funds, the borrowings turn out only to have hurried them more rapidly to disaster.

(Aggressive managers as a class lose more money than they make, because you can only raise money for aggressive vehicles, such as venture-capital new-issue accounts, when the pot is boiling, and the lessons of the last collapse a few years earlier have been forgotten. Thus, this kind of money is by it nature collected when the cycle is nearer its end than its beginning. So relatively little money is in the aggressive pools of capital on the way up, and a lot more on the way down.)

The torrent crashes down the falls. In the final plunge some stocks give up in a day their gains of a year, and drop 30 percent in a week. Frank Fishstory pushes his customers to sell before they lose everything. It is so sudden and so awful that for a while many investors can't quite believe it.

When the smallest investors finally throw in the sponge and sell out, it appears in the newspaper figures on odd-lot short sales. The man who can't afford to deal in hundred-share lots goes to his broker so sure that the end is at hand that he sells short seventeen shares, say, of U.S. Steel, hoping to buy it back for a lot less after the cataclysm. This paroxysm of odd-lot despair takes place right at the bottom of the market. (See Figure 6.)

So here we are again, four years or so after we started out, half drowned, half our bones broken, all passion spent, washed out. (For a "cardiogram" of this four-year cycle, see Figure 7.) The summer of 1982 is an example from recent memory. For a detailed discussion of that moment—and a prediction—the reader should turn to Appendix IV on page 250.

# Secular Movements

In addition to this standard short-term cycle, there are much longer-term cycles operating in the market. These too are based on the bandwagon principle. They are sometimes called secular movements, and seem to last twenty years or so.

*1907.* At the turn of the century, bonds were still considered the basic form of prudent investment.

*1927.* Time passed and the merits of equities became more and more understood, until in the latter 1920s the "growth" mania began to take over and stocks became over-

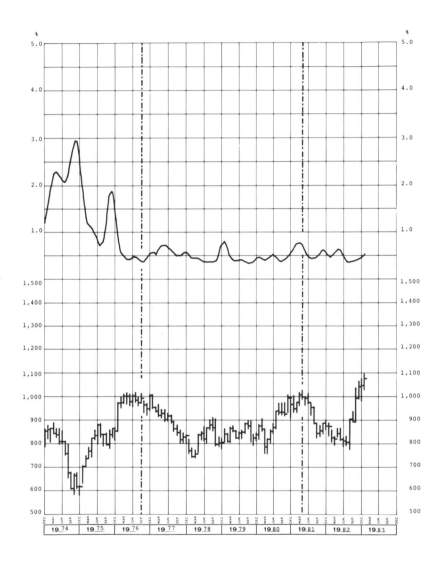

**DOW JONES INDUSTRIAL AVERAGE—MONTHLY**
**Odd-Lot Short-Sale Ratio**

**Figure 6**

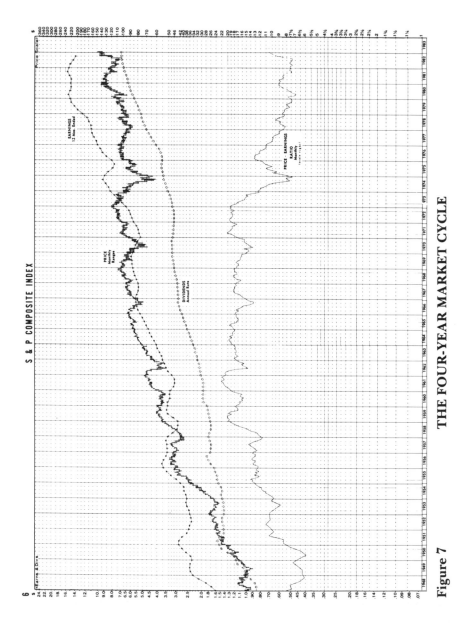

Figure 7

THE FOUR-YEAR MARKET CYCLE

28

valued. "No price is too high to pay for RCA" was the famous cry. Then, of course, came the collapse, and for years stocks were under a cloud.

*1947.* This attitude persisted into the 1940s. At the end of World War II the Dow Jones yielded 6 percent and U.S. Government obligations around 3.5 percent. People still respected the relative security of bonds and were fearful of another debacle in equities. A conventional bank trust portfolio in those days was at most 50 percent in stocks. Pension funds were about 15 percent in stocks. That, of course, was the top of the bond market, and a great buying point for stocks.

*1967.* Thereafter stocks slowly rose in popularity until by the latter 1960s a usual proportion would have been 75 or 80 percent in stocks and the rest in bonds—a ratio of three or four to one. This went on and on until instead of a 6 percent yield on stocks and a 3.5 percent yield on bonds, the yields reversed: 7 percent (or even more) on bonds and 3.5 percent on stocks. "Never sell IBM," one said.

So there we were back to the relationship between stock yields and bond yields that existed in the late 1920s.

What next?

In the early 1970s I wrote that for a number of years the tide would run against stocks and in favor of Treasury bills and the like, as soon as people realized that the mass of stocks had not been growing for some time. (See Appendix I, p. 239.) Runaway inflation plus the convenience of the money funds as an alternative investment helped hold down most stock prices for the next ten years. In 1983, ten years later, all one can say is that the next cycle is coming closer.

However, one can't be sure. In the meantime the violent shorter-term cycles are where money is to be made and lost, and it is to them that the active manager should give most of his attention. Summer is a lot warmer than winter even if an ice age is coming on.

# Crises

Sudden disasters and crises usually knock the market down too far, for anything from a few days to a few weeks. Examples might include the sinking of the *Maine,* the occupation of the Rhineland, Pearl Harbor, the Suez war, the Cuban missile crisis, or the Kennedy assassination. Professionals always buy at these times, as the market always recovers. The news is never as bad for stocks as it seems at the moment of a disaster.

That, then, is the morphology of market cycles. I suspect that the pattern would remain valid even in an unchanging economic environment. The speculative frenzy can take possession of investors in commodities, after all, or in art, where there are no intrinsic earnings and where the total supply available for investment is quite well known. As wild a market boom and crash as any in history centered on speculation in tulip bulbs in seventeenth-century Holland.

The basic concept is that the easiest move upward is when there are almost no sellers and a few pioneer buyers who know what they are doing. A little interest then produces a big percentage gain, just because there is nothing to stop it.

The easiest move downward is when large numbers of later buyers ("followers," you might say) have copied the pioneers and have pushed prices way up, buying out the pioneers in the process. They are now potential sellers in their turn, but at some point there are insufficient additional "followers" for them to sell to. In due course they give up hope and throw in their hand.

So the cycle repeats itself.

# The Contagion of Concepts

Mankind craves simplified explanations.

Not only old wives propagate tales: also priests, doctors, politicians, intellectuals, professors, and indeed you and me.

Perhaps in the end, like the Irish elk, whose horns grew so long they rendered him helpless, the human race will be done in by its propensity for ideologies.

Certainly one sees this human failing wonderfully well in the stock market.

Although scattered, investors—including their leaders, the institutional money managers—are a mob, governed by mob psychology. (So is the electorate, also widely separated, but united, like the investors, by the media.)

If the investor looks at the Most Active List of the American Stock Exchange he can see any day the contagion of ideas at work. Year in, year out, one fad follows another. The brokers beat the drum for it a while before dropping it and moving on to the next.

One year the electorate demands stringent laws against air pollution by automobiles, which cuts the mileage down. Putting on its investment hat, the same body bids up oil drilling and pollution-control stocks. Then the electorate demands higher mileage, and oil and pollution-control stocks go down again. Then, during the period of waiting in long gas lines, the oil drilling stocks soar. In 1980 there's an oil glut and the energy group collapses again.

Highway fast-food chains, transistor manufacturers, computer software companies (hundreds of them), above-ground swimming pool makers, outboard motorboat companies, air-conditioner makers, computer software houses, prefab house builders, land developers, textbook publishers, gambling houses, toy manufacturers, mutual fund distributors, C.B. radio manufacturers, digital watchmakers, home computer companies, computer videogame purveyors—the stock market fads are like popular tunes: How many you remember only depends on how old you are.

Each time they are supposed to represent a unique and lasting innovation, which should sell at many times asset value and lofty multiples of earnings, even if the companies started yesterday. They are all deflated again in due course, by increased competition or changing trends.

Very few fads last, and very few fad stocks are worth high multiples.

Distrust attractive concepts—and "concept" stocks.

# "Glamour" Stocks

There is no economic category of glamour stocks, the way there is of automobile stocks or chemical stocks. A glamour stock is just a growth issue that is in the limelight, and is therefore probably overpriced.*

Very few human endeavors are worth twenty times earnings, however (the typical "glamour" multiple), and almost none over thirty times. At such multiples you are betting heavily on conditions that lie many years in the future, which may be all right, but with very unfavorable odds, which is not.

The essence of "glamour" in stocks is precisely that: The odds become unfavorable.

It is usually a poor policy either to buy or sell glamour stocks.

---

*In 1972, 160 top financial institutions gave their favorite stocks for 1973 to *The Institutional Investor.* If you had put equal amounts into each, you would in the following year have lost 44 percent of your money.

That, of course, sounds strange. Clients often carefully explain to their adviser, who they assume enjoys superior wisdom but perhaps not sufficient zeal, that if he no longer considers a stock a buy, then he should sell it.

The difficulty is that nobody can know how far a trend will continue. An institutional darling like Schlumberger may stay overpriced for decades and yet go right on up during the period, with perhaps a two- or three-year rest from time to time. If one has the stock at a good profit, meaning a significant tax liability on selling, the safest policy is often just to stay on board.

"Well, then," says the client, "if it's not a sale, shouldn't we buy it?"

No, because the uncommitted investor should try to go that strategy one better. He should seek out a stock with equal prospects that at the moment is *out* of favor and therefore underpriced; that is, he should try for the "double play." Let the glamour premium come after you've bought the stock, rather than before.

# Wrestling with the Inner Hercules

When sudden terror seized travelers in a lonely place, the ancients said that the god Pan had come upon them . . . whence our word *panic*. Very simple. We moderns—from politicians to investors—instead produce odd rationalizations of our feelings. The fleeing army shouts *"Nous sommes trahis!"** In a falling market the frightened broker, his soul

*"We've been betrayed!"

on fire like Saint Theresa's inside his pin-striped waistcoat, pleads with his customers to sell everything at twenty cents on the dollar because it's all going down to ten cents . . . or to nothing at all.

Under the skin of every investor there is an inner man, small but immensely strong. He yearns to be one with the crowd. And what he wants he gets.

He is only happy marching in step, singing in unison, and betting on the favorite.

Since the favorite never gives the good odds, this is a way of saying that our little inner man wants us to lose money. Indeed, he commands, he imperiously requires, like a Great Dane on a leash dragging a child into the gutter, that we lose money.

## The Line at the Buffet

*Place:* The country-club dinner dance—in the dining room.
*Time:* 7:00 on Saturday night. People are sitting at their tables drinking cocktails they have brought over from the bar. Along one side of the room the buffet is spread on long tables; cauldrons of soup, shrimp cocktails, chicken, roast beef, gravy, vegetables, several desserts, coffee. There is nobody at the buffet. At about half the tables the following dialogue is taking place:

*Lance:* Well, let's eat!
*Nicole:* Not just now . . . there's nobody *there.* They'll think we're pigs.
*Lance:* Why don't you just admit it?
*Mother:* Really, Father, you ought to speak to Junior.
*Father:* Take it easy, you two.

(7:05 P.M. There is still nobody at the buffet.)

*Lance:* Well, how about now?
*Nicole:* Oink-oink.
*Lance:* How did you get that way?
*Mother:* What's the matter with you two?

(7:07 P.M. H-hour! There is a roar of chairs pushing back like an artillery barrage, a whoosh of dresses and tuxedos like a rocket taking off, and suddenly there is a line of 150 people in front of the buffet.)

(7:10 P.M.)

*Nicole:* Oh, there's Tracy in the line . . . and there's Beverly and Kimberly! Save a place for me, Kimberly! Let's go, folks!

(7:50 P.M. After forty minutes, the family has worked its way nearly to the head of the procession.)

*Lance:* God, I'm hungry. Why did we have to wait until there was this enormous goddamn *line*?
*Nicole:* Dry up, you drip.
*Father:* Cut it out, you two.

## Beating the Market

*Place:* Lunch at the Civic Club.
*Time:* 1:30 P.M. Wednesday.

*Walter Grunion, Sr. (a lawyer, partner of Grunion and Onion):* What do you think of the market, James?
*James Sounder (executive vice-president of the Fourth National Bank):* We think that this pessimism has been overdone.
*Henry Haddock (president of Haddock's, the department store):* But do you think it's time to buy?
*Mr. Sounder:* Well, it's certainly no time to sell, just when everybody else is.
*Ebenezer Wartkopf (a wealthy investor):* You know, gentlemen, I can't help thinking of something my father used to say. He used to say, "You can't go broke taking a profit." I keep wondering if we're not in for something really bad.
*Mr. Sounder:* Of course, if the game plan fails, or if the Democrats get in, then all bets are off.
*Mr. Grunion:* I sometimes get a letter put out by a fellow who tells you what everybody is thinking around the country, so that you won't get caught in the contagion of crowd psychology. It's quite helpful.
*Mr. Wartkopf:* Yes, but everybody thinks that way now. I found out in 1930 that it's not always that smart to buck the main trend.
*Mr. Haddock:* My brother showed me an article by that guy, what's his name? You know, the one who said the Dow was going way, way down.
*Mr. Grunion:* He was wrong last time. He said we were in for a depression.
*Mr. Wartkopf:* Maybe we are! Has anything changed? Mountains of federal debt, all the cities are bust, people won't work anymore, foreign competition . . . And as for the kids! What hap-

pens when *they* take over? It'll *take* a depression to bring people to their senses.

(Both HADDOCK *and* WARTKOPF are big accounts of SOUNDER's, and GRUNION is a trustee of the hospital endowment and the teachers' pension fund. SOUNDER resolves to tread warily.)

*Mr. Sounder:* Of course, we do feel in the bank that it's important to use a time like this to upgrade portfolios. Selectivity's as important as ever. If there were to be trouble we wouldn't want to be caught with our pants down.

*Mr. Wartkopf:* That's the truest thing I know. Stick to real quality. None of this second-rate stuff that drops right out of sight in a real downtrend. I remember there were no bids *at all* for lots of things in 1962 and 1974! That's how you end up in the poorhouse. What was it my father used to say?

(SOUNDER returns to the bank after lunch and eliminates from the portfolios of HADDOCK and WARTKOPF the only two really intelligent speculations they hold: One is a specialty chemical company, which sells at twenty times earnings and which SOUNDER has never understood. It has doubled from its original cost, but is down 30 percent from its high. The other is a Japanese electronics company, which seems too good to be true and makes him uneasy. He puts the proceeds into Water Works preferred. He is pleased. The next day he will call the others to tell them what he has done. He knows they will approve. He decides to go home. It has been a satisfactory day.)

So the different sides of human nature contend with each other, like an octopus using judo throws on itself.

The average investor is hopelessly in the grip of the herd instinct when he tries to be innovative in the stock market, as whenever he tries to act (or dress) in an original way. (People are never so conventional as when they try to be original.*) He is also too busy to stand outside himself and comprehend what is happening to him. He finds out the hard way. Here is a last playlet:

---

*When we named our youngest daughter Lisa, I knew exactly one other Lisa in the whole world. Now my Lisa complains that half the girls in her class share her name. Jung's idea of synchronicity certainly works in matters of fashion.

# Outguessing

*Place:* GEORGE is at his desk at Blatter, Clatter & Company, members of the Stock Exchange. The phone rings. It is CYRUS, a doctor, GEORGE's customer and lifelong friend, calling from his office in the Medical Center.

*Time:* 11 A.M. Monday.

*Cyrus:* George? Cyrus. I've only got a minute. You know that woman I sometimes tell you about? The one who wants to have all the operations? She just went out the door. Fantastic! Now she's after me to go in and take out her spleen. Her spleen! Where did she ever *get* the idea? Anyway, that's not what I'm calling about. Where's ITT?

*George:* It's at 27.

*Cyrus:* What did I buy it for?

*George:* I suggested it about two years ago at 35, and when it went to about 40 you put an order in to buy some at 37, but it went straight on to about 60, so you didn't get any. Then it came back to 39 and you bought a hundred, and another hundred at 29. Then it got down to 27 on all that bad publicity and you sold it again. Then it got to 24, and we both agreed it was cheap and you bought back two hundred shares. Then came the washout, and you switched everything into Treasury bills. Then it got back to 31 and you bought a hundred shares back. So now you have a hundred shares at 31.

*Cyrus:* But how much have I lost on the other trades?

*George:* I hate to think.

*Cyrus:* I guess I'm the ideal customer, right? In and out . . . lots of commissions!

*George:* It's not how I like to live. A broker has a nice life if he has a lot of happy customers, and they're happy when he's made them money.

*Cyrus:* Anyway, what should we do now?

*George:* Well, the stock's still a gift. If you broke it up, it would be worth twice what it's selling for.

*Cyrus:* So you'd buy back the rest of the stock?

*George:* I'd rather have done it at 24, but it's still cheap at 27. It's a growth stock, and it yields 5 percent. Most of them yield less than 1 percent.

*Cyrus:* Well, okay. You've always been right on this one, I must admit. Let's pick up another hundred shares, and maybe it'll get back to 25 or thereabouts so we can fill out the last hundred. Sound okay?

*George:* Sure, if when it gets down there you really do buy it. It's not that easy to make yourself buy when the market's going down.

*Cyrus (aside):* All right, Nurse, show him in. *(To George.)* Listen, George, I have a patient. Buy the hundred shares and call me if anything happens.

*George:* Right. 'Bye, Cyrus.

*(Ten days later.)*

*George:* Cyrus, it's George. You asked me to call you if ITT got down to 25, and here it is, almost. The last sale was at 25½.

*Cyrus:* What'd we buy it at?

*George:* This last time, 27.

*Cyrus:* And now it's 25½?

*George:* There it is again . . . Four thousand shares just traded at 25¼.

*Cyrus (dismayed):* 25¼?

*George:* What difference does it make? It was 60 a few months ago. It'll get there again. There go a thousand at 25.

*Cyrus:* Jesus Christ! What's happening?

*George:* Well, the company's raised the dividend, but on the broad tape it just said that Ralph Nader wanted to reopen the suit to make them divest Hartford Life. He lives up that way . . . somewhere near Hartford.

*Cyrus:* Will they make them do it?

*George:* We don't see how the merger could be reversed at this point.

*Cyrus:* But it *could* happen, couldn't it? Wouldn't that be bad?

*George (testily):* Anything *can* happen. Yes, of course, it'd be bad. It's a question of odds. ITT is being thrown away in here. There it goes at 24½. I may buy some myself.

*Cyrus:* Well, I know, George, but we've been crossed up before, and it's been expensive. Nobody's infallible . . . we doctors know that! I think I'd feel a lot more comfortable if we just dropped it off and switched into some of those high-yield Treasury bills, and then when the dust settles we can decide what we want to do. Okay? After all, an awful lot of people have the stock at a loss and will just be waiting for a chance to sell, won't they?

*George:* Why not just sell a hundred?

*Cyrus:* No, I'd really feel more comfortable not having to worry about it. When I'm inside a patient I don't like to have any more on my mind than I have to. It's not a lot of money either way. Go ahead and sell it, and then when things calm down we'll see.

*George:* You're the boss! Thanks for the order, anyway. Will we see
    you Monday?
*Cyrus:* On Monday? Oh, yes, of course. We're looking forward to it.
*George:* So are we. Well . . . have a good weekend!
*Cyrus:* You too. 'Bye, George. *(Hangs up, feeling better.)*

Most people, the mass, by the very nature of the mass,
will continue to get stuck in the line at the buffet and go on
selling stocks just before they double.

The mass cannot escape from itself, any more than a
man from his shadow. The talk, the thinking, the foxiness,
are all rationalizing, are all in vain.

# Cowboy Investing

In World War II, if you visited a high U.S. Army headquarters you could see bustle, running around, bells ringing, and
a great show of activity at any time of day or night; while at a
British Army headquarters at teatime everything stopped for
tea, people got enough sleep, and frantic bustle was taken as
a sign of failure to delegate properly, so that one could focus
on the larger questions. Once in Edinburgh I called on the
manager of a Scottish trust whose performance I had long
admired. I did not find him shouting into two telephones
while fussing with ten bits of paper, like some of his Wall
Street counterparts, but rather in the drawing room of an
Adam house, legs up on a footstool, gazing into the fireplace
while pulling meditatively on his pipe.

Flopping about, rather than masterful inactivity, charac-
terizes the proceedings of many American portfolio managers, to the considerable disadvantage of the funds under
their care. It reminds one all too much of a rodeo. The newly
appointed money manager bursts from the pen digging in

his spurs, waving his hat, and shouting about his grand designs. He buys, he sells, he changes, he installs computer programs, he announces new philosophies—usually, just about when the other investment cowboys are adopting similar philosophies.

Here are some of the typical moves and countermoves:

- The Midas Memorial Fund switches to a policy of "quality growth." The results are good, since the growth issues have been neglected for some years. After a while the pack comes pounding after, so there are in due course no good values left.

- Midas now adopts a strategy of selling out to the others after its "quality growth" issues are bid up beyond a certain point, and substituting new ones. The pack catches on and starts doing the same. The idea of hiring a "spread" of hot managers to manage divisions of the portfolio begins to appear attractive.

- Midas holds a demure press conference to describe its new computer system, which will enable it to detect with great precision when to buy the neglected issues and then, when they have run up, when to sell out to the others.

   The Holy Father Foundation hires the manager of the Midas Memorial computer setup and starts a similar one. So do one hundred and then two hundred other groups.

   There is a huge increase in portfolio turnover and after a while all the performances are equal once again, except that they have been nicked for the amount of the brokerage, the spread between bid and asked, and the transfer taxes (which can come to quite a sum).

- (A heresy) The new president of Merlin College demands and gets from his trustees a free hand to try and "build" its portfolio fast. He hires a flashy young manager who shows spectacular results by going into less seasoned issues (which his and his friends' buying pushes up) and a proportion of letter stock, over-the-counter numbers, and private deals. He shows an appreciation of 35 percent in eighteen months.

His brother, father, and niece are all hired by rival funds and enthusiastically start in on the same game.

- (A heresy) Midas Memorial, noticing that it isn't getting anywhere anymore, fires its manager and hires the assistant of Merlin College's hotshot, who puts the portfolio into "emerging growth" companies. Many institutions follow suit.

- At some point in all this the market takes one of its regular fourth-year tumbles, and the "heretics" discover that they have lost 50 percent in one year; indeed, that there are no buyers at all for many of their holdings, some of which turn out to be without intrinsic value.

- These institutions fire their managers and switch to conservative trust companies for advice. The trust companies, gratified, put the money into their standard buy lists, which in due course are run up beyond their normal values and have nowhere further to go.

- After a while the institutions notice that their portfolios aren't "getting anywhere"—that is, are only making a normal stock return on the stocks and a normal bond return on the bonds.

- Fitzfrank Fosdick, the new president of Utopia Institute, publicly chides the educational institutions for timidity in their investment policies. The wisest pay no attention, but his blast tips the balance in the investment committees of some of the others toward the young Turks who want to be more venturesome, and bit by bit the same old sequence is repeated.

What, then, can large institutions do to come out ahead of the market? Probably nothing.* They are the market. All

---

*There is, however, a sure losing strategy available: Buy "trendy" issues when they are popular and sell them later at a loss to chase the next trend.

of them as a class are like logs floating down a river: Day in, day out, they will progress at the speed of the river.

In the language of the day, big institutional money is pretty much a "zero-sum system" as far as beating the market goes. There is an old joke of the host at a poker game saying, as he puts out the pretzels and beer, "Now let's all play carefully, boys, and we can all win a little." No way! The whole market should rise by the amount of the companies' earnings that are reinvested, plus inflation, but beyond that, Fitzfrank Fosdick to the contrary, the gain of one must be the loss of another; the game (or system) comes out to zero.

# What Is Left?

The institutional brokerage houses will probably have a dull time. Institutional research has become a commodity, and pretty well cancels itself out anyway. It is almost illegal to know something in Wall Street today that everybody else doesn't know. I would think that the institutions could more and more go back to running their own money. Cut out the brokers, shrink the staffs, lower the turnover, pigeonhole the snazzy gimmicks, and be content with moderate objectives. If they hire outside advisers it could be for very slim compensation.

# The Hemline Indicator

For decades market theorists have been baffled by the correlation between the length of women's skirts and the Dow Jones Average.

When skirts get low, as in the 1930s, shortly after World War II (the "New Look"), or in mid-1982, then the market is low* and you can buy with confidence, in expectation of a long-term rise. When skirts get very high, as during the flapper era of the late 1920s and the miniskirt period in the 1960s, then the market is high and will decline.

The skirts and the stock prices are not directly connected, like the steering wheel of a car and its front wheels, or the price of steak and the amount of steak people eat. Rather, they are both expressions of human behavior. High skirts (or exposed bosoms), speculative markets, and high interest rates are manifestations of one *Zeitgeist*; covering up the body, a conservative attitude to investment, and low interest rates are manifestations of another. I will call them the "grasshopper" and "ant" syndromes.

A simple sketch of each might go like this:

### GRASSHOPPERS

1. Short skirts and/or low necklines expose the body.
2. Men's clothes are flashy.
3. Education is permissive. Junior knows best. What use is spelling?
4. Gratification now. "Do your own thing."
5. Diligent work and duty to society are avoided.

---

*Relative to usual standards of value, that is, not necessarily to a particular level in the Dow. The market was "low" in 1950 at eight times earnings, with stocks yielding more than bonds, "high" in 1961 at twenty-two times earnings, with bonds yielding twice as much as stocks, and "low" in mid-1982 at six times earnings, with many stocks yielding more than bonds.

6. Businessmen and investors expect to make money easily, and so borrow freely.
7. Bankruptcy carries little social stigma.
8. The government runs a deficit, financed through excessive bond issues.
9. Business and the stock market boom on borrowed money.
10. High demand for loans, to cover both government and private spending, plus inflation and frequent bankruptcies, push up interest rates.

### TRANSITION

High interest rates and sloppy work choke off the boom and the stock market. There is a severe shakeout. The corporate manipulators and market speculators are disgraced. Companies can no longer afford shoddy workers, and lazy executives are fired. Banks suffer heavy losses and become careful whom they lend to. An image of seriousness and responsibility pays.

### ANTS

1. Women dress modestly.*
2. Men's clothes are sober.
3. Children are taught.
4. Build for the future: insistence on honesty, seriousness, and concern for society.
5. The loafer is not wanted.
6. Life is hard; stay out of debt.
7. A bankrupt is disgraced unless he discharges his obligations.
8. Sound money and a balanced budget are demanded.

---

*What has once been in fashion will again be in fashion. After the no-bra look has lost interest, women will again wear corsets.

9. Business activity is moderate. The market is cautious.
10. Slow loan demand, low inflation, and prudent lending practices keep interest rates down.

An economist might use interest rates as the central variable. High rates choke a business boom and collapse the stock market by pulling money out of equities into higher-yielding fixed-income securities.

I suggest that interest rates, in turn, are an index of social morale. When life becomes a carnival and people put on fancy dress, so to speak, the prevailing high interest rates reflect widespread borrowing, inflation, dishonesty, and risk of loss.

When life (and clothes) are sober and serious, people hesitate to borrow and are careful to repay punctually, inflation is less of a factor, and interest rates come down.

Thus clothes, interest rates, and the stock market reflect the grasshopper-ant alternations in our affairs.*

### POSTWAR BLOWOFFS

It seems to be a general rule that at the end of major wars, such as the Napoleonic Wars, our Civil War, and both World Wars, women's clothes and morals both get skimpy. There is a libertarian reaction to all that discipline and martial fervor.

During a war women are called upon to accept sacrifices for their absent men, who are sacrificing so much for them. Women become surrogates for men, and their clothes often echo the design of uniforms. Thus in World War II women wore tailored suits with broad shoulders and wide lapels.

In wartime a barrage of propaganda extols the heroes of the home front and berates the sluggards. Year after year the population slaves away, sustained by idealistic slogans.

---

*When the Russians restore the stock market, they will not want to call pessimists—who will be jailed for economic sabotage—"bears." They have a special feeling for bears, as of course Spaniards do for bulls. They should start thinking now about using the terms "grasshoppers" and "ants" instead.

The momentum of this effort carries on for quite a few years after the war is over. Eventually there is a reaction, however. The idealistic aims are disappointed, and the fervor wears off. The age of the grasshopper returns.

After the coverup—the tailored suits with broad shoulders or the long skirts—comes the striptease. Grandmothers start dressing the way tarts did in the previous cycle. Sex becomes free and easy, and the carnival spirit spreads. The economy booms on borrowed money.

It is often observed that a number of years after a major war there is likely to be a severe economic dislocation or collapse. (Vietnam followed World War II and Korea, so our postwar collapse only began at the end of the 1960s.) I do not know if that is because of the problems of shifting from a war economy to a peace economy, including altered markets and unemployment, or because of the ant-grasshopper cycle, including the bust that usually follows a boom, or other reasons.

Anyway, the "grasshopper" syndrome we experienced in the late 1960s and early 1970s seems to characterize the aftermath of most wars. The same postwar rejection of discipline may have resulted in the young people "doing their own thing," and the grasshopper cycle. Pop everything— easy virtue, easy credit, high interest rates, frothy markets . . . and short skirts.

As the reaction runs its course, as is happening now, men want to dress as much as possible like J. P. Morgan and women like Queen Mary. *Penthouse,* we trust, will be replaced on the stands by *Commentary*. Bonds will yield less than stocks, and the stock market will be a buy.

# II.

# Good and Bad Advice

# How to Find an Investment Adviser

In the 1930s there came into existence in America the profession of investment adviser (still little known in Europe). Like a doctor or lawyer, he accepted the responsibility of being primarily devoted to the interests of his client, instead of having an essentially commercial relationship with him, like the stockbroker.

Perhaps in an ideal world the professional adviser would on the one hand deal with the client and then turn around and deal with the stockbroker, with whom the client would *not* be in direct contact, just as in England one's legal affairs are looked after by a solicitor, who in turn engages a courtroom pleader, a barrister, if necessary. In part that separation is to minimize the risk of a barrister's encouraging a client to litigate. Similarly, the ideal arrangement would make it harder for a broker to encourage a customer to trade. This would reduce the total volume of trading (and thus the breadth of the market), but that is no more valid a counterargument than to argue against civilian control of the military on the ground that it should reduce the number of wars. After all, at one time (and indeed even today in some countries) a doctor made his profit on the medicines he sold. That is now seen to be unwise. The patient is today felt to be better served if his physician's income is not linked to the volume of medicines consumed.

Anyway, until this separation takes place the investor should at least know that the two systems exist side by side: He can go for advice to a broker, who gets no fee and is compensated on turnover, or, if his portfolio is of a certain size, he can go to an investment counselor, who receives a fee and is obliged under the Investment Advisors Act to put his client's interest first, above his own, like any professional, disclosing all conflicts of interest, and also taking account of his client's entire financial circumstances in developing an investment program. The adviser's fee usually runs from .5 percent to 1.5 percent per annum and is tax deductible. I suspect it pays for itself in most cases in lower brokerage commissions (which are not tax deductible) and in lower turnover, quite aside from the hope of better performance and, as indicated, the advantage of a program based on the investor's entire situation. A good counselor will have adequate knowledge of trusts, insurance, real estate, tax shelters, and such matters, and can steer his client to the right specialists.

The advisory organization (unless it is a captive subsidiary of a brokerage house) has the great advantage, furthermore, of being able to use the research and best ideas of lots of different brokers.

I do, therefore, recommend dealing with a Registered Investment Adviser. He should be able to do two jobs for you: help you work out your overall financial planning and appropriate investment objectives—the financial architecture, one might say—and then execute this plan. The architecture is done at the outset and then reviewed every year or so. The execution goes on every day.

Where, then, do we look for this interesting figure?

A logical way to start collecting names is to study the long-term performance figures of the mutual funds that are run by advisory firms as showpieces and as vehicles for smaller accounts. There are exceptions, but a firm's record will usually be shown by the performance of its fund through several market cycles. If you are impressed by one, it is a good idea to send for the fund prospectus and reports to see how the performance is achieved. The safe and elegant way is to purchase stocks of what turn out to be prime companies and hold them for long periods. The jazzy but potentially dangerous way is to trade in lower-grade issues. When you find a good firm in your area—or somewhere you go regularly—that also runs individual portfolios, you can visit it. (The travel cost is tax deductible.)

Another way of finding an appropriate adviser is, of course, to ask around locally. Here I have only three pieces of advice. (1) Ask about the adviser's intellectual honesty as well as his cleverness. (2) Seek advice from friends and professionals in related areas, like trustees and company treasurers, rather than brokers (who have reciprocal arrangements). (3) Identify the man as well as the firm. A star in a dull firm can often do more for you than a nine-to-five pedestrian in a top one.

It is reasonable to interview several firms and try to get to know the man or group that will actually handle your account. If the "vibes" aren't right, ask to see somebody else. That is important, because if the professional does not inspire your confidence he will not be able to do his job easily and fluently. He will, in fact, be tempted to deform his policy to accommodate your concerns, which will affect the results. To please you he may sell at the bottom, or change his technique just when it's about to pay off.

You shouldn't expect to find an arrangement that will last forever. Human affairs are mutable, and unless you are choosing a trustee or executor you are not locked in. Indeed, you should keep the relationship under review. In investing, as in any highly competitive game, a man or a team may not maintain its quality or, even if it does, may get so busy that it becomes hard to deal with. So just look for an organization that seems appropriate for the present and reasonably near-term future.

You should ask for any written *internal* statements of philosophy and policy. (The regular brochures for clients are usually pablum.) A firm with distinction usually does have a philosophy. To channel and focus its members' efforts it needs an intellectual framework, a discipline.

# Investment Techniques

There are many possible approaches to investing. For what I consider good reasons, I favor the growth orientation, which is in any event probably the only practical one for a do-it-yourself investor, but a good firm can go about it in many other ways.

There are, in fact, about as many other valid investment techniques as there are techniques of courtship. One admirer will send around the Rolls with a diamond carnation under the lap robe. Another just puts down the milk bottles and tows the housewife off to the cellar. Anything works if you're good at it. So too the investment firm should follow whichever technique it knows. They might include:

Three types of "value" investing:

- The "Graham & Dodd" approach, emphasizing balance-sheet analysis and low price-earnings ratios. You try to buy a company for less than a bank would lend on it, and preferably for less than working capital alone. Growth is unimportant. This is the safest technique, and the dullest.
- Takeover situations, in which a company selling below its intrinsic value is broken up and turned into cash or securities of another company. Here it is safest to be a member of a group that is actually in a position to carry through the takeover.
- "Asset" investing, particularly in real estate and the extractive industries, where a company's land, timber, oil, or minerals are worth much more than the market price.

- Then there is growth investing. One tries to buy a company whose growth is not reflected in its market price (not the "official" growth stock that commands a high price because of its establishment status, but whose best growth was in the past).

Three different trading philosophies:
- Following changing public enthusiasm as it rotates from group to group.
- Buying depressed issues (or the whole market) in expectation of a recovery—a variation of the "double play" strategy (see p. 123).
- The Swiss technique of buying the largest and best-known companies in whatever countries seem most attractive at the moment.

- "Turnarounds," or troubled companies where new management has changed things for the better.
- Perhaps the most spectacular of all, investing in small specialty companies, usually with new processes or products in high-growth industries.
- In general, what Wall Street likes to call "special situations."
- Hedged investing, including the convertible hedge. You try to go long an issue that will go up and short one that will go down, so that you make money regardless of the movements of the general market.*
- Merger (also called risk) arbitrage. Two companies are supposed to merge on agreed terms. You buy one stock and sell the other so as to make a profit. It's fine unless the merger is canceled; then you lose money.
- Speculating in commodities and options. These are gambling games, not investing, set up by brokers to fleece the customers, not to make money for them.

Any of these approaches *can* work out well if done by a specialist. The problem is that except for the "value,"

---

*Hedge funds are acutely conscious of each other, like rival actresses. The result is that they rarely sell prudently at tops, but instead try to squeeze the last few percent of profit out of the market, and almost always go over the waterfall in a bear market.

"growth," and "Swiss" approaches, they are so risky, complicated, and competitive that they are only indicated for professional investors, and put exceptional demands even on them. They are no way to run a family's assets.

The trading approaches are particularly hard, incidentally, because they are costly in commissions and in the spread between bid and asked prices, so the odds start out against you. Also, they are acutely competitive. Roughly speaking, the term "successful trader" is an expression for which, like the unicorn, there is no corresponding reality. Few amateur collectors think they could make a practice of going to an auction attended by dealers and experts, buying several objects, and then selling them at a profit a day or two later in the same auction gallery. One would lose money following such a procedure, and that is in fact how the in-and-out stock trader loses money.

Knowledge is the key to it all. You have to know more than the man from whom you are buying the stock, and yet you cannot afford to develop and maintain the necessary degree of knowledge except about a small number of very interesting situations.

It follows that you have to concentrate your attention on the smallest appropriate focus with burning-glass intensity. There is no hope of being superior all over the board. You will just be a random plunger. A firm's "philosophy" is just a statement of what it is trying to focus on. No philosophy, no focus. No focus, no superiority.

# Using Your Adviser

It is by no means certain that the firm you prefer can in fact give you superior performance. Indeed, it is not even very likely. What it should be able to do is save you from expensive blunders and to help you choose the type of investments appropriate to your situation. Almost never, I find with surprise, is a new client's existing portfolio exactly tailored to his needs. Sometimes investors in the upper tax brackets have a number of holdings that pay out high taxable dividends, rather than plowing profits back for relatively tax-free growth. Often a portfolio was originally developed by a businessman or trust officer who froze it in the most promising areas at that time, which have in the subsequent decades become mature industries, so that such important growth sectors as personal computers or monopoly newspapers are unrepresented. The income rises, but the forward movement stagnates.

Usually an older person has much more to lose than to gain, and should shift his investment philosophy to put maintaining the value of his capital ahead of possible growth, particularly if retirement has put him in a reasonably low tax bracket.

Often when a client is well off and in a high tax bracket, it makes sense for him to invest only for growth, minimizing dividends, and put himself on a "salary," as it were, of 6 percent or so of his investment assets per annum. The investment adviser is then told to generate that amount in the way that will impose the least tax burden, emphasizing "plowback" stocks. This might result in 4 percent in dividends and interest, and 2 percent in capital growth, for instance.

The adviser should take account of real estate and art holdings, and also of eventual expectations through inheritance. He should do a comprehensive plan of all the present and future assets in the family, together with the amounts needed for living expenses. It sometimes turns out that thanks to the appreciation of some country real estate, the older members of a family are better off than they were conscious of and can reasonably afford to live on a somewhat better scale than they realized.

One must consider the nature of a man's work and how the needs of the different generations should dovetail. A program of regular giving may be desirable. Sometimes a man saves for years to benefit his children and then gives back many years of those savings in unneeded taxes. The adviser should understand the operation of revocable and irrevocable trusts, insurance, and such arrangements so as to be able to recommend a specialist when appropriate and work with him.

The adviser should carefully collect this information and assemble it in an orderly way, drawing the client's notice to areas in his financial planning that require attention.

This type of overall financial architecture is often as much as half of the adviser's job, and if one considers that he can't guarantee to deliver superior performance, perhaps the most important half.

Properly organizing a client's financial affairs is like designing a house. If the architect does his job in a workmanlike fashion and if the materials and labor are adequate, the house will be suitable in design for the family living in it.

On the other hand, building a better house than the neighbors have with the same materials is something that a contractor cannot ordinarily promise to do. Similarly, an adviser cannot promise that your portfolio will outperform the market, only that it will be appropriately designed for your financial circumstances.

As you talk to a possible adviser you should be aware of these two sides of his work, and try to make sure he is competent in both. Or, if you are dealing with an investment specialist, then also engage an accountant or lawyer familiar with insurance and estate planning. If your principal adviser is an accountant or lawyer, then you also need an investment specialist. His training and mentality is different from the other two.

Having agreed with your investment counselor on the strategy of your account, you should give him discretion in executing transactions as long as he stays within the guidelines. If you second-guess him, the relationship is unlikely to work well. The best stocks often make the client uncomfortable, because neither he nor the public quite understands them yet. As they become understood, they go up.

One should not criticize the adviser for short-term adverse fluctuations in stocks that may be bought. Short-term movements are unpredictable and are not worth worrying about. The questions to ask are: Is the company prospering? Will it go on prospering in the future? If the answers continue to be yes, then the price will probably take care of itself.

Here is a bit of rather technical advice about dealing with trust companies. They themselves will be the last to deny that they have a tendency toward mediocrity, and yet there is usually talent somewhere in any organization. If there is an exceptionally able man in a trust company, he or his group will be much in demand, and used as bait for the largest and most demanding clients. You can usually find out his name through friends who know the company, but the problem is to get assigned to that section. If the account in question is an irrevocable trust, there's not much you can do. Since it's captive business and can't escape, there's a risk that eventually it will be assigned to some unimaginative younger officer. By assigning hundreds of trusts to each such officer, who incidentally is poorly paid, the trust company itself makes quite good money.

I know of a few "counters" to this situation.

1. Have the trust instrument specify that an outside individual or committee, or a committee of the adult beneficiaries, can remove the corporate trustee and substitute another. If the trust company's performance is too dismal, you can use the threat of such action to bring about a change. If the trust company is taken over by outsiders, as happens more and more these days, it may become important to have this power.

2. Have the trust come into the bank on the coattails of a corporate pension fund and be handled by the same manager. Corporate treasurers know all about performance, and keep the manager on the *qui vive*. They are also constantly comparing one bank's performance with another's and analyzing the reasons for it. Since banks know that, and also know that a corporate pension fund tends to grow and grow, they usually give them the best handling they are capable of.

In a very few investment counsel firms and trust companies a high degree of discipline over the various managers is maintained and all, or almost all, of the accounts with a given objective and tax status march in step, so to speak. When Kodak goes on the buy list, the manager of every growth account must buy some or produce a valid excuse: e.g., too much Polaroid in the account already, no free cash, or whatever. If the stock selection process is outstanding, then this arrangement produces the best results, and the best-performing firms are usually run this way.

More usual by far, however, is a mediocre stock selection process, which means that there is no reason not to give considerable latitude to each manager. This is even truer of brokerage houses. I have never heard of one that did not allow its reps to recommend more or less what they liked, within reason, unless the firm had developed a specific policy against some stock or industry group. In dealing with a brokerage house, then, it is more important than ever to find the right man. (In an investment advisory subsidiary of a brokerage house there is more control, of course.)

It doesn't happen often, but theoretically makes good sense for a group of knowledgeable investors to form a pool to hire superior management and, by collectively being an important mass of capital, keep that management on its toes. One disadvantage is that a group so constituted is likely to enter the short-term performance derby, which can rule out the best long-term results, as in so many areas of life. (Trading secondary and new issues produces the biggest gains during certain periods, or selling out completely; but either strategy prevents the portfolio from settling down semipermanently with a collection of great long-term winners.) An advantage of the group approach is that one moves more quickly to get away from bad management. Having been burned, one is less likely to be turned over and roasted on the other side, as sometimes happens to good-natured individuals. Some members of the group are bound to blow the whistle. On the other hand, these arrangements make the manager nervous.

For a family to move one by one into a serious counseling firm (assuming superior results) makes for a particularly satisfactory relationship on both sides. If a reasonable amount of capital is involved, the counselor will make a special effort to understand how the trusts and property arrangements work, how everybody thinks, what they need, what provisions should be made for which children, and so forth. A relationship of confidence and indeed affection can be built up which enables the counselor to do his best work. He can permit himself to make intelligent speculations knowing that the ones that do not work out will not be held against him because all concerned know his record.

Most clients—particularly those who are successful in business, for some reason—are very conscious of the losses, even if the gains are outstanding. By analogy from their business experience they may feel they should rub the adviser's nose in each of his mistakes, to show they are on top of things. In such a situation the adviser may feel that the safest strategy, in terms of his own interest, is not to play the game he knows best and that will in fact make the most for the client, but to invest defensively. Babe Ruth stops swinging for the fences and starts bunting. His batting average improves, but the team is worse off. The adviser's duty is to explain to the client what his attitude may bring about, and resist departing from the strategy he knows best.

# Performance

It's fine for an investor, or an investment committee, to be concerned about performance. That's what it's all about, after all.

This concern has to go one step further, however, or it will do more harm than good.

The worst approach, although very widely followed, is to

split the fund into several parts, farm them out to different investment advisory firms, worry quarter by quarter about what is going on, and then once or twice a year cut back or fire the worst performers and build up the best ones.

That is much too simple.

In the first place, the comparative results will probably just reflect the kind of market it's been recently. The growth stocks will have two or three good years, and the growth addicts will look wonderful. Then those issues will have gotten so high they have to have a rest, so perhaps the low price-earnings issues or the energy stocks have a run, and the specialists in those issues get the applause. The strength rotates among the various philosophies, and in those periods the manager with that approach looks best.

The truth is that these vogues usually last only two or three years. Then so many revelers pile on the carousel that it breaks down.

So jumping from one area where the action is to the next will often result in tying onto the tail end of each fad and participating in one shakeout after another.

The correct approach is to analyze a successful manager's technique for the last ten years or so. If the results have been achieved in a first-class way, then you should ask whether the kind of stocks he specializes in have had a big play recently or whether on the contrary they are in the discard and represent outstanding value.

If the latter, then perhaps you have something. You make sure the manager in question is still employing his perennially successful but recently unpopular method, and then hire him. You should participate strongly in the recovery that will be along sooner or later.

The same manager will probably just have been fired by an overly performance-conscious institution because of two bad years—the same bad years that have coiled the spring for his type of issues to rebound.

# No Amount of Tanzanians Can Put a Man on the Moon

Fairly early in the space race I remember reading with satisfaction an announcement by a young government minister of Tanzania that his country would soon have a man in orbit.

After a while reporters were invited to witness one of the high points in the program. A husky citizen was placed in a barrel, to which was attached a rope looped around a stout tree. Strong assistants then whirled the barrel around and around the tree, like a dancer whirling his partner off her feet. It was explained that this experience would familiarize the man in the barrel with some of the discomforts of orbital flight.

Little more, alas, has since been revealed about this important conception, doubtless because of security considerations.

Anyway, I mention it, not to slight Tanzania's cultural and scientific achievements or its proud role among the nations, but rather to explain the background of my reflection that no amount of Tanzanians can put a man on the moon.

The application of the principle to portfolio investment is as follows:

*No amount of mediocre researchers can find you a great stock.*

Picking stocks that will go up from the mass of stocks that will not requires an exceptional mind, not a large number of average minds. (Mozart was not a committee.) So when you hear a brokerage house or trust company talk about investment selections "backed by our twenty-man research department" or "our team of fifteen top-flight analysts" you do not really know more than you did before about the likelihood of their selections working out well, any more than if a college you never heard of was playing Notre Dame, say, in football. The fact that Incognito U. has a team does not necessarily mean that they are likely to win. On the contrary, there is a presumption they are going to lose. If they were hot stuff you would probably have heard of them already.

A big research department should in theory be able to predict how the companies it follows are likely to do in the immediate future, and to buy (or sell) those whose prices do not reflect their prospects.

What happens is quite different. Strange as this will seem to the non–Wall Streeter, most researchers increase their earnings estimates as a stock's market price rises, and reduce them as it falls. Some few analysts really make informed guesses as to next year's earnings, but for a large, complicated company without a regular growth pattern, that's exceedingly difficult. So the general practice is as I describe—understandably enough.

How well a given research department's recommendations work out will depend on where its researchers rank in quality among the twenty thousand U.S. security analysts—nearer to the top or the bottom; how the department deploys its men (twenty researchers giving some coverage to the entire range of U.S. industry means a very faint penetration indeed); and how the firm uses its research ideas. In theory, it should follow up the correct research data and ignore those that are mistaken—a division that unfortunately is most apparent only quite a while later.

The actual stock picker in the average investment organization knows that the average researcher in his firm is often wrong—perhaps more often wrong than right.* In the few cases where the stock picker finds winners it is likely to be because he is an outstanding man himself. He may develop his ideas on the basis of widely known, unargued facts, which

---

*So is the average retail broker. One big, successful investor, dealing through one broker, buys at the bottom, say, from hundreds of small, uninformed investors, each dealing through his own broker. So to the extent that a small investor trades, as distinct from buying and holding, his broker is likely to be on the wrong side of each transaction.

he interprets differently from the mass of investors at that time, or indeed he may get information from friends in other houses, which he may not share with the rest of his firm.

And in a huge firm, you can't make much use of most ideas, even if true, because they have to be so widely shared.

What about the individual investor? Does it get him very far in practice to "investigate before you invest"?

Except to determine the suitability of the holding in general terms (income, growth, high-grade, speculative), probably not. The individual investor is almost certain to rank near the bottom of the twenty thousand analysts and in the lower ranks of stock pickers. He has neither superior information nor seasoned judgment. Would the man in the street's judgment be of interest in guessing next year's prices of rococo furniture or German Expressionist paintings? He, too, is a Tanzanian.

What he should be able to do, if he disciplines himself, is establish a reasonable investment philosophy and see that his adviser carries it out carefully. There are few Thomas Jeffersons who can design their own Monticello, but a lot of us can find and work with a competent architect.

# Icarus

More money is eventually lost by hot managers than they ever made, since it is the very fact of their expansion that brings them down, like an overloaded airplane.

We have touched on one of the ways a great stock picker is brought low: He becomes the center of an organization, with interests and prejudices of its own, which he then has to wrestle with. Eventually, it gets so big it necessarily becomes mediocre.

There are a number of other typical variations, however. Almost all of them are simply the predictable results of success moving the key man up beyond his ability to cope with things: A brilliant professor can't necessarily run a university. Here are some pseudonymous but real cases.

*Tom Trotter.* Tom was a wonder at technology stocks. He was with a prestigious house that had large accounts and many correspondents in the United States and abroad, and they made the most of him. After four or five companies he had carefully researched worked out according to plan, the stocks soaring, Tom was one of the most listened-to men in the financial world. He began pulling in $500,000 a year in commissions. As he talked on two phones at once, a vein bulging in his forehead, and with other phones ringing on his desk, his desperate secretary, hand over the mouthpiece of still another, would say, "Mr. Trotter! Hong Kong's been waiting on the open line for forty minutes!" With a groan, Trotter leans over the telephone held by the secretary and bellows, "BUY DATCOM!" "Aw li'," the tinny Oriental voice rises from the instrument—Trotter no longer there but the secretary listening—"Aw li', we buy fi' million dollahs!"

No more research trips, no more meditation, no more technical journals—just commissions, commissions, commissions.

First the ideas fell off, and then, still young but burned out, he dropped dead.

*F. O. Smith.* A distinguished market theoretician, he assembled some friends and started a limited partnership to see what he could do in practice. He did wonders: 700 percent in seven years. His partnership grew, and he started another; later, an offshore fund. He brought in brilliant young men to run sections of each fund. Spurred by an incentive-fee arrangement, the young men began chasing each other out on thinner and thinner ice. Shortly after the funds had attained vast size, the ice cracked. The funds lost 30 percent in one year and 20 percent the next. Overzealous managers were fired and new ones brought in, just in time to buy into the latest popular trap. The capital withered away.

*Ivan Vladimir.* An unquestioned genius, he could play the economy like an accordion. He loved knowledge, spoke many languages, and did not tolerate fools. Soon after he created the firm that bore his name, his reputation began to spread. Business grew and grew. He checked every letter, approved all transactions in every account, and researched every stock idea. He started a mutual fund and managed it personally; then another. He handled new business and administration. He was far too fastidious to risk imperfection by delegating anything. The firm mushroomed. His family hoped he would have a heart attack to slow him down before he worked himself to death. Alas, it happened as they feared.

*King Kung.* The first of the postwar crop of Chinese investment wizards, he was talented enough to make a name (an unusual, Oriental name in fact, which helped) as a manager of one of the Codman Funds, out of Boston. It was a good life for one of studious bent, except that one did not get much of the gravy, or first billing on the prospectus. One day he quit and hung up his own shingle. He found an underwriter and launched his own fund on the crest of a bull market: "Superfund." The result amazed everybody. Hundreds of millions of dollars came in, far more than King had ever managed before. Then there were salesmen to hire, vice-presidents to motivate, a large *apparat* to administer. It was a flop. The performance was mediocre. After all the buildup, people had expected the Second Coming. In desperation he stuffed the fund with speculative cats and dogs to catch the last surge of the bull market. He was late: All the "concept" stocks and hot new issues started to fall. The shareholders began to sell out, and King did too: He swapped his shares in his own fund management company for millions of dollars of stock in a financial conglomerate, of which he became director of planning, a congenial post. After a few years Superfund had lost 60 percent of its value per share and only a quarter of its original capital was still in it.* The planning turned out not to be too impressive either.

*If you invested $1,000 in the capital shares of Gerry Tsai's Hemisphere Fund in January 1969, by mid-1970 you had $30 left.

King went weeping to the bank, as they say, with his millions of dollars of conglomerate stock. The shareholders went weeping too, but not to the bank.

In all these instances something happened to change the game, to take the unique figure away from the function only he could carry out. All the stories illustrate the Parkinsonian principle: growth brings complexity, and complexity, decay. There are dozens of ways for a superior investment firm to become mediocre, but most of them are variations on this one rule. Unless carefully guarded against, corruption of the original basis for superiority will follow from too rapid success.

Hemingway noticed a similar thing about American writers: often they enter the literary arena with calloused hands, fresh from the waterfront or the lumber camp. They know an interesting side of life and have something to write about that the public finds fresh and lively. Then the money begins rolling in. The leather jacket is exchanged for a Cardin suit, the Cherokee girlfriend is exchanged for a Vassar grad, the trailer turns into a residence in Connecticut, and the time once spent in adventures goes to lecturing, TV interviews, political pontificating, and publishers' signing parties. They lose touch with their material, with mother earth. They and their books become flabby. Pretty soon success has prepared the way for defeat.

# The Peaceable Kingdom of the Wall Street Opinion Makers

People are sometimes surprised to get contradictory investment advice from different qualified sources. That, however, is in the nature both of markets and of advisers. Furthermore, as I will try to show, when market advice is virtually unanimous you can steer in the opposite direction with almost perfect safety.

## The "Standard Forecast"

The messages on the stock market outlook one receives from stockbrokers and trust companies often begin with a "macroeconomic" prophecy of conditions in the coming year, and then draw the appropriate conclusions for certain industries and for the companies within those industries.

This "overview" of the bank or securities firm is usually based on the opinions of its particular economist, who often has government or university credentials, or both.

The economist generally starts his prophecy by referring to the government's announced objectives and recent actions, current economic statistics, and industry or company statements. He then describes his "model," on which the bank or securities firm's conclusions are based.

Unfortunately, it is not possible to look a year into the economic future, and to that extent long-range economic forecasting, like weather prediction in the 1930s, can only be called a pseudoscience. Too much depends on imponderables, such as consumer confidence, politics, foreign governmental and military events, and projections from large amounts of imperfect data.

Magazine writers brush over this problem. They will run an article based on interviews with several economists, try to find some sort of consensus, and then print it as a statement of simple futurity, e.g., "Unemployment will drop from 8.6 percent to 8.3 percent," or "Plant utilization will rise from 74 percent to 77 percent," or "Inflation, seasonally adjusted, will slow from 9.7 percent to 9.2 percent."

Alas, these figures are not known with that kind of accuracy. When later on you read the revised figures, it often turns out that the inflation rate was really 11 percent at the time of writing (and would have been quite another figure if the elements used in the tabulation had been differently weighted); then a run on the dollar or an impending election forces economic actions that invalidate the prediction. This type of figure probably cannot be known, and certainly not projected, beyond the first digit.

Reported unemployment in America has recently been running over 9 percent, for instance. If one tries to draw economic conclusions from that figure one immediately discovers that as much as 20 percent of the whole labor force has jobs they do not report, including most of the permanent 10 million illegal immigrants. So total real employment may be at an all-time high. Then, the Consumer Price Index, by which inflation is measured, is constructed as though one bought a new house and got a long-term mortgage on it every year—which is scarcely the case for most people—thus exaggerating the effects of both house prices and interest rates.

It seems logical that the price of IBM next year should depend largely on its profits, which in turn should depend on how many computers are sold next year, and that those sales should in turn relate to the economic environment. In fact, however, things rarely work that way. IBM, propelled by a consensus of the Wall Street opinion makers, may already be so high that it is discounting—that is, reflecting—improved earnings for many years to come. Similarly, the market as a whole may be discounting an improved economy.

So the macroeconomic projections, models, and overviews, to the extent they look beyond six months or so, are essentially hypotheses, and best ignored.

The exception arises when there happens to be general agreement among them, which gives rise to the "standard forecast" situation. Here the strategy is fairly obvious once it is pointed out. I will give an analogy.

Before the war I once crossed the Atlantic on a Cunard liner in which a horse-race game was played in the evening. The horses were numbered from one to seven. Each horse was moved along a green baise "track" according to a throw of the dice when its turn came. Those who backed the winner divided the pot, minus a cut for the old sailors' fund or whatever.

Before each race the participants went to one of seven positions at a long table to buy tickets. Watching all this I noticed that some numbers were more popular than others. Three was usually the favorite, and the winner of the previous race was generally avoided.

After a while I realized that if you waited long enough you could improve your odds by simply going to the position with the shortest line. All the horses were equally likely to win, but the shortest line meant the biggest reward if that horse happened to be the winner. The longer the line, on the contrary, the worse the odds for the gambler.*

In reality the long-term economic future is not knowable because so much depends on politics and other imponderables. The old term "political economy" had much to recommend it. So the one thing you can say about the standard forecast is that you aren't getting good odds if you bet on it.

Now let us consider the main sources of Wall Street opinion and their characteristics.

Unlike a good dictionary, Wall Street advice almost never seeks to be authoritative. Rather, it is like the opinions

---

*This is even truer of economists than of the shipboard horse-race game for the reason that the economists act *en masse*. Like five Eskimos in one bed, when they turn, they all turn together.

of busy politicians: based on limited knowledge and intended to serve the speaker's purposes.

Another comparison would be with the creatures of the forest. Each sings its own song. The stately evergreen Ponderosa Trust Company intones: "Observe how grand I am, how fundamentally stable. I do not fidget back and forth in the wind or frivolously shed my leaves periodically. Let us all raise our voices in 'O Tannenbaum.'"

"Pompous ass," sniffles the low-multiple mole. "I'm warm and dry and snug down here, while you have icicles in your beard!"

"A second-rate point of view," quacks the brokerage-house duck. "Only my setup really makes sense. I enjoy the summer here, and then I buzz off to my place down south when it turns cold. I don't see how you stand it."

The special-situations fox smiles, winkles off another chicken, and says little.

Moral: Any adviser tends to favor the strategy implicit in his situation, and the services he can provide.

## Trust Companies

Thus the giant trust company, no more able to go indoors in a storm than the Rock of Gibraltar, cannot in practice do anything except play "Nearer My God to Thee" when disaster strikes. How does $10 billion scurry down a hole for safety? There is no way. Large trust companies are therefore perforce long-term investors in major companies: nothing exotic or unpredictable—set the course and stick to it.

They do not necessarily *talk* that way, however. Their ads emphasize what the public thinks it wants. In boom times, investors want to dance, and the Rock of Gibraltar bedecks itself with lights . . . dresses ship, so to speak. The ads begin to show idealized customers who turn out to be ocean yacht racers or debonair tennis players who fly their own jets to Acapulco. The ad introduces them as "The Performance People" and explains that "They Want the Bank That Performs." Or the trust company announces that it, and no other, "Works Harder to Make Your Money Grow," or whatever.

In fact, of course, they are all about the same, and once they buy a stock it is usually many years before they sell it. If one bank finds a wizard to set investment policy, the next bank can for the price of a good salary hire its own wizard. A rash of competitive wizard hiring some years ago brought in a troop of clean-cut younger wizards, still in their thirties, as top investment officers of some of the largest New York institutions. They then justified the confidence of their directors by all buying the same "favorite fifty" stocks, which went up and up and up. The accounts looked wonderful. Those stocks became way overpriced compared to the rest of the market, but nobody could sell or they would collapse. What to do? Before the answer was found, they collapsed.

I favor immobilism in trust companies. They are so big they *are* the market, and they should act their size, just as it would be unseemly for Madison Avenue buses to tear up and down like chariot racers. Furthermore, trust company officers are not all Bernard Baruchs, not by any means. To the extent they did actively trade their accounts they would almost certainly lose money, run up huge brokerage commissions, and incur unnecessary capital gains taxes.

# Stockbrokers

The broker, on the other hand, is in the opposite situation. Movement is his breath of life. Like the shark, he will drown if he lies still. He is therefore little disposed to seek out the "one-decision" stock that so pleases the trust officer. In general, mutual funds run by stockbrokers have twice the turnover of portfolios run by institutions with no stock exchange affiliation.

Also, the advice one receives from the stockbroker will

usually relate to "value." General Metropolitan is overvalued and is therefore a good switch into National Cosmopolitan, which seems cheap. The fact that neither company is of long-term interest is not emphasized. There is obviously an almost infinite opportunity for action (that is, movement) in this approach.

# The Constraints of Size

If a giant trust company—or indeed investment adviser or broker—is by its nature increasingly condemned to immobility, how large can a firm be and still move its accounts from a fully invested position to one with significant cash reserves?

My guess is that it stops being likely after the total amount the firm manages passes about $700 million. I cannot demonstrate that statistically, however. (Mutual funds never do it in practice. Brokers almost never: While the cash is sitting there burning a hole in the customer's pocket, another broker calls up with a hot idea and gets the business.)

The next question, of course, is: Does it really make money for the client to move from stocks to cash and back to stocks? Usually, no. By the nature of markets, they will usually buy high and sell low. Only a very few firms regularly do it successfully.

# Subscription Services

Another class of informant whose nature and interests should be understood is the market letter writer, or subscription service. Here we come to a puzzling subject, which I will first sum up briefly and then try to explain:

- Some (a very few) subscription services are usually right, or at least serious. The best thing they can do for their customers is urge them to sell near a top, when the mass of investors are buying, and urge them to buy near a bottom, when the mass of investors are selling.

- Most subscription services have to live (like stockbrokers) by reinforcing their customers' impulses. In panics, they print ads showing how for months they have been bearish and are tonight predicting the end of the world. (Twenty-five dollars for a three-month trial.) In booms, they describe their recent winners and urge the timid to jump in.

There is a simple Darwinian reason for most phenomena of behavior. If the service isn't popular, the subscriptions won't be renewed and the publisher will go out of business. He won't be there anymore, and his place will be taken by someone who *is* popular.

At any given moment a large number of subscriptions are up for renewal. If the readers are not happy with what is served up to them, they will vote with their feet. That means that the services, like short-term politicians, have an incentive to echo and reinforce their listeners' enthusiasms and despairs.

I once knew a market letter writer named Paul Dysart in Louisville, Kentucky, who was for years almost always right on the major market turns. It was uncanny. As I gained respect for his work, I started to talk to him, which I often do in such cases. He told me that he usually lost 40 percent of his expected renewals each time he anticipated a major change of market direction. His readers were so disturbed and annoyed by his heretical ideas that they preferred to shut him off.

Incidentally, knowing this fact, I still on two occasions over the years did the same thing myself. "The old boy really has gone dotty," I'd say, and let the subscription lapse. Then, once again, he'd turn out to be right, and six months later I'd come crawling back into the fold. (For some useful services, see Appendix IV, p. 250.)

Here are some further curiosities.

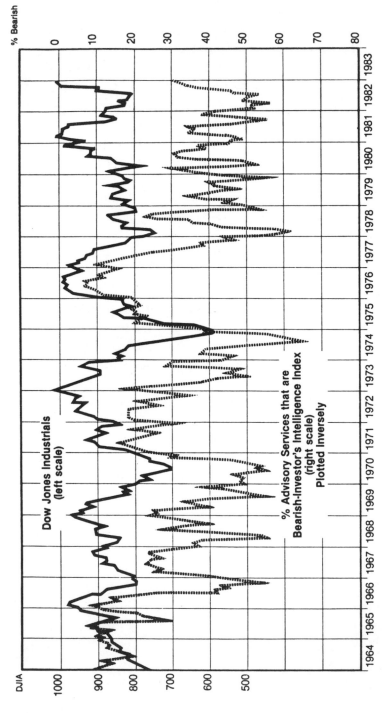

Figure 8

SENTIMENT INDEX OF THE LEADING
INVESTMENT SERVICES

74

First, there are now franchise organizations that will set anybody up in the market letter business. If you have the cash and the dream, they will provide a fetching title, find you some promising mailing lists, a printer, and a fulfillment service, and hire you a fellow to write snappy paragraphs.

Second, I have charted the consensus of advisory services and found with interest that they coincide perfectly with the least-informed segment of the investing population: the odd-lot short sellers. It turns out that if 60 percent of the subscription services are bullish, a significant market decline is imminent, and that if only 15 percent are bullish (that is, if 85 percent are pessimistic), a major up-move is about to occur. (See Figure 8.) That is the very nature of markets. If all the kids get on the south end of the seesaw because it's supposed to go up, it can't possibly go up. When "everybody" is desperate, selling dries up and the market is likely to rise from that point.

Finally, a few subscription services are *always* bearish. They appeal strongly to older investors and develop a faithful flock of good Calvinists who enjoy hearing that the wicked world is destined to perdition. It is like old Grandpapa at the end of "Peter and the Wolf." The procession, led by a joyous Peter, emerges from the forest with the wolf strung on a pole. Grandpapa brings up the rear. "This is all very well," he grumbles, "but what if Peter had *not* killed the wolf? What then?"

Look at it this way: A burglar must among other things be a man that dogs don't bark at. A professional oracle, to be a financial success, has to be *plausible*. Most of the time, a false prophet will take the trouble to be more appealing, and thus more plausible, than a real prophet. Real prophets do well to escape with a whole skin (witness Cassandra and Laocoön). So the cynical prophets will be in the vast majority. In fact they are experts not in truth but in competing, like the cuckoo, which is born with a special muscle in its back for heaving its foster brothers and sisters out of the nest.

Even the real prophet has a very hard job. He must serve

up a lot of stuffing with the turkey. He really has something to say about once or twice a year. (Ideally it would be two messages—a "buy" and a "sell"—in every market cycle, or about two messages every four years.) However, he needs to collect about $150 a year from each reader, and a reader will not pay $150 for one or two letters a year, so the market service has to appear weekly, fortnightly, or at least monthly. That means that most of the content has to be, and alas visibly is, stuffing: plausible chaff that just confuses and distracts the subscriber. As a result the ordinary subscriber can only rarely distinguish between the few valuable and the far more numerous merely popular market letters.

Then you have the hot advisers, who become news themselves. Since their tips knock the market off balance, if you act on the news you'll get a bad price and show a quick loss as the market recovers. These hot operators always lose their touch in time.

I hope that the reader will have gotten from all this the feeling I am trying to convey about the immense flow of bulletins and exciting phone calls, of stories, opinions, forecasts, figures, computer printouts, and reports that Wall Street pours out every day of the year. Is it all true? No. Is it all false? No. It is, so to speak, the murmuring of the forest, the sounds each creature makes as it pursues its function in the larger design.

# Investment Nonmanagement

In addition to his own money, the reader may be concerned with the management of his pension fund or the endowment of a school or other institution he is involved with. Such portfolios are often run by outside organizations specializing in that work. These organizations have their own life cycles, though, just like other companies, so in the rest of this section I will describe some of their problems so the reader can be on the lookout. One of these problems is an aversion to hard, often painful, decisions—the kind of decisions that make money.

A committee—and the reader may well have been part of one—in search of exceptional management for a portfolio usually prepares a checklist of desirable criteria to help it winnow out the possibilities. Then, like the Magi, or like Tibetan priests seeking the latest incarnation of the Dalai Lama, it journeys from place to place with patience and humility, seeking a sign. The pilgrimage is often interesting and instructive. It is helpful to jot down what the putative Lama says and then see how the utterances look a year or so later. That, of course, would be a bit slow for such a committee, unless it is maintaining an inventory of possible lamas.

One criterion that usually turns up in these checklists is "depth of organization." As the committee of Magi files into the offices of Abracadabra & Company, one of them draws their contact aside and explains: "We've heard very fine things about Dr. Abracadabra, and we understand that your work for the Euthanasia Foundation, of which our Mrs. Bunyan is also a trustee, is excellent, but we were wondering, while we were here, if we could meet, or preferably interview, a few of the other principals? One or two key people? After all, we are looking for a long-term relationship, and supposing someday something should *happen* to the doctor?"

This reasonable request has, not surprisingly, been foreseen, and in addition to encountering the great man the committee meets several mature, pleasant, balanced, well-connected, and fully informed colleagues, whose manifest sincerity and professionalism largely offset the puzzled feeling that their exposure to the doctor himself leaves them with.

But portfolio management is a competitive game, not a common effort like firefighting or chamber music, where a gain for one is a gain for all. Champions at intellectual games tend to be unusual people, to say the least. Is Bobby Fischer a regular fellow?

Really good portfolio men, in my observation, usually have a mental kink, perhaps because the essence of the game is to oppose the crowd. Horace's *Odi profanum vulgus et arceo*—"I dislike and avoid the herd"—could well be the motto of a Bernard Baruch (who after a while got rid of all his clients so he could think more independently), a Jesse Livermore, or any other great speculator.

A bit of personality theory may help explain why that almost has to be true. One of the variables of human character is what some writers call the internalizer-externalizer or ideational-perceptual contrast. (They are not too far from Freud's introvert and extravert, but these terms have been so deformed through vulgarization as to be almost unusable.) Which type you are can be established very early in life. The internalizer likes to think, analyze, organize concepts. His satisfactions are those of a real philosopher: within himself. The externalizer needs to interact with people and to operate in the outside world. For him, often, action *is* truth. He is constantly sensing the feelings of those around him and making adjustments accordingly. He is sympathetic; people like him. An externalizer is often better at math than an internalizer, but if a tester tries to see who can remember a string of figures better, the internalizer is likely to come out way ahead, because he is less conscious of the tester.

Obviously the internalizer is the one who is more likely to outthink the crowd and buy tomorrow's concepts at a bargain price today. The externalizer takes pains not to offend people, and considers it bad manners to have unusual ideas. For the internalizer it is as obvious that original, true ideas are the point of life as that the top of the mountain is where you want to climb to . . . alone, if necessary.

Clearly it takes one of these original spirits to develop exceptional stock ideas, which are the useful ones, and clearly he will not win many popularity contests.

Furthermore, when because of the evolution of the

group he is surrounded and eventually smothered by externalizers (who in a practical situation tend to rise to the top), the excellence of his firm's ideas is likely to be weakened.

Stock-picking is really not that overwhelming a subject. A superior man, not a committee, is needed to set the policy, and assuming he has access to good information, which can certainly be arranged, one man can set the "buy list" for even the largest firm. *The whole thing will stand or fall on whether once or twice a year or so he can spot a potential Schlumberger, and then avoid being pressured into selling it.* If a Churchill can preside over a nation—indeed, an empire—at war, cannot one man pick a number of stocks and hold them? Neither Napoleon nor Wellington asked for advice or held "councils of war." They would have regarded a general who required such councils as incompetent. Similarly, no first-rate investor wants to filter his ideas through a committee.

One solution is to find the great stock picker, the Bobby Fischer, and put him off by himself in an isolated box on the organizational chart: no administration, no contact with clients, nothing to distract him from his specialty.

Returning to our patient committee, toiling through the countryside looking for a savior, it should recognize that with a few exceptions any professional has a life cycle, like an artist. In his prime a first-class representative of either category can handle the largest transactions, whether a $2 billion portfolio or the Sistine Ceiling. The question, therefore, should be, "Are you in fact Michelangelo?" and not, "May we interview the rest of your management team?" When Michelangelo falls off his scaffold, never presume that his colleagues can continue the work. Start looking all over again.

The committee's natural desire is to find a respectable solution that will last for many years. If that is its real wish, it should go straight to a large committee-run investment counsel firm or trust company and accept the probability of mediocre results. That is, in fact, the most prudent solution. But if it wants something outstanding, then it should expect to find an "original" in charge, and it should watch things carefully, and start to move out by degrees if hubris or institutional sclerosis sets in. Parkinson's Second Law operates infallibly in the investment business, I believe: "Growth means complexity, and complexity, decay." If the committee spots a real go-getter and decides to take a chance, it won't be too long before another committee finds the same go-getter, and then another and another. Pretty soon the go-getter, now running over a billion dollars, either attempts risky stunts, trying to maintain his performance superiority (including delegating authority over parts of the portfolio to hyperaggressive junior go-getters), or else accepts the fact of middle age, and gets tangled up with research departments, strategy committees, and so on. The new institutional *ethos* settles for sound mediocrity and steady profitability.

Does this mean that all outstanding smaller firms must inevitably grow too fast, and thus either get tangled up or else puff out into mediocrity?

Not necessarily. Some small firms remain at a manageable size—where the able people can run things—and thus retain their distinction for decades.

It's extremely hard to institutionalize the superiority of any competitive organization, however; perhaps impossible. Either the brilliant successor is tempted to save ten years by breaking away and hanging up his own shingle, or else there isn't one, in which case the firm falls off after the original animator moves from the scene. Eventually a man takes over who is dedicated not to the ideal on which the organization grew great (e.g., service to the client) or even to the organization itself (the bottom line), but rather to his personal advancement, at the expense of the other two objectives. After a while smaller and keener organizations start carving slices out of the old one, which degenerates.

Generally, then, outstanding investment management, like many other things, is likely to come from a few individuals, and too much success, too much growth, can easily mean that their talent is diverted to corporate concerns and away from their basic skill.

As to larger institutions, although some remain exceptionally professional and "correct," eventually they tend to grow more and more alike. To use the jargon, they "regress to the mean."

# Performance Monitoring

A variation of the nonmanagement principle has blossomed into an industry all its own. It has a demure appeal that makes it irresistible to corporate treasurers.

The idea is that there are now so many performance-oriented money management companies that you cannot keep track of them. Each has printed brochures, including a statement of principles roughly equivalent to the Declaration of Independence, an impressive performance record (the manager with a bad record joins someone else), and a dignified, understated office.

Our well-intentioned corporate treasurer invites presentations by a dozen of these firms and selects a couple, including the trust department of his company's lead bank and an outfit recommended by his company's most cantankerous outside director. He now pauses, musing. How do you choose several fish out of all the fish in the sea?

Fortunately, his corporate training has programmed him to accept the pseudosolution that presently appears. How do corporations do things? How does a corporation find a new treasurer? How was he found himself? You hire a consultant.

Dozens of firms now exist that will help you select a team of outside managers and will then monitor their performance, stuffing you with computer-prepared, alpha-weighted, beta-sensitive, and gamma-selective higher math. (What you actually learn is how the market's been doing. Nobody's bright enough to operate effectively in more than one or two categories of investment, so rotating group strength in the market will make the cyclical-oriented manager look good as the cyclicals get a play, then the growth-oriented man when the growth stocks are picked up, and so on.)

This number-intensive approach to things is just what the treasurer has been trained for all his life. The idea's appeal for him is instantaneous.

He probably does not even finish his coffee, but hurries back to his office and has his secretary put in a call for the name he got at lunch.

At the very most, he calls a crony who is treasurer of another company.

"Mike? Bill. Listen, you know these people that you can hire that keep tabs on how the people are doing that you hire to run the employees' pension fund . . . you know what I mean? Yeah, that's it . . . performance monitoring. Do you know a good one? Who have you got? Is that so? Great! Okay, let me get it: ECO-TECHNICS. Thanks a lot. Hank had one, too—Robinson and Associates. Okay, sounds like just what I want. Great . . . thanks! See ya!"

The chances are he hires the first one who shows up, since they are indeed just what he wants, what everybody wants: someone to do his job.

More precisely, he has already gotten approval to have someone do his job of managing money, so now he gets someone to do his job of supervising that manager. He has found a respectable substitute for hard work and real thought: the nonmanager's dream.

But will it indeed purchase better performance? Most unlikely. The treasurer does not realize it, but he has just hired the commanding general of the pension fund on the basis of a tip over coffee and a telephone call to a pal. The performance-monitoring firm is in business too. They know a great deal more about what they are doing than he does, and like any adviser tend to favor the solutions that perpetuate their own tenure. They will thus always favor dividing the portfolio among several managers, will probably urge selection of managers that have varying investment philosophies, and work up a complicated mathematical formula for the whole thing. These are all operations that they can carry out much more efficiently than our friend the treasurer.

They have, in other words, successfully installed themselves as the high priests of a cult, like the high priests of any cult, including government, teaching, penology, law, medicine, and interior decorating.

"Naughty! Don't touch," the earnest layman is told if he tries to do anything for himself. The introduction of higher mathematics to embellish that modest commodity, a few young men "following" a number of companies and meshing them with a hypothetical "macroeconomic model," is mere theology, like the disputations of the Schoolmen over the *logos.* One can say of such machinery, as one should have been able to say of the *logos,* "That's not where it's at!"

Taking all performance-monitored outside-managed funds as a class, I am inclined to predict that their performances will be slightly inferior over the very long term to outside-managed funds not so monitored. They in turn should be slightly inferior to funds managed in-house. Among those managed in-house, those with high turnover should be inferior to those with low turnover, and those managed by a committee slightly inferior to those managed by an individual.*

In all the alternatives except the last, the difference is just the costs involved. Turnover does not improve things, and it costs money; outside management costs more money; performance monitoring costs still more money. Whatever anybody says, the corpus of the fund ultimately pays that money.

---

*Incidentally, it's time—and should be fun and not expensive—for someone, presumably working for a newsletter, to monitor the performance of the performance monitors.

# Social Responsibility

"Corporate responsibility" pressure groups can cost you money while doing more harm than good to society. Often a group of enthusiasts start clamoring for a voice in a college or church endowment's investment committee so that they can make moral judgments on the companies selected.

Thus, Ford does business in South Africa (where admittedly, it pays exceptionally high wages); Kodak hires few blacks (although, admittedly, its training programs for blacks are better than anybody else's); U.S. Steel charges too much for steel (although, admittedly, it only makes 2 percent on capital); ATT has women as operators and men climbing the poles instead of vice versa; Control Data sells to the Defense Department (only partially excused by its deals with the Kremlin); General Motors makes cars that run over people (although, admittedly, they rarely start themselves and chase pedestrians).

Nothing is more satisfying than to take a lordly tone about someone else's life by applying your, not his, criteria. The Victorian lady with ten servants knew herself to be superior, because physically cleaner, than the chimney sweep: the poet finds the admiral lacking in esthetic sensibility; Henry James finds Mr. Morgan a trifle commercial. And students, needing like all of us to be important, bite the hand that feeds them by demanding that the fiduciary running the endowment should be unfaithful to his trust. They want to impose restrictions on his work based on moral theories that even if valid are outside his responsibilities. The doctor cannot refuse to treat a patient on political grounds, nor can a lawyer fail to give his client his day in court because of his religion. The fiduciary has a clear obligation to the capital he manages. Legislation is the remedy if Ford really should get out of South Africa, not making the endowment sell the stock. Such private pressures deprive their victims, both the corporation and the endowment manager, of due process.

Both are entitled to rely on settled doctrines of law or on national policy solemnly promulgated.

# The Computer Trap

Once every three months or so I pass a pleasant afternoon with a bright man who got an engineering degree and then became intrigued by the application of the computer to predicting the market. (Not the same bright man . . . different ones each time.)

He has usually spent about three years building his data base and playing around with different regression series, and maybe eighteen months simulating various market strategies: What happens if you buy low price-earnings stocks that have just skipped a dividend? Or stocks whose earnings growth is accelerating?

You can always retroactively produce an investment decision-making strategy that paid off splendidly up until yesterday. The necessary computer time will cost you somewhere between several tens of thousands of dollars and several million.

I doubt, however, if the computer system can provide a consistent winning strategy for the future, and the reader should be wary of such claims.

Certainly none of the gentlemen I spend these afternoons with has ever called me two years later to show me how well he did. When I run into them later they explain how they are just putting the finishing touches on a new and better method.

Why is this? Is it somehow in the nature of things?

I think it's another example of the difference between theory and practice, like the disappointing results of so many promising educational or economic notions.

It seems to me that my engineering-oriented friends neglect the competitive or market characteristics of the problem. In determining an objective truth, such as the angle to point a rocket to hit Venus some months later, a computer is indispensable. But one recognizes instinctively that the computer can't write a great novel, unless the programmer happens to be called Leo Tolstoi.

When it comes to the stock market we're in a human and competitive environment, more like art than astrophysics. Flair and intuition become central.

Furthermore, I (and every other professional investor) am also a computer. I may well read a hundred pages a night trying to stay ahead of the crowd, and then consult my psyche to guess what the pack will do when it comes pounding along in subsequent days or months. By the following morning I (and my peers, who have also not been idle overnight and who manage tens of billions of dollars) have made our dispositions.

My friend with his computer program has not sat up overnight factoring hundreds of pages of new data into the system and checking its impact on a simulated cybernetic psyche. Differently put, his model is always too simple. It is not sensitive to the endlessly changing currents of mass emotion.

The reason all this is a trap, as distinct from merely being inadequate, is the same reason astrology or alchemy is a trap. It doesn't work, but more important, it takes you away from what does work.

It's like a mad student who instead of actually studying for an exam spent the time trying to work out a formula to anticipate the order in which the right answers to the multiple-choice questions occurred.

Similarly, my engineering friend, in the thousands of hours he spends manipulating one or another mathematical simplification, could put on his hat, set forth into the great world, and discover something true and useful that might aid him in his profession.

Is that experimental drug really working out? Is the new Japanese copier as reliable as they claim?

A good investor mustn't be afraid to roll up his sleeves and dig into the primary matter. A reporter has to get out and unearth the facts, to quiz people who have information. So does a detective. An investor is a little of both. There is no easy way. The computer is a godsend in holding and manipulating huge amounts of data, but the day the computer will relieve the analyst of the need for shoe leather, plant inspections, character assessment, industry knowledge, and a lifetime's experience and flair will be the day the birds become willing to fly up the barrel of your gun.

There was once a "quant"—as the computer-bug type of nonanalyst is called—who day after day, year after year, sat at his console in a pleasant trance tapping out questions.

100 LOWEST P/E STOCKS WITH FIVE-YEAR EARNINGS PER SHARE GROWTH OVER 18 PERCENT, SALES OVER $200,000,000, DEBT LESS THAN 20 PERCENT OF BOOK VALUE

Lists would come pouring out, displayed in rapid strips on a screen. Our quant, who was always neatly dressed and slightly pale, since he had little cause to go out of doors, enjoyed this game, but was occasionally rendered uneasy by the thought that several thousand other quants were at all times doing exactly the same thing.

Finally, after many years, he one day questioned the computer as follows:

WHAT IS BEST DEAL OTHER PEOPLE HAVEN'T ALREADY FIGURED OUT HOW TO DEVELOP USING THIS PROCEDURE?

The machine replied:

AHA

The quant, puzzled, typed in:

REPEAT

Again the machine replied:

AHA

Troubled, the quant then typed:

EXPLAIN

The computer hesitated. Then it replied:

YOU ARE CURED.

DISCONTINUE TREATMENT.

RETURN THIS EQUIPMENT TO LEASING COMPANY.

YOU WILL BE BILLED ON YOUR CREDIT CARD.

GOOD LUCK IN REAL WORLD.


# Technical Analysis

The study of value is the basis of stock investment. There are no shortcuts. The technician, however, tries to predict stock movement through the shapes on a stock's chart, without reference to value.

It is not knowable from what a stock did last month or last year how it will do next month or next year. Brokers' pronouncements on this subject are tea-leaf reading, fakery. Imagine a bookstore in which the salesman didn't know what was between the covers, and instead offered guesses on next year's prices for the merchandise! What a broker can and should do is establish facts and values, so the customer can decide if he wants to buy what has been described. This involves legwork, study, interviews with a company and its competition, consultation with industry experts, and the like, the whole then to be presented in a form which permits an investment valuation, but also where errors will stand out.

How much easier and what tripe to say that a stock at 50 "seems to be poised for a breakthrough to the 54–56 area, although a stop-loss order should be placed at 47." One reader-adviser can issue pronouncements on hundreds of stocks on this basis, instead of clearly revealing his competence (or incompetence) on one.

I have a naughty bet that I offer any "technician" I meet and that none has accepted. It goes like this. He is asking his readers to accept his word for it that if they do what he says they will make money; that is, if he says Polaroid is "technically" a buy, and they buy a hundred shares, then they will come out ahead reasonably soon, after round-trip commissions and taxes. That is no joke. If Polaroid costs 50, they are supposed to put $5,000 at risk, equal to the price of a good used car, on the strength of the wizard's readings of the wiggly lines.

Why not let him take a chance too?

So my bet goes like this: Somebody digs out some charts done on a daily basis from a few years back. He removes any identification and cuts each chart in the middle. He gives the first half to the technician.

All that worthy has to do is tell me, on a $100 bet, whether a stock was higher or lower at any specified point in the second period than at the end of the first. Since he claims the ability to prophesy, and is willing to have the rest of us take a substantial risk on his say-so—paying brokerage and tax whether we win or lose—he should be confident enough of his powers to give modest odds. Three to two seems fair enough.

So far, as I say, no "technician" has ever accepted the offer.

Personally, I do not think the S.E.C. should allow any registered investment adviser to put out advice on stocks based on technical analysis. I consider it unprofessional.

Brokerage firms that I know have spent millions of dollars (literally) on computer programs for technical stock analysis and then quietly scuttled them.

If one has been around for some years, one remembers any number of famous "technicians" who eventually became partly or utterly discredited. In the 1970s the big names were

James Dines and Howard Ruff, who made too many boners. By the early 1980s a new swami had arisen, Joe Granville, whose words alone could make the market plunge—a self-fulfilling prophecy. Granville announced that he never again expected to make a wrong market call. Then came the great bottom in the summer of 1982. Granville not only had his followers out of stocks, but *short*, as the Dow staged one of the greatest rises in its history. Misery!

Next came William Finnegan Associates, of Malibu, California, which ran ads in business magazines saying, "If you happen to know what the Dow Jones Average will be eighty trading days from now, you could make quite an impression on your friends. Not to mention your banker. Well, you can know."

The reader was invited to buy a module, to be plugged into a Hewlett-Packard MP-41 Calculator. The module contained a program that, after you punch in some market information, would tell you what the market would do in the next eighty days.

Beginning on August 13, 1982, the start of the spectacular 1982 rise, each and every daily forecast for the following eighty trading days was for a decline, starting with the first one, which called for a drop of 7.5 percent, instead of the advance from 767 to well over 1,000 that actually occurred.

# III.

# Investment Strategy and Tactics

# Why Buy Stocks?

In seeking a home for one's excess savings, one basically has two pairs of alternatives: property—income-producing or nonincome-producing; or marketable securities—equities or fixed-income.

Foreigners feel at home with property and are often suspicious of securities, since foreign law generally gives an investor poor protection. Thus, in England, Italy, Greece, and Austria, respectively, such income property as a farm, an apartment building, a merchant ship, or a forest, is considered as normal a holding as stocks or bonds. Nonincome-producing property, also called "hard assets," includes gold and other precious metals, gems, art, and "collectibles." These are portable and easier to keep confidential than income property, and are discussed later in Part III, in the chapters called "Speculating in Art" and "Commodity Speculation." Over the long term they tend to keep up with inflation. Their drawback is that they are not inherently building value the way a good business is: If you live by selling pieces from a collection, you will run out of money sooner or later unless you are unusually lucky.

A grave disadvantage of most property, except precious metals, is that it is cumbersome to buy and sell. If times are hard and you need to raise money by selling your farm or your collection of photographs you may find that even after waiting six months for a buyer you only get half what you expected. Indeed, if you buy a work of art or a piece of jewelry in one store, cross the street, and offer it for sale in another, you will do well to get half what you just paid for it. Also, the management of income-producing property— farms, rental buildings, or a ship—makes heavy demands on the owner. Finally, there are times—and today is one of them—when many business assets sell in the market for substantially less than an informed buyer would pay for them. Indeed, in the summer of 1982 the whole stock market was selling for about half its replacement value. When foreign clients who are familiar with timber ask me if it is an attractive investment in America, I reply that it is most satisfactory; but you can get it at half price or even less by purchasing shares of Weyerhaeuser or another well-managed timber company. Furthermore, if you need to sell some again, you can do so in minutes, not months, and probably without affecting the price noticeably. And you don't have to get involved in constant business decisions or, indeed, litigation. So as a practical matter one is better off buying the stock of Weyerhaeuser than some particular tract of forest. At other times, of course, the market will price assets at more than an informed private buyer would pay for them, and in that case one might consider switching from the stock to the underlying asset.

The advantages of owning assets in the form of a listed security are multifold, and for most readers of this book overwhelming. First, you can buy and sell quickly and anonymously. Second, if you are abused by management you can obtain redress far more readily than from a private company. The S.E.C. will fight many of your battles for you. Third, if you know what you are doing, you can take advantage of the public's alternating optimism and despair to buy or sell a little at favorable prices, improving your average cost. Fourth, you can hire advisers and custodians to look after your property for you at a very modest cost and with greater assurance than if you had to find managers for specific businesses or pieces of property. In sum, financial assets, also called portfolio securities, are passive investments. They make few enough demands on you so that you can contemplate them almost on a philosophic level, rather than getting embroiled in detailed business concerns.

Financial assets—securities—divide in turn into two categories: equities—stocks—which represent the ownership of shares in businesses; and fixed-income securities, notably bonds and other evidences of secured and unsecured indebtedness.

At one time only bonds were considered prudent investments. Companies could lose money and go bankrupt, but in the ensuing liquidation the bondholder was likely to come out all right. Then came inflation and high income taxes, which together have had a murderous effect on bonds. Also, there have arisen huge diversified enterprises that continually migrate toward areas of economic growth and opportunity. It is quite hard for most people to say what 3M, General Electric, or Procter & Gamble "make." They make thousands of products, in all sorts of fields; essentially, they make money. Such a company is unlikely to get left on a sandbar as the economic tide ebbs out of some particular industry. So the recent experience of investors has been that in practice one is safer as the shareholder of such an enterprise, whose steady progress seems to continue decade after decade, than one is as a bondholder, since inflation makes bonds less and less valuable in real terms, even without considering the high taxes on bond interest. (The buildup in the value of a good company is not taxed until you sell, and then at a low rate.) Even more rewarding to the investor than large, diversified growth companies—but also harder to get right—is the occasional company that gets a lock on some specialized high-growth area. Here one receives a splendid return on one's investment—if one does not pay too much for it—during the dynamic phase of the enterprise. As it matures, however, one has to be careful not to overstay the situation. Some companies of this sort develop into large, well-managed, steady growth companies of the 3M type; others move to excessive premiums in the market because they become household words, and thus become dull investments even though they are successful enterprises; still others become large, heavy, and capital-intensive. Only a few can keep alive decade after decade the high return on invested capital, the dedication to innovation and growth, and the management leanness that made them attractive in the first place.

So all in all, I conclude that in an inflationary era one should put most of one's savings in marketable shares of outstanding businesses, with some kept in other assets, as discussed later on. How one goes about becoming a shareholder of an outstanding business is our next subject.

# Buying Strategy

The reader should by now have a good feeling for the regular and violent emotional currents that sweep the market up and down, this way and that. If he can develop an instinct for these cycles, and no more think of buying a widely touted stock during a bull market blowoff than of going clamming at high tide, then he is half saved. He will not lose money the way most investors lose money, and, indeed, if he can nerve himself up to buy when everybody is desperate, then he will make money the way the professionals make money.

Next comes the other half of the problem: *What* should he buy when the market is cheap because everybody is desperate? The first answer is that anything will do; the rising tide lifts all the ships. But one can do better than that. You should either try to buy what is *particularly* cheap, with the thought of selling again when it gets expensive, or else pay a bit more for a share in a company that gives promise of growing and growing and growing, and which you can therefore, with luck, hold for many years.

For a variety of reasons, I think that trust companies and other institutions with portfolios managed by professionals should generally give more attention than they do to buying stocks that are simply cheap: those that are selling at low price-earnings multiples, are at a discount from liquidation value, that have high net current assets per share, and so forth.

Benjamin Graham's *The Intelligent Investor* shows how to recognize bargain issues, giving a number of simple tests. *Forbes* prints lists of what it calls these "loaded laggards," as do other magazines. If you wait for the panicky phase of a bear market and then buy a selection of these companies that are selling in the market for much less than they are worth *in toto* to a private buyer, then you won't go wrong.

When things get really bad, it may become possible to buy assets at half their hard liquidating value, or even half their cash in the bank, net of all charges, with the whole company free. In the trough of any four-year market cycle, many such opportunities appear. Many oil, forest products, and real estate property companies are down to fifty cents on the dollar as of the time I am writing, for instance. Buying that kind of bargain is a valid strategy, if you have knowledge and patience.

However, after many years of studying the achievements of successful private investors—and, indeed, of participating in the process—I can say that by far the largest number of individual investors who do really well follow the growth philosophy. Indeed, one rarely encounters a successful individual (as distinct from institutional) practitioner of the cheap stock philosophy. I don't know what it is that goes awry. Often a stock that looks cheap to a stockbroker has things wrong with it that the broker isn't penetrating enough to spot, so that it isn't really cheap at all. Often the buy cheap–sell dear approach results in overtrading, fatuous chipping and chopping, so that the portfolio is eaten up by commissions, which can be a much bigger drag on perform-ance than most people realize.

My suggested strategy for individual investors is to *wait for periods of market weakness*, and then (and only then) to buy *seasoned* stocks of *leading* companies with *high profit margins* in *rapidly growing* industries, and hold on to them. That may sound simple, but it isn't. Every part of the for-mula must be followed. However, it works very well indeed. This book will give you a good idea of how to go about it: first, how to recognize where you are in a market cycle, and then, how to identify a good company, either on your own or using an adviser.

# How Do I Find a Good Stock?

The individual investor, then, should get on the up escalator and stay there. That involves two operations, both of which this chapter discusses: collecting likely candidates, and test-ing them to be sure they are authentic. Very few readers of this book will be able to collect potentially interesting stocks on their own. The time and experience they can bring to the task will get them nowhere against the millions of dollars a year of outstanding talent deployed by their professional competitors. So the easy way is to get the ideas from the first-class competitors, test the ideas yourself, and wait for a washout to buy the stocks. Once you know a lot about a lim-ited range of stocks, you will find it possible to buy them when they are cheap, instead of being panicked into selling. In other words, knowledge is the key to controlling emotion;

but in a limited time one can only know a few things well. For the average investor, the thing worth knowing well is perfect medium-sized growth businesses that he will be happy owning for a long time.

Over the long term, a stock's market price and dividends will rise at about the rate that its earnings rise. (For a very fast-growing company, dividends are modest at first, because management has so many opportunities to reinvest earnings; then as the company matures, the dividends catch up with a rush.)

If the earnings do not rise by at least the amount of inflation, you are actually losing ground, destined to be squeezed by labor costs, competition, and the like. So stocks with long-term growth trends are essential. Whenever you are interested in a stock, the first thing to do is look at a chart of its earnings to see what the trend is. (There are some examples of this in Figures 9–9e.)

There is no special reason why most companies' earnings should rise. You may therefore often be better off in short-term bonds than in the mass of stocks.

It is easier for most people to pick a good no-load mutual fund than a good stock. The best funds tend to have consistently superior records. Get the annual *Forbes* issue showing the fund records (see Table 1), pick several consistently outstanding no-loads, send for the prospectuses, discuss them with informed friends, and buy three or four. Review the results once a year. If one fund does badly, sell it and buy a better one. Give preference to funds that are run by established investment counsel firms, not by companies that are only in the fund business, and particularly not by brokerage houses. The best funds tend to have low portfolio turnover.

It is often said that closed-end funds selling at a discount are attractive long-term investments. I agree, if one buys close to the maximum historical discount. However, the absence of competition (the money is locked in) and the lack of new money for which new opportunities must be sought

## Table 1. Forbes Fund List

| Name | Type | Market ratings UP | Market ratings DOWN | Annual return | Assets (millions) |
|---|---|---|---|---|---|
| **Diversified stock funds** | | | | | |
| AMCAP (4) | load | A | B | 14.3% | $394.0 |
| American General Comstock (2) | load | B | A | 15.4 | 153.4 |
| American General Pace (1) | load | A + | A | 17.0 | 129.7 |
| Charter (5) | load | A + | B | 18.0 | 44.7 |
| Fidelity Magellan (1) | load | A + | B | 19.0 | 146.8 |
| Janus (1) | no load | A | A | 18.4 | 44.9 |
| Mutual Shares (7) | no load | B | B | 18.6 | 130.0 |
| Nicholas (1) | no load | A | B | 15.4 | 56.1 |
| Petroleum & Resources (6) | closed end | A + | C | 15.2 | 183.0 |
| Pioneer II (1) | load | B | A | 18.5 | 485.1 |
| Putnam-Voyager (1) | load | A | C | 14.7 | 87.9 |
| St Paul Growth (1) | load | A | B | 15.0 | 36.7 |
| Sigma Venture Shares (1) | load | A + | C | 14.0 | 22.7 |
| Templeton Growth (9) | load | B | B | 17.3 | 508.2 |
| Twentieth Century Growth (1) | no load | A + | C | 21.5 | 261.9 |
| Twentieth Century Select (5) | no load | A + | B | 17.9 | 49.4 |
| Vance, Sanders Special (3) | load | A | C | 15.2 | 86.4 |
| **Funds for investing abroad** | | | | | |
| ASA Limited (4) | closed end | B | A | 17.6% | $301.9 |
| International Investors (3) | load | A | A | 19.0 | 203.3 |

Note: Number in parentheses is number of times on honor roll.

sometimes produce dull performances. Some good ones are Source Capital, General American Investors, and Niagara Share Corporation. Sometimes the manager of a closed-end fund thinks of his position as a sort of political plum, instead of a fiduciary office, and abuses creep in.

If you do buy individual stocks, you should give careful attention to each, so you have to keep your list small. The candidates should be long-term growth issues, which with luck can be held for decades, rather than stocks that are supposed to be undervalued right now, although not necessarily of perennial interest. In playing the "value" game you are competing with very able opponents, who in practice you probably can't beat. Holding Hewlett-Packard year after year means not competing with anybody.

Size is a problem. Except for the rare specialty company, a candidate for selection should be big enough (over $100 million in sales, say) so you can know a lot about it. It should also have a privileged position in the world, meaning that it has grown and should continue to grow unusually fast. It

## PATTERNS OF EARNING TRENDS

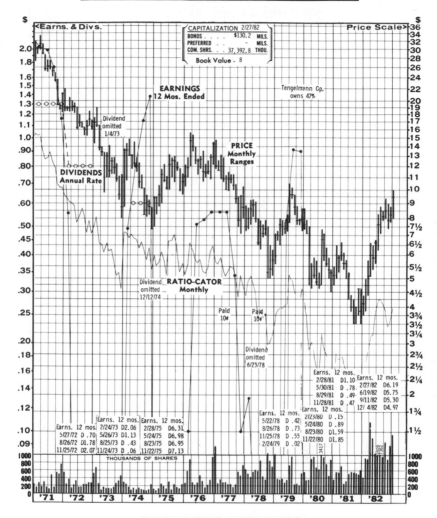

**DECLINING EARNINGS**
Great Atlantic & Pacific Tea Co., Inc. (GAP)

**Figure 9**

should not be so big that its growth is made unlikely by its size. Few companies with over $2 billion in sales can maintain an exceptional growth rate.

A broker can present a case for almost any stock's becoming a fast grower in the future. Almost none will actually make the grade. Insist on a record as well as a vision.

Where do we start looking? A highly effective approach is to get the prospectuses of some successful funds that follow the long-term growth approach (Rowe Price New Horizons or Putnam Investors) and see what they hold and what they are doing. You can, for instance, make a list of all their big holdings and recent purchases, and ask your broker to send you the small Standard & Poor's sheets on each. Sort them into industry groups (consumer, high technology, financial, and so on) and try to understand the thread of reasoning that runs through them. Quite often the managers write annual summaries of their thinking, including what they foresee for the next few years.

Several publications now tell you what the larger mutual funds and investment counsel firms are buying. A broker or banker can get them for you. Vickers Associates (see Appendix IV, p. 251) puts out the most useful of them.

This procedure gives you an invaluable head start. The organizations that run these funds have dozens of in-house researchers and vast experience of the field, and are the preferred customers of every top institutional broker. What you see in their portfolios is a distillation of the best wisdom in the securities business, and a priceless source of leads and ideas. If you confine your list of possible buys to stocks chosen from successful fund portfolios, you will save an extraordinary amount of time and lower your risk greatly.

It is, of course, useless to pay attention to the holdings or transactions of funds or advisers with inferior records.

So now you have a list of a few dozen purchase candidates. How do you test them for authenticity and suitability for your particular point of view?

There are two steps: theory and analysis.

First, each stock should have a strong long-term concept. Rising earnings derive from rising sales, which are usually found in industries with rapidly expanding markets, which in turn can usually be classified under such concepts as "oligopoly," "franchise," and "Gresham's Law company" (see pp. 113, 116, and 119).

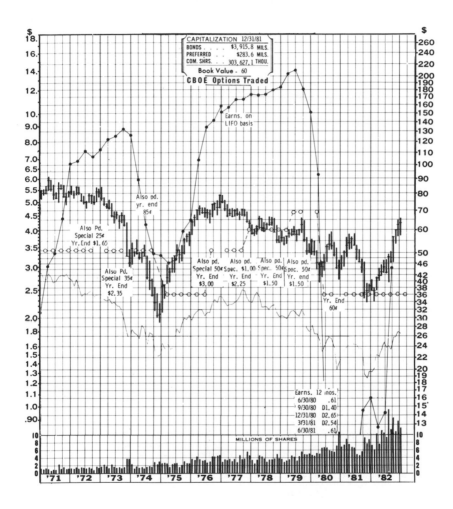

**CYCLICAL EARNINGS**
**General Motors Corp. (GM)**

**Figure 9a**

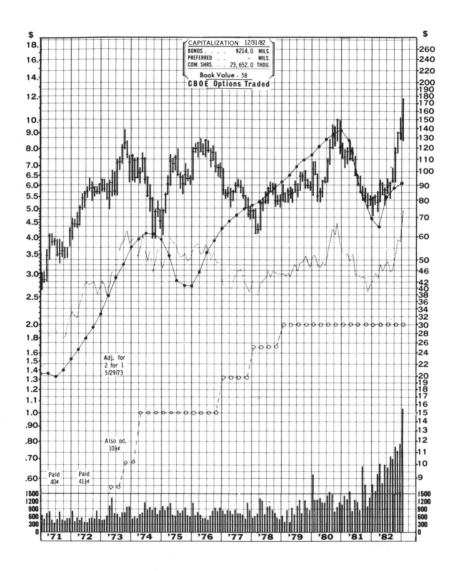

**CYCLICAL GROWTH**
Texas Instruments, Inc.

**Figure 9b**

To check the concept one should know a company's place in its industry (including growth of sales, earnings, and profit margins), both domestic and worldwide, and understand how it proposes to defend and expand its position. (By expand, I do not mean through diversification. You are safer with a portfolio of a number of companies that are each unbeatable at one particular thing than with a smaller number of companies that do all sorts of things but are outstanding in nothing.) The annual report usually gives management's long-range strategy.

I do not, incidentally, think it is always such a good idea for the ordinary investor to meet the management of companies he is interested in or even to go to annual meetings, particularly if he buys stocks chosen from serious fund portfolios, where he can be confident of the research. He is more likely to be brainwashed than to learn something not available through the published material.

On this subject people often cite the statement of Billy Rose that he wanted to know every director of any company he invested in. Fine—but it is also often mentioned that Billy Rose's largest investment was ATT, of which he was the largest stockholder. You would have to get up early in the morning to find a duller holding than ATT, although it has a highly prestigious board.

Consider also the case of "Brother" Parker, a distinguished Boston investment manager, who built up a large and respected fund. He habitually got very close to the companies the fund owned, sometimes going on the boards, and in one case even becoming chairman. That was fine in the early days, but as things got more competitive it inhibited flexibility. The performance sagged. The odd climax of a most respectable career was that his fund's shareholders voted him out as manager! An investor should be like a judge: objective and unattached. Otherwise he loses the greatest advantage of portfolio (as against direct) investment—freedom to act.

There is one exception. Sometimes there are really good

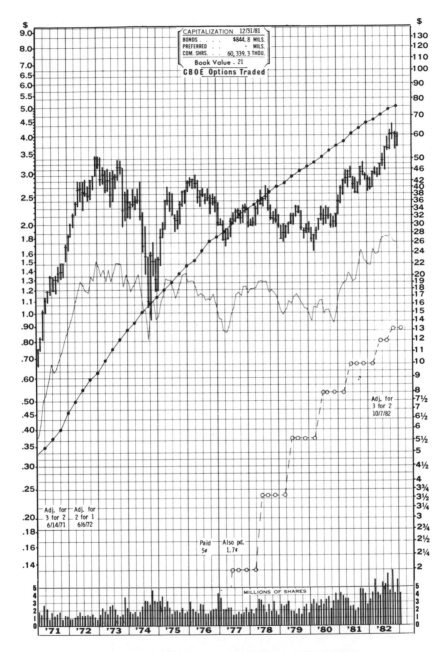

CAPITALIZATION 12/31/81
BONDS . . . .   $844.8 MILS.
PREFERRED . .      -  MILS.
COM. SHRS. . .  60,339.3 THOU.
Book Value - 21
CBOE Options Traded

Adj. for
3 for 2
10/7/82

Adj. for
3 for 2
6/14/71

Adj. for
2 for 1
6/6/72

Paid
5¢

Also pd.
1.7¢

MILLIONS OF SHARES

**RAPID GROWTH—MEDIUM QUALITY**
**McDonald's Corp. (MCD)**

**Figure 9c**

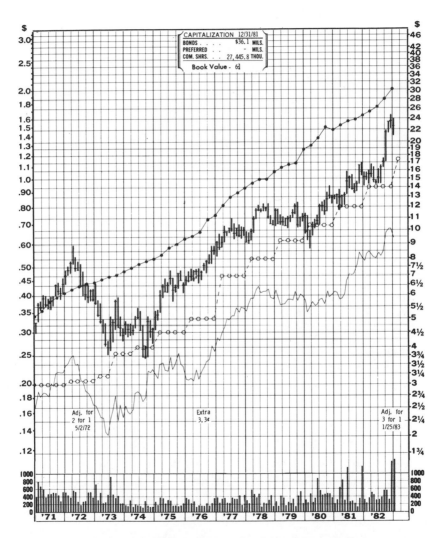

**STEADY GROWTH—MEDIUM QUALITY**
U.S. Tobacco Co. (UBO)

**Figure 9d**

local companies that are already understood in your area but not yet in Wall Street. Xerox made a lot of money for people in Rochester, and Odeco for people in New Orleans, for instance, before the rest of the country believed in them. Sometimes the local investor can know enough about the management and business of a regional company so that he gets a valid head start on Wall Street.

All right: You have worked up a list of interesting stocks, each sanctified by inclusion in outstanding fund portfolios and backed by a powerful concept. You have applied such touchstones as "oligopoly," "franchise," and "Gresham's Law company" to them, and they qualify. It is extremely helpful if there is an understandable "double play" aspect to the stock: if you are taking advantage of an error or oversight in crowd thinking.

The second step is to tabulate on a single large sheet the most significant figures on all your stocks of interest. By far the most important elements, in my opinion, are growth and profitability.

These figures can mostly be put together from the standard manuals, such as *Moody's* or *Value Line,* if you don't want to dig them out of the annual reports. *Business Week* runs many of the figures each quarter. Your bank or broker certainly has the necessary sources.

The percentage of sales devoted to research should be noted. Imagine what it is like to compete with a company like AMP or Lubrizol that dominates a whole field of industry and spends up to a dollar on research for every dollar it shows as profit! Or to be a small competitor of IBM, which spends $2 billion a year on research and development.

Under "growth" you can show the past five-year compound rate. I also like to show the "intrinsic" growth—the same figure minus inflation and earnings bought through new financing.

To indicate profitability, show the operating margin and the return on the invested equity capital.

I also like to make an adjustment to the apparent price-earnings ratio to reflect a company's excess or deficiency of

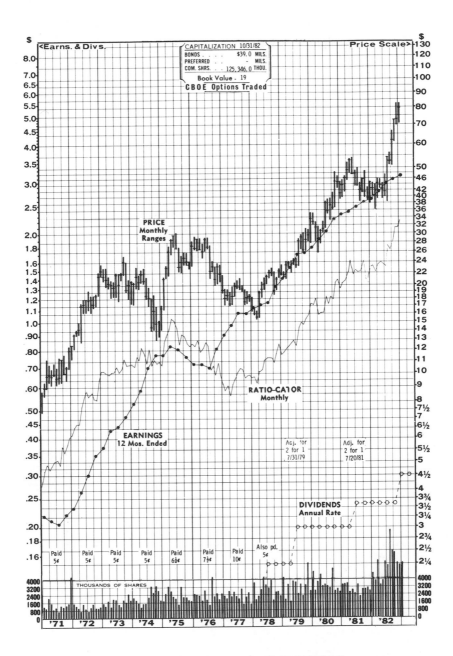

**RAPID GROWTH—TOP QUALITY**
Hewlett-Packard Co.

**Figure 9e**

## Table 2. Some Selected Growth Stocks

### August 1982

| | Stock Price | | | | # Shares Million | Mkt. Capitalization $ Million | Approx. Revenues $ Million | Mkt. Capitalization/ Revenues Ratio | % Labor Cost/ Revenues |
|---|---|---|---|---|---|---|---|---|---|
| | Jan. 1, 1982 | March 1, 1982 | June 1, 1982 | August 1, 1982 | | | | | |
| American Int'l Group | 64 | 66 | 61 | 57 | 57 | 3,250 | 3,000 | 1.1 | - |
| Bandag | 25 | 23 | 24 | 25 | 12 | 300 | 350 | .8 | 15 |
| Capital Cities | 73 | 72 | 73 | 69 | 13 | 1,000 | 650 | 1.5 | 25 |
| Cross (AT) | 27 | 26 | 27 | 23 | 8 | 190 | 140 | 1.4 | 12 |
| Electronic Data Systems | 24 | 21 | 27 | 26 | 27 | 700 | 550 | 1.3 | 70 |
| Fort Howard | 40 | 35 | 36 | 34 | 27 | 920 | 550 | 1.7 | 24 |
| Harland (John H) | 24 | 18 | 21 | 23 | 8 | 190 | 160 | 1.2 | 35 |
| Harte-Hanks | 32 | 25 | 24 | 24 | 10 | 350 | 400 | .9 | 44 |
| Hewlett-Packard | 39 | 42 | 41 | 39 | 124 | 4,800 | 4,000 | 1.2 | - |
| IBM | 57 | 62 | 60 | 63 | 594 | 37,000 | 32,000 | 1.2 | 35 |
| Nalco | 25 | 24 | 23 | 20 | 40 | 800 | 700 | 1.1 | 23 |
| Pioneer Hi-Bred | 25 | 24 | 23 | 21 | 32 | 670 | 550 | 1.2 | 16 |
| Premier Industrial | 21 | 21 | 22 | 18 | 21 | 370 | 350 | 1.1 | 25 |
| Raytheon | 37 | 32 | 34 | 34 | 84 | 2,900 | 6,400 | .5 | 32 |
| Schlumberger | 55 | 48 | 40 | 34 | 289 | 9,800 | 6,600 | 1.5 | 27 |
| US Tobacco | 47 | 46 | 44 | 45 | 9 | 400 | 300' | 1.3 | 15 |
| West Co. | 19 | 17 | 16 | 13 | 8 | 110 | 190 | .6 | 30 |

| % Research & Dev./Revenues | % Foreign Earnings | % Tax Rates | Earnings per Share Latest 12 Months | Price-Earnings Ratio Latest 12 Months | Price-Earnings Ratio Corrected[1] | Estimated Earnings per Share 1982[2] | Annual Dividend | Consecutive Years Sales Growth | Consecutive Years Earnings Growth | 10 Years EPS % Compound Growth | 5 Years EPS % Compound Growth | % Operating Margin[3] | % Return on Equity | Intrinsic Growth Rate[4] |
|---|---|---|---|---|---|---|---|---|---|---|---|---|---|---|
| 0 | 60 | 18 | 6.56 | 9 | 9 | 7.10 | .48 | 15 | 15 | 24 | 23 | 16 | 21 | 12 |
| - | 9 | 48 | 2.62 | 10 | 8 | 2.80 | .90 | 14 | 4 | 17 | 15 | 22 | 20 | 12 |
| 0 | 0 | 48 | 6.49 | 11 | 12 | 7.00 | .20 | 27 | 27 | 22 | 20 | 32 | 20 | 13 |
| 0 | 7 | 43 | 2.23 | 10 | 9 | 2.45 | 1.10 | 20 | 20 | 21 | 17 | 27 | 29 | 12 |
| - | 0 | 40 | 1.72 | 15 | 12 | 1.90 | .64 | 13 | 6 | 12 | 22 | 15 | 25 | 16 |
| 1 | 10 | 45 | 3.24 | 11 | 11 | 3.40 | 1.08 | 25 | 15 | 21 | 16 | 36 | 23 | 12 |
| 0 | 0 | 46 | 1.85 | 12 | 11 | 1.95 | .62 | 32 | 28 | 20 | 21 | 19 | 24 | 13 |
| 0 | 0 | 49 | 2.67 | 9 | 10 | 2.75 | .90 | 10 | 10 | 19 | 17 | 23 | 19 | 11 |
| 10 | 35 | 46 | 2.78 | 14 | 13 | 2.95 | .24 | 16 | 6 | 25 | 25 | 20 | 18 | 13 |
| 6 | 37 | 45 | 5.99 | 10 | 11 | 7.00 | 3.44 | 0 | 35 | 11 | 6 | 30 | 19 | 8 |
| 4 | 12 | 43 | 1.85 | 11 | 10 | 1.80 | 1.12 | 29 | 3 | 17 | 12 | 24 | 25 | 11 |
| 3 | 4 | 49 | 2.54 | 9 | 8 | 2.65 | .72 | 11 | 3 | 28 | 16 | 28 | 24 | 14 |
| 1 | 0 | 44 | 1.66 | 11 | 10 | 1.70 | .42 | 5 | 16 | 20 | 23 | 19 | 26 | 15 |
| 3 | 12 | 40 | 3.94 | 9 | 10 | 3.95 | 1.40 | 11 | 11 | 23 | 22 | 13 | 23 | 8 |
| 4 | 66 | 31 | 4.82 | 7 | 7 | 4.95 | .96 | 18 | 18 | 37 | 29 | 38 | 34 | 15 |
| 0 | 0 | 48 | 5.25 | 9 | 9 | 5.60 | 2.80 | 9 | 21 | 15 | 14 | 34 | 25 | 10 |
| 2 | 18 | 46 | 1.64 | 8 | 8 | 1.70 | .36 | 6 | 6 | 18 | 21 | 24 | 20 | 11 |

[1] The corrected price-earnings ratio is computed by adding long-term debt and deferred taxes to market price per share; deducting net quick assets; and dividing the results by latest 12-months' earnings. This adjusts the price-earnings ratio to reflect excess liquidity or significant debt.

[2] The earnings estimate for Pioneer Hi-Bred is for the fiscal year ending August 1983. All other earnings estimates are for the 12 months ending December 31, 1982.

[3] The operating margin is calculated before depreciation, amortization, interest, and taxes.

[4] The intrinsic growth rate is the product of two ratios: (a) the retained operating margin on sales, and (b) the turnover rate of gross operating assets (a measure of the capital required to produce a dollar of sales).

cash. A house under a large mortgage is worth less than one free and clear, which in turn is worth less than one with some extra land you could sell off. So conceptually I sell stock in an underfinanced company to pay off the indebtedness, or conceptually use excess cash to retire some stock. Conceptually changing the number of shares also changes the earnings per share and thus the price-earnings ratio. The resulting corrected ratios are more nearly comparable to each other: apples and apples, as it were.

To do all this requires quite an effort. The whole job from start to finish takes several days, once one has gathered the material. But what an education! You will be forced to measure your selections against each other as businesses. You will understand far better the real, hard facts about each: the essential qualities by which all business endeavors can be compared. And for such important matters it is time well spent. Would you begrudge two or three days spent in looking for a new house? Furthermore, you can keep such a rating system up to date fairly easily.

By the end of the process you will have a highly reasoned and carefully filtered buy list, whose logic you will understand completely and which will contain some of the prime names in all industry.

At this point you need a professional's analysis of each stock. Such problems as unfunded pension obligations,* accounting changes, deferred items that should have been written off, inadequate depreciation, and the like may constitute serious weaknesses. Your bank or broker should get hold of an authoritative study for you.

You should now try to list the possible negative arguments against each company: too big, too small, competition or regulation bound to increase, or whatever. Then, you should list the answers to these arguments, remembering that a plausible adverse story could be enough to collapse the stock during the next bear market. A market cycle is like a love affair: At the start, all doubts are resolved in favor of the object, and at the end, against.

*Which are sometimes larger than a company's market capitalization.

After all this, four or five stocks whose ratings are among the highest can be purchased in the knowledge that they are the result of a systematic, disciplined procedure. You will also understand the reasoning behind the selection well enough so that you won't worry too much about short-term swings. As conditions change, you can see if the original logic is still applicable.

You should not, however, change the portfolio more than once or twice a year.

Remember, there is no obligation to buy at all, so you can and should be extremely choosy.

Some of the ablest investors maintain that if a stock becomes overpriced, one should start selling it. In my opinion, however, it is rarely good business for most investors to sell out a successful selection solely because it has become too high-priced. In theory, you buy it back cheaper. In practice, you usually don't.

The Swiss often have their clients sell enough to get the original capital back after a stock has gone way up. That fortifies the investor's willingness to hold on to the rest through thick and thin.

# Investing in Oligopoly

As I've pointed out, for most investors the only way to make large profits in a portfolio is to buy prime growth stocks in periods of market weakness and hold them for long periods of time. It is difficult to catch turnarounds in cyclical issues, and even if successful, one pays capital gains taxes on each transaction. Over the long term, most conventional cyclical industries are slowly squeezed by the unions, government regulation, higher costs, and the Japanese. Only the exceptional growth companies can leave these constraints far behind.

A prime growth stock should have most, or if possible all, of the following characteristics:

- A dominant position in a growth industry, and a good reason why the position should continue: preferably what might be called an unfair advantage. Examples are IBM's huge sales force and research budget; Schlumberger's technical skill and head start in a super-growth area; or Gannett Newspapers' regional monopolies. The dominant company usually understands the industry best and profits most from opportunities.
- A long record of rising earnings, with sustained high-profit margins. These high margins, e.g., U.S. Tobacco or the pharmaceuticals, are a sure tipoff that you are in the presence of an oligopoly, a market with a limited number of sellers.
- Superb management, in sufficient depth, with a substantial ownership stake. Business management ability is fundamental; technical ability can be bought. Financial and marketing skill and integrity are essential.
- A commitment to innovation, and a research program sufficient to bring it about.
- The ability to pass on labor and other cost increases to the consumer. This follows from a dominant position in an industry.
- A strong financial position. (Growth stocks usually have little debt. A heavy debt load usually suggests low profitability.)
- Ready marketability of the stock, preferably on the New York Stock Exchange. It helps to have an attractive, understandable "concept"; for example, a stock whose name is that of an outstanding product, like Coca-Cola, Disney, or Sony.
- Relative immunity to "consumerism" and government regulation. The government's natural instinct is to hold down prices in order to buy votes, which can bankrupt the object of such regulation.

If one buys such a stock at an acceptable multiple of earnings (presumably ten to fifteen times, and if possible substantially lower than the company's own growth rate) and the growth in fact continues, then the multiple should be maintained or increased. The stock price should therefore rise over the long term at least as fast as the earnings do: with luck, 15 percent a year or more. One should not be prepared to pay extremely high multiples for even the finest stocks, because in all human situations there are changes and surprises.

There are probably less than two or three hundred companies in the country that satisfy these criteria, and there are far fewer that can actually be identified and about which one can get regular access to first-class information. The rewards of finding and keeping a Schlumberger are so enormous, however, that one should concentrate on this search. Even the largest investment firms cannot afford to follow all the standard industrials and still do an authentic job on the growth issues. My firm therefore concentrates its research effort in the growth area, which is an important market in itself: The top growth issues have a market capitalization of well over $100 billion.

We avoid the large, cyclical industrials (the heavies, as we sometimes call them) even if they are supposed to be ripe for an upward swing. As mentioned above, usually it does not occur; and if it does, then sooner or later you must sell, pay taxes, and try to buy back the growth stock you really wanted, quite possibly having lost ground against it in the process.

The number of prime growth stocks is so limited that they are the pearls of great price of portfolio investment. One can be sure they will always be in demand and fetch top prices. (In bear-market bottoms they may become reasonably priced for a while.) One should not ordinarily sell a stock with a high built-in capital gain merely because the multiple is high (unless it becomes simply outrageous, where pruning may be justified). One should sell it if the whole market has started to slide and the company's earnings are flattening. That is the moment of maximum market vulnerability.

Once one has developed a portfolio "core" of prime growth stocks that have appreciated substantially, then one can try for larger—and riskier—gains in "emerging" growth stocks. Several may have to be tried and discarded (probably at a loss) for each one that proves to be a big winner.

# "Franchise" and "Commodity"

Beware of the company with a franchise that has turned into a commodity. I do not mean a franchise in the sense of a specific license, like a royal monopoly on salt, or a Ford dealership, but rather in the sense of a built-in favorable situation. The "franchise" is usually the essence of an oligopoly, and its degradation into commodity status signals the end of it.

Sometimes, for instance, a company finds itself in such a favorable economic environment that it can reach great size quite fast. Then the economic situation changes, and it is impossible for other companies to catch up with the first. That is a valid "franchise," if the industry is a good one to be in. Leading local banks or newspapers or the first big hotel in a city often reach this position. (You may then have an oligopoly situation.) It can change, though, and the franchise can lose its value. Often this happens when the particular thing the franchise had that was rare and valuable becomes generally understood and widespread. At one time, for instance, a Howard Johnson's was something special. Now there are dozens of highway food chains, and Howard Johnson's is just one more; their situation has ceased to be outstanding and has become something anyone can buy if he wants to: a "commodity."

Sometimes a company scores a technological breakthrough and finds itself running with the ball down a clear field, so to speak. The development of the transistor by

Texas Instruments is a famous example. For a while the company had a very strong lead over all competition and the stock got over seventy times earnings, in recognition of what the market hoped was the company's commanding "franchise" in that business. Inevitably, however, other companies were attracted to the field, competition developed, and profit margins began coming down. Then the Japanese got into the act, and the former specialty became a "commodity" in a highly competitive field, with margins under constant pressure.

A curious example of this transition is W. R. Grace, one of the few companies that has lost its franchise twice over. Before World War II they were in a unique situation in South America because of their generations of experience and their well-entrenched local businesses in many parts of the continent. Then they decided that South America was becoming unstable and competitive: that their franchise was losing its value. They determined on a complete metamorphosis. Attracted by the high profit margins then prevailing in the chemical industry (around 14 percent), Grace took on a huge debt load plus a large equity dilution to enter it—just in time to see formerly specialty chemicals become a commodity in turn, and profit margins fall to about half their former levels. The franchise proved to be temporary, although it may return.

The long, slow decline of A&P has points of similarity. Profit margins and the price-earnings ratio both decayed steadily as the company's formerly excellent franchise—its four thousand stores—degenerated into a mere commodity, and in fact were in many cases left stranded by inner-city decay, and the advent of a specialty, the discounters, who will in turn become a commodity.

From very recent history, a striking example of the undermining of a franchise, at least temporarily, is DeBeers. For generations it exercised an iron grip over the volume of diamonds going to market and the price structure of gem stones. It even got the Russians to join its system, which looked eternal. Then, as a result of uncontrollable speculation, pushed largely by fly-by-night American boiler rooms, an enormous price bulge began, which resulted in disorder in the diamond market. Leaks began to spring up as some countries refused to accept the DeBeers monopoly. The price collapsed.

Perhaps the most discouraging examples of franchises that lost their value are the railroads. Nine of the original eleven stocks in the Dow Jones Average were rails. They were money machines. Like kingdoms, they were the objects of vast struggles between armies of tycoons. In this century, though, every transcontinental line except one has been in bankruptcy. Competitive transportation, plus government regulation and union featherbedding, did them in.

A recent instance is the Stock Exchange member firms. Once a prosperous cartel, they were put through the wringer in the 1970s when the fixed-commission structure was abolished. Hundreds of them folded or had to merge. A still later example is the wave of airline bankruptcies that followed their return to competitive conditions after deregulation.

Size is also a factor. The most satisfactory franchise should neither be so large and conspicuous that it attracts political opposition nor so small that it can be overwhelmed by a much larger competitor. A medium-size enterprise is best.

In any case, a good franchise, like a country, must be defended or it will not endure.

# Investing in Gresham's Law

For better or for worse, the great current of our time is the mass man assuming control of politics and economics. Even if he is not enthusiastic about this process, the investor must understand it.

Investors fortunate enough to have a certain capital will in the nature of things presumably have an interest in quality and an awareness of the good things of life. They may therefore be surprised by one of the central truths of investing in the fourth quarter of the twentieth century.

1. *The best companies often make things the investor wouldn't buy himself.*

Few readers of this book will live in mobile homes; none, I daresay, roars around on a Japanese motorcycle; few indeed eat regularly in such highway fast-food chains as McDonald's or Kentucky Fried Chicken; probably none relies on a Timex watch; few get their ideas from *Playboy*, have discovered double-knit leisure suits, or buy their furniture from factory-outlet stores. They probably drink more claret than Dr Pepper.

Alas, my readers are not a multitude, and the big money is not made in catering to their tastes. Let me give some more examples. (The young may not remember some of the "quality" names, and older persons may not recognize all the new ones.)

The general reason for all these disappearances is that the quality company—the old Ritz, or Black, Starr & Gorham, or whatever—has to compete for managerial talent, real estate, and TV time with mass-maket companies enjoying a vastly higher turnover and therefore able to spread their overhead over a much broader sales base. The quality company tends to get squeezed out of business as the number of buyers who can pay for top quality declines and the number who can buy lower quality increases. Obviously, the

119

**Table 3. Some Great Mass-Market Companies**

| Consumer Industry | Quality Company | History | Mass-Market Company |
|---|---|---|---|
| Entertainment | D'Oyly Carte | Folded | Disney, Atari |
| Restaurants | Pavillon | Gone | McDonald's |
| Jewelers | Black, Starr & Gorham | Gone | Zale, Josten's |
| Hotels | Ritz (New York) | Gone | Hyatt |
| Shirts | Charvet | Insignificant | Arrow |
| Vehicles | Packard | Gone | Honda |
| Publishing | Alfred Knopf | Merged | *Penthouse* |

trend to higher wages accelerates this process: It means that the cost of a Sulka shirt becomes prohibitive, but that the cutter himself can afford more Arrows.

Remember, we are talking about the consumer sector. For industrial products the principles are a bit different.

2. *Successful mass-market companies must be superbly managed, and particularly they must be tigers in marketing.* Incidentally, Disney and McDonald's are among the best-managed companies in America.

It is no longer true, as a general rule, that if you build a better mousetrap the world will beat a path to your door. Unless you can license it to Avon or Sears, you will end up with an impressive heap of dead rodents, but no cash. In the first place, how does the; world get to your door? You need ample parking space, which means a lot of rent, which requires a very high volume. You can sell it by mail, but that means capital for TV spots. The days of Fabergé and Haydn are gone with their patrons. The new patrons look to Krementz for their adornments and for their music to the Grateful Dead or the Stones.

How does one invest in all this? Quite difficult. In the world of the consumer, nothing stays put. As mentioned above, marketing is the essence, and it can't be patented.

There are, nevertheless, a few *de facto* oligopolies in the consumer area, which year after year build higher sales and profit margins. Disney and Avon did it; some of the pharmaceutical companies seem to be unbeatable; people can't stop smoking and for years Philip Morris has hogged the center of the road with extreme skill; and so have a few of the soft-drink companies. There are a number of such examples. Their products would not look at home in Mount Vernon or the Frick Museum, but they give the mass man what he wants, in huge volumes, at low prices. They elbow the quality products off the shelves: Gresham's Law.

I am sure the reader has got the idea.

There is another dimension to it too, though: politics. In the days when a Washington or indeed a Hoover could be

President, and a Hamilton or a Mellon be Secretary of the Treasury, a sound currency was a prime governmental objective. Now, with the unions crucial in every election, hard money is a political impossibility. That is the influence of the mass man in politics and economics—Gresham's Law in another form.

Monopolies have become illegal. Nevertheless, one monopoly is tolerated: union labor. Thus U.S. Steel and General Motors may sell lots of steel and cars, but the shareholders make less and less profit. Therefore:

3. *Avoid labor-intensive industries.* (Some specialized service companies are exceptions.)

We must also face still another implication of the same trend. It is that the legal position of capital is undermined, by taxes, regulation, and (particularly in the extractive industries abroad) outright or disguised expropriation.

For instance, "capital gains" today often just reflect inflation, like the price changes on the menu while you were looking at it in a German restaurant during the '30s. To tax such "gains" is to a considerable extent a capital levy and perhaps unconstitutional—but there it is.

Higher taxes, "consumerism," and regulation may be good politics and possibly even good for society, but they mean misery for the manufacturer.

To sum up:

4. *Avoid industries and countries where the workers and consumers wield quasi-governmental power to beat down the producer.*

Before abandoning all hope, however, please reconsider the right-hand column in the table of great mass-market companies (Table 2). These companies have been wonderful investments. There have been many, many more, in such areas—not too likely to be familiar to most "quality" buyers—as auto replacement parts (Monroe), tire retreading (Bandag), regional retailing (Petrie), door-to-door selling (Mary Kay), do-it-yourself home repair (Loew's Companies), flavored wines (Taylor), and the like.

# "Double Play" Stocks

The "double play" in portfolio investment is my term for finding an outstanding growth stock whose value is not generally recognized. As its quality becomes apparent, it sells at a higher multiple of higher earnings and thus scores a spectacular gain. When executed in a top-quality stock, this is one of the most elegant operations in portfolio investing. In the old days the typical double play was in a stock whose hard assets were undercapitalized in the market. Now it is likely to be in a stock whose earnings growth turns out to be faster and more certain than had been realized.

If all goes well, the investor will make not one but two profits, since the company, and the price of its stock, will grow, and the institutions will catch on and pay a higher multiple (e.g., twelve times instead of eight times) for those higher earnings.

To illustrate this process, let us assume a stock earning $1 a share and selling for $8, or eight times earnings. After a few years its earnings grow to $2 a share, and it gets bid up to twelve times those earnings, or $24. That is, the earnings have doubled but the stock has tripled. It may even rise to sixteen times earnings, or $32, meaning it will have quadrupled.

It is in reality more conservative to buy a stock where this seems likely to happen than one where it already has happened, since if one buys a stock that is already an institutional favorite, selling at a fancy multiple, and anything goes wrong, the whole process may reverse and the stock collapse. If on the contrary something goes wrong with a low-multiple stock, there is usually not so far to fall.

It is, of course, a lot more work to find companies on the threshold of institutional acceptance than to buy the ones that are already there. One traditional technique is to buy a sound, otherwise eligible company that, however, does not yet pay a dividend. (Non-dividend payers are avoided by trustees because the income beneficiaries complain.) Then when the stock goes on a dividend-paying basis its market broadens and the price should rise.

Another way is to buy a stock that is not understood, or under an unjustified cloud.

Disney, for example, was for years considered an essentially quaint affair, until the analysts awoke to the immense value of its library of past hits, which can be re-released every five years or so forever, as new generations of children come along. Then the success of Disneyland and its implications became understood. Disney is now regarded as a prime Gresham's Law or mass-culture company in the entertainment field.

Japanese companies, even the greatest, were for years considered vaguely inscrutable, even as they blandly took over whole industries within the United States itself. "Ah, but the Japanese market is very speculative," the trust officer would say, or "The companies are undercapitalized," or "Yes, but their growth will have to slow down sometime." Alas, some years later he pays fifteen times earnings for an "established" company now down to 12 percent growth that has at last gotten on the "approved list," while before, when the name was less familiar, he could have paid twelve times earnings for 30 percent growth. (I well remember a 1950 report from the largest investment counseling firm in the world announcing sadly that they had "missed" the Japanese market, and it now seemed to be "too late.")

Another example is Philip Morris. In 1970 three things happened all at once: There was a market decline, the Surgeon General determined that smoking was risky, and TV advertising by cigarette companies was halted. The tobacco stocks slumped.

It did not take too much research to find out that:

- The dangers of cigarettes had long been known (they used to be called "coffin nails") but their consumption went right on rising steadily.
- The media ban was actually good for the cigarette com-

panies: They already had very high market penetration, just like marijuana or the numbers game, which get along swimmingly without any advertising. (Everybody who offers the pack to his neighbor is a "pusher," after all.) The companies advertise chiefly to maintain their competitive positions vis-à-vis each other.

It turned out that in several foreign countries where TV advertising of cigarettes had never been permitted, the sales growth was even higher than in the United States. Furthermore, denying new entrants access to TV means much less chance of new competition to the established brands. Oligopoly! Briefly, the only real result of the TV ban was to save the companies a quarter of a billion dollars. (It also, as I expected, killed off *Life* magazine by creating a void in TV prime time that advertisers rushed out of the magazines to fill—an example of the unintended results of tinkering with the environment, economic as well as natural.)

Anyway, we bought Philip Morris—by far the best cigarette company, and superb at marketing—in all accounts. The earnings continued to grow at the same steady pace, the price-earnings multiple rose, and the stock rapidly tripled. By 1982 it had quintupled, but its intrinsic growth rate was slowing, and we were doing some selling.

A wonderful example of a "double play" opportunity was American Express during the Tino de Angelis salad-oil scandal. An artful con man borrowed a fortune on the strength of a vast inventory of "salad oil" stored in the tanks of an American Express subsidiary—tanks that turned out to contain water with only a thin layer of oil on the surface. The lenders sued everybody involved. This was one of the great uproars in the whole history of American business, and for a while people were most reluctant to touch American Express because of it. In terms of financial danger to the company, however, the risk from the salad-oil lawsuits was very limited. The problem was settled, and after a time the extraordinary earnings growth of the company and its high-quality management reasserted themselves. The stock in the next few years rose several hundred percent.

More recently, Ross Perot's Electronic Data Systems, the leading computer software service company, collapsed in the market after it sustained heavy losses trying to bail out two large stock exchange firms. The stock remained under a cloud for years, even after the brokerage adventure was written off, and the growth of the basic business could be seen to be flawless. When light dawned, the stock tripled.

To sum up: One feels safest buying a potential double-play stock when one can see just what it is that seems to be holding it down—temporarily bad earnings, seemingly adverse developments that in fact are ephemeral, or whatever.

The same is of course true of the market as a whole. An example vividly remembered by lots of investors was the Cuban missile crisis of 1962. With Khrushchev and Kennedy huffing and puffing and a military showdown imminent, many investors understandably panicked and dumped millions of shares, which the professionals coolly swept in at bargain prices. One recognized a unique opportunity–in Wall Street terms, that is. If there were a limited conflict, stocks would resist the resulting inflation better than a bank balance; if there were an all-out nuclear exchange, one might as well go to one's reward clutching IBM as greenbacks; and if, as seemed likely, things blew over, prices would leap up. (To buy a double-play stock during a panic gives one a chance at a really spectacular gain. It is also a useful act, since one helps stabilize the market when it really needs it.)

One curiosity in this area is that a stock becomes more eligible for trust-company investment by the mere fact that its price rises. Institutions prefer not to fuss with stocks with small market capitalizations, since even if they like them they can't buy enough to justify the research effort needed to keep on top of the situation.

For instance, an outstanding but unrecognized company might have $200 million in sales and $20 million in profits, and sell for eight times earnings, or a total market capitalization of $160 million. For a trust company managing, say, $10 billion spread among ten thousand accounts, there is no use getting involved, since the most they would be able to buy would probably be $15 million or so. Activity in the stock would probably be low. There is not much point in buying and following a stock that will represent only one- or two-tenths of 1 percent of the managed assets.

If, however, the stock catches fire and is run up to fifteen times earnings, or $300 million of market value, then it is worth looking at. Turnover is likely to be high, and one could put a respectable amount of capital to work in the issue; perhaps $40 million over a period, and more in time as the company grows and the stock works higher.

Obviously, at that price-earnings ratio, the "performance" of the investment has to come from the intrinsic growth of the company. The institution reasonably cannot hope for the "double play" of a higher multiple as well. The investor they bought it from has already gotten that!

Often one has a better hope of executing a double play in a stock that almost no one has heard of than in a famous stock that has collapsed for the wrong reason. That's because the famous stock may have been "over-owned," as one says in Wall Street, before its decline, so that even if the misapprehension is corrected, there will still be a supply of sellers who have a loss in the stock or are worried that its aura of invincibility has been punctured. A forgotten or little-known stock, on the other hand, has only one way to go if its fundamentals improve: up.

# Sol y Sombra

Some time ago at a mutual fund directors' meeting the new head of research was produced to explain how things were going to be even better in the future.

He described how he was reorganizing the department so that the people available would follow fewer stocks more closely. From about five hundred companies the analysts were going to concentrate their focus down to only about three hundred.

As I listened to this plan I reflected that the disappearance of the other two hundred companies into limbo was a good example of a bear market in action.

A few weeks in the future a pension fund analyst would call up to ask why Federal Sign & Signal was selling at six times earnings, no more than the cash in the bank, or why Handy & Harman was down in the market to little over half the value of its inventory, and would in essence get his inquiry back stamped "Address Unknown." Alarmed, he would presumably switch to something he could continue to get documentation on, and the stock would decline even further.

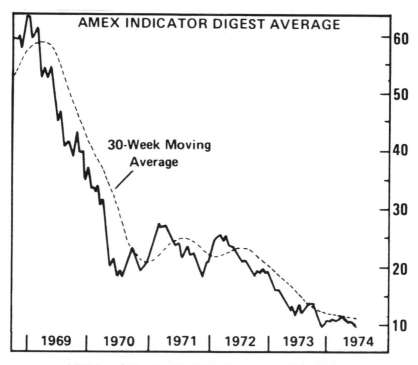

**OVER 1,200 AMEX STOCKS UNWEIGHTED**
The Cats and Dogs Go to the Pound

**Figure 10**

The extreme example of this effect is the less active over-the-counter stocks, on which all bids dry up completely during a bear market. You can't even get someone to take the shares off your hands to record a sale for tax purposes.

On the other hand, when a bull market starts you can get astonishing bargains by picking up some of this abandoned merchandise at thrift-shop prices six months or so before brokerage houses resume the search for not yet over-exploited stocks. In a bull market you can't go too far wrong on a stock selling for half its liquidation value.

A simple analogy for this phenomenon will be familiar to anyone who has bought tickets to a bullfight (or indeed the U.S. Open tennis matches).

There are three areas in the bull ring: *sol,* which is in the sun; *sombra,* or the shade, and *sol y sombra,* where the shadow moves during the afternoon so that after a while what started out in the sun ends up in the shade, as the sun sets.

In the stock' market it works both ways. There are perhaps a thousand names in the *sol y sombra* section. At all times several hundred companies are either moving into limbo *(sombra)* or emerging from it into the sunlight of institutional interest.

The most ghastly trap a small investor can fall into is to heed the blandishments of a friend in a brokerage house and take some issue off his hands just before night descends on it for several years. (Alas, a much more important customer has probably forced the broker to bid on the stock; he then has to get rid of it.)

Conversely, one of the most spectacular gains that a masterful speculator can rack up comes from buying heavily into the third-tier issues while they are still selling at *sombra* prices, before they go back on the brokers' active lists.

Since you cannot as a practical matter analyze these companies, you should use shortcuts in identifying areas of interest. Here are two:

1. Start buying an aggressive no-load fund specializing in smaller companies run by a good investment counseling

firm after it has gone down 40 percent or so in a washout. Suitable names might be Rowe Price New Horizons or Scudder Development.

2. After a major market bottom find out what is being bought by the so-called special equity funds of the big banks, such as Morgan Guaranty or Bankers Trust, and get some too. A knowledgeable broker can often tell you.

In both these strategies the pent-up buying power of the institutions and their investors is so huge that such issues are very likely to double in a bull market.

Conversely, when the market peaks, the investor in *sol y sombra* issues should run for the hills. Volatile money moves out of the more speculative mutual funds as their prices fall. As a result, the funds have to dump their holdings to meet redemptions in less and less receptive markets, dropping stock prices (and the fund's own value) further, which exacerbates the problem. You are doing yourself and the market a favor to sell around tops and buy around bottoms.

# Trends

Market trends often go much further than one would ever think.

Some of the trends that continued to amazing extremes were the infatuation with stocks in the 1920s, the unwillingness to buy them at any price in the 1930s, the enthusiasm for cyclicals as against growth stocks in the 1950s, and for growth stocks as against cyclicals in the early 1970s, and for energy stocks at the end of the decade. One should usually expect a trend to continue, regardless of whether it seems to have gone too far by the standards of the recent past.

If you look at a book of charts (such as those found in Figures 9–9e) both of stocks and of the market as a whole, you will be struck by how obvious major trends usually are when viewed from a distance, and how persistent. They often go on for years. At the time, though, the investor does not have the feeling of their great sweep. He thinks they may reverse tomorrow or next week.

An important application of this to investment is that you should not set a selling target in advance when you buy a prime growth stock. If you buy such a stock at 20 with a target of 50 and sell out, you may be dismayed to see it at 100 a year later and 1000 ten years later. I well remember a market pro saying to me years ago in his whispering voice, "John, we old speculators have a saying: 'Wait and see where it's going to go.'" How right he was.

Is the reverse also true? Should you hold off buying a stock when it gets down to the point where it is an unquestionably good value to see if it may not go even lower? Here, of course, the fundamentals are different. A true growth stock tends to increase in value as the earnings rise. It may fall much more than one would expect, but probably not to zero, whereas it can go up ten times in ten years.

So I'd say that the easiest technique is to buy a little when it gets in range, so that you'll feel better buying a little more later if it climbs back above your original price. Otherwise you may hold off and hold off as it rises, waiting to get a second chance that never comes. Having that first commitment in place gives you a platform or marking point, so to speak. Of course, if a prime growth stock collapses to a real bargain level before recovering, then you can complete the position at leisure.

One must, naturally, distinguish between a true long-term trend that continues for decades or more—inflation, for example, with all its consequences—and the standard pendulum of popular enthusiasm, first for one thing and then for another—such as the market cycle itself. If you have had three great market years, you know that the odds in favor of a fourth are poor, and the same is true of runups in specific groups: electronics, pharmaceuticals, cosmetics, or whatever. (A given group almost never has several good market years in a row. After one or two, everyone is aboard who's going aboard.) You know they can't turn into real growth areas because production can be expanded until the margins come down. That sort of trend is intrinsically limited. So if a cyclical group that doesn't enjoy an oligopolistic position becomes a popular favorite, then you should start remembering the Chinese adage that the trees don't grow up to the sky.

# How High Is High?

This book says a lot about the psychological climate of an overpriced market and little about objective measurements of value. That's not an accident. There are whole libraries of studies on the subject. Unfortunately, they are hard for the nonprofessional investor to use. Here are some touchstones:

1. In recent years the Dow has tended to fluctuate between seven and fifteen times earnings. A reasonable investment range might be eight to ten times. Of course, one has to reduce the nominal earnings of the Dow by underdepreciation, inventory profits, and the like. In other words, the real price-earnings ratio is higher than the nominal price-earnings ratio.

2. Those few stocks that have outstandingly high profit margins and year after year enjoy consistently high growth are, of course, in a special category. On average, such stocks rarely sell below ten or twelve times earnings. They will probably fall back after running up over twenty times earnings.

3. Tangible value is a useful measure. The Dow Jones Industrial Average often comes back to about 125 percent of its own book value. A much higher valuation is probably unsustainable, and a significantly lower one is probably a bargain. (See Figure 11.)

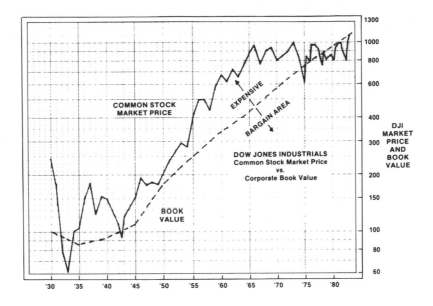

RATIO OF STOCK PRICES TO BOOK VALUE

**Figure 11**

4. Finally, when many stocks are selling below their working capital value you can almost always afford to take a constructive attitude toward the market.

Generally speaking, however, the nonprofessional will have to be guided by the specialist in determining absolute values.

Sometimes, though, he can—better than the specialist, who is likely to be preoccupied with narrower concerns—feel when the whole investment scene is going crazy. He knows about overexcitement from his business or personal life, even if he can't evaluate a mining company's depletion policy. So in practice the substantial investor is likely to have to impose his market judgment on the specialist.

As I note elsewhere, large institutions usually make little attempt to catch market swings . . . rightly so, in my opinion. When they try, it usually costs them money.

# Reserves

In general, ownership of growth stocks is more profitable for a substantial investor than ownership of bonds, particularly after taxes. (Only about half the earnings of most companies are distributed to the shareholders as taxable dividends. The other half goes to build up the company and thus in due course to make its stock more valuable.)

In certain situations, of course, bonds are better than stocks: when stocks are so high and bonds so low that you wait much longer to get your money back from stocks than from bonds; in a depression, when companies lose money and indeed collapse; or during severe bear markets. The most important single objective in portfolio investment is to avoid going over the waterfall.

If for any of these reasons the investor decides to get out of stocks, the next question is, what does he buy instead?

The answer flows from his reasoning in getting out of the market. If he is trying to scramble up the riverbank to avoid the cataract, then Treasury bills are the answer. They provide a reasonable yield and are perfectly liquid. Longer-term bonds are likely to be a trap. The reason is that while at one time money tended to slosh back and forth from stocks into bonds and bonds into stocks, so that their behavior was reciprocal, of late the money has gone right out of the system, so that stocks and bonds go up and down together.

An example will make this clear. The most usual species of bear encountered these days in one's investment safari will be the inaugural-year credit squeeze. The incoming President wrings out of the economy the excess liquidity that was pumped into it during the election year by the incumbent. This operation brakes the economy and deflates the market. But the same credit squeeze also puts bond interest way up, and so drives down the bond market at the same time as the stock market. When the job has been done and the credit spigot is opened again, bonds and stocks recover hand in hand.

Short-term Treasuries fluctuate very little in market value, since they are paid off so quickly, and therefore are a better refuge than bonds for this situation. If there is a collapse, they are a great deal safer.

Another solution is to switch into more or less recession-proof groups of stocks, since sometimes, particularly if such a group is reasonably priced when the recession starts, enough institutional and professional investors may switch into it from more volatile sectors so that it will actually rise in the market against the general trend. In the old days food companies often acted this way; also ATT, a traditional security blanket.

Occasionally gold issues, which some investors feel comfortable with in bad times, move up when the market is weak.

I do not know any general rule for choosing stocks that will buck the trend—or decline less—in a bear market. I think it is an example of an "outguessing" situation: You just have to look around and see if any of the standard defensive groups are underpriced enough to make them worth the gamble as an alternative to Treasuries for part of your reserves.

The trouble with this strategy is there is always the chance of another 1962 or 1970 or 1974, when virtually nothing holds up.

A paradox of portfolio investment, by the way, is that a great stock picker is usually very bad at catching downturns. A few investors I know, for instance, figured out Schlumberger early and held it through thick and thin. That means that they made ten or twenty times on their money, just as they hoped. I find there is not much use talking to such people about a suspected bear market, even though the stock is smashed in the market from time to time. (Xerox, an earlier superstock, was roughly cut in half in 1962, 1966, and 1970.) Their burning conviction of the stock at 1000, like the early Christian's vision of paradise, is far more real to them than such hypothetical perils as a 50 percent price drop or being eaten by lions. It takes the utterly cold-blooded market analyst, who preferably does not even know what the companies do, to enforce a reserve-raising program in an investment firm. To require the dedicated stock picker to raise 50 percent in reserves is about as congenial a mandate as telling a mother to turn out half her children. At the end of each washout, his list down 40 percent, holding his head in his hands, he'll agree to do anything, next time; but when next time actually comes, then, flushed with the prestige of a 70 percent rise in two years and thirsting for more, he resists like Hector before Troy any pressure to abandon his positions.

A plausible trap is convertibles. When a bull-market blowoff is in progress, brokers can quite often get investors—particularly Europeans—to switch from stocks into converts on the reasoning that the higher yield will cushion their decline. This proposal is attractive because of the European investor's greater attention to yield, and also because he knows he is usually wrong anyway on the market swings, and likes the idea that the conversion feature means he is not entirely out of the ball game if the stock continues to rise after all. If the market does drop, however, the foreigner is likely to take a drubbing, for several reasons. First, the premium over conversion parity that the convert sells at will narrow, so it actually goes down more than the underlying stock, instead of less; second, convertibles often have particularly thin markets, so that when panicky investors start dumping they are crucified by the specialist; and finally, the somewhat higher safety of the convertible is often taken by the investor or his banker as justification for lingering in unseasoned companies whose weaknesses are exposed in a downturn: One thinks of the massacre of the foreign holders of Gulf & Western, LTV, Litton, or other conglomerate paper in 1970.

Another trap is thinking that it is enough to switch from higher-multiple stocks to lower-multiple stocks in anticipation of a bear market. In even a moderate bear market the public is likely to stop buying, which means that there may be no bids for issues that do not enjoy institutional sponsorship. The institutions, on the other hand, have money coming in continuously—a couple of billion dollars a month, say, year in, year out—and so will usually be there to pick up bargains in their types of stocks even in bad times.

One thinks of a bear market in terms of declining values, but an equally important part of it for many people is partial or complete loss of liquidity in many issues.

So if you switch from an overpriced institutional favorite into a lesser-known secondary issue you may be making things worse. You may find that the institutional favorite declines only 20 percent in a bear market and the secondary issue two or three times as much, as it goes to a lower multiple of lower earnings and the institutions decide they don't want it anyway.

Thus, other things being equal, although they are better values, low-multiple stocks should by no means be considered reserves, or even decline-resistant. The easiest demonstration of this is that the American Stock Exchange generally sells at a substantially lower multiple than New York does and yet goes down more sharply in declines.

There is a category sometimes called "semi-upstairs money"—e.g., high-quality preferreds, short-term liquidating situations, or the like—but in most investors' hands they too are traps, since you quite possibly cannot use them when you want them. They are not true reserves. The greatest value of reserves is to give you something in hand to buy real bargains with on the occasions when good stocks are knocked down by half or two-thirds. Those moments are usually brief. To have the money coming in later on, or find that the "reserves" are as badly bruised as the things you wanted to buy, is not very useful.

No, Treasury bills are for most investors the correct reserve holding.

What if the economic or market downturn degenerates into a crisis? That leads us to what one might call last-resort reserves.

# Crises

Financial crises are of two sorts: economic and political. It is important to distinguish between them, since they call for different strategies. Gold, however, is the best thing to have in either case.

## Gold

Depending on how bad a crisis gets, gold ranges between being the best answer and the only answer. When people see everything collapsing around their ears they become more and more eager to exchange paper—any kind of paper—for the one imperishable, portable, easily hidden value that has always been accepted by mankind.

One can try to demonstrate that perhaps men *shouldn't* always want gold but should instead agree to accept wampum or some other commodity in limited supply. If you try to think up alternatives, though, you soon see the disadvantages they all have.

(From the eternal desire for gold arises the fact that gold mines are about the most depression-proof industry, since with luck the percentage of their own output that they have to pay their workers actually declines in very hard times, so there is more left over as profit; and sales go right on.)

The most convenient way to own gold is widely traded coins that sell for about their bullion value, notably the Maple Leaf and the Krugerrand. A rare coin sold with a numismatic premium over its bullion content may lose some of the premium if the price of gold declines. Also, such coins are subject to forgery and alteration, and are routinely sold by dealers in a higher quality category than they belong and repurchased in a lower one. One should keep all coins in their original wrappers or packages, and retain the dealer's statement of the quality category.

138

# Economic Crises

In an economic crisis people will accept money in exchange for value, but will distinguish between kinds of money. Coins with a high bullion content are preferred to those without; any coins are preferred to paper money; paper money is preferred to bank deposits (which may become inaccessible). Stocks and bonds are suspect. Barter goods are highly acceptable, and gold is the best of all.

Of course, you have exceptions, including periods of heavy Russian selling, the aftermath of overspeculation, and liquidity squeezes; but the general rule is usually valid.

# Political Crises

In a political upheaval, such as a revolution or an invasion, portability is of the essence. Gold, precious stones, and small, valuable works of art are desirable, while barter goods, non-gold coins, and bulky art objects are of less interest.

Precious stones are portable, but hard to negotiate in small amounts, and of fluctuating value.* Also, the spread between buying and selling is huge—often 50 percent—and more if the stones are in the form of set jewelry. That means that if you buy a stone from a dealer it may take years before you can sell it again for a profit. The alternative is to bypass the dealer, but that calls for real expertise.

Vladimir Nabokov's family sustained life in exile for a number of years, incidentally, on the proceeds of the sale of a single diamond that his mother had slipped out of Russia in a jar of talcum powder.

Rare stamps are portable and are satisfactory over the long term. Here again, expertise is needed for effective buy-

---

*The building that now houses Cartier's in New York was bought by Pierre Cartier from the Plant family in 1915 for the price of one exceedingly fine pearl necklace. Never again! The pearls were auctioned in 1957, over forty years later, for $315,000.

ing. They have one unique merit, which is that even if one is trapped by invasion or revolution one may be able to get them out of the country and turn them into cash, with the thought of following later oneself. You can do it by sending them abroad individually in innocuous letters mailed to foreign accommodation addresses. They can be glued under the regular stamps. Some will be lost, but not all. Or a visitor from abroad can take some back out, perhaps added to the envelopes of his business correspondence. They can be hidden more easily than almost anything else, do not appear in X-ray analysis, and are not what the customs people are looking for anyway. On the other hand, in an unstable situation they are not as easy to exchange as gold. One has to wait for things to settle down.

The head of the Vienna branch of the Rothschild family was a good friend of mine. He had escaped just ahead of the Nazis with the clothes on his back and his stamp collection in a suitcase. It supported his family here for years, until they were able to get some of their property back after the war.

# Flight

If it is a question of packing a few things to get away from the Cossacks, say, then in addition to gold and stamps, old-master drawings or perhaps etchings are acceptable. They tuck away into a very small space, such as in the shaft of an umbrella or the lining of a small bag.

The father of one of our colleagues was, in the 1930s, the London representative of an affiliate of the Warburg bank in Hamburg. Once in the principal offices of the bank he commented on the old masters on the walls. He learned that they were in special mountings, so that in an emergency they could rapidly be detached from the frames, placed in tubes, and spirited off.

Incidentally, large amounts of gold become quite hard to carry. A few hundred thousand dollars' worth weighs as much as a full Army field pack, and is the most one could carry at all conveniently; whereas you could put $3 million of the most expensive art in a briefcase.

In this type of situation, neither paper money nor (still less) securities are the answer, since outside the country they are hard to negotiate. The values are contingent on the good will of the government, but that is just what is in question.

Sooner or later every country is invaded or experiences a political convulsion. It's even happened two or three times in America—the Revolution, the Civil War, and the Depression. If one wants to set something aside for stormy weather, he should get some assets abroad while it is still legal, and in addition have something he can take along to live on if he has to go in a hurry.

The time to do all this is when there is not a cloud in the sky.

# Dividends

Wall Street opinion on the importance of dividends to the investor has fluctuated over the years.

Sometimes the dominant feeling has been that dividends are helpful in sustaining the price of a stock. The argument is that growth is a most uncertain affair (which is in fact true for the mass of stocks) and therefore a company with a settled business and a continuing stream of dividends will at least give the investor something in hand. Also, stocks that pay dividends have better markets and thus do not fall so far in bad times. (That, of course, means that one has more opportunities to buy low-dividend stocks on favorable terms.)

The contrary position is that a good company can usually invest its available cash at a higher rate of return than the investor himself can: 20 percent, let us say. Furthermore, runs this line of reasoning, in order to pay a dividend the company has to pay full tax at the corporate rate, usually around 50 percent, and after that the shareholder has to pay personal income taxes on the dividends received. In other words, a dollar of operating profit distributed out as dividends may lose seventy-five cents in tax before the shareholder can spend it, leaving him with twenty-five cents or less. How much better, therefore, one can argue, to rely on the corporation to invest most of this same dollar in research and development, the building of new markets, or some other pre-tax purpose, which will in due course be reflected in a higher stock price. In this situation the investor can sell some of his stock from time to time, paying taxes at the lower capital gains rate, rather than living off dividends.

For smaller investors who don't make a specialty of the subject, I think the pro-dividend school has the safer position, as long as the dividends rise as fast as inflation. Preserving capital in real terms is very hard. Most people are kidding themselves if they think otherwise. So let them invest for preservation of capital, and regard their dividends as the fruit from the tree, which they can consume. If they also chop up branches for firewood, there may eventually be no fruit.

For the high-bracket investor, though, I favor the second strategy. It is unavailable to most investors, and therefore in following it the substantial investor is taking advantage of his situation, like a giraffe browsing higher on the tree than other animals can reach. The small investor and the trustee are both pretty well precluded from investing in stocks that pay almost no dividends, the former because he lives off the income, and the trustee because he may not distribute capital gains to an income beneficiary. That means that, other things being equal, low-dividend stocks should be better values.

What doesn't work at all is buying stocks with high taxable dividends that don't rise as fast as inflation. This is essentially a taxable return of capital, just as bonds are; the capital declines in real terms at the same rate as inflation.

# Market Growth Follows Earnings Growth

Very roughly, the rate a stock's earnings and dividends grow will also be the rate its market price rises over a long period. Similarly, the rate a portfolio grows is likely to be similar to the rate the earnings of the stocks in it rise, assuming they are not bought at excessive price-earnings ratios. Growth-stock investment thus tends over the long course of time to be the most profitable investment strategy, and also to produce low yields, since growth stocks normally pay low dividends until their growth tapers off, when the cash is less needed for corporate expansion to keep up with growing markets, and the dividend rate can be increased.

Although a stock that pays no dividend usually enjoys less favor in the marketplace than one that does, if earnings are comparable then the non-dividend payer may be a safer buy. For instance, assume the following two situations: Company A's earnings grow at 14 percent a year and it sells for twelve times earnings because it pays a good dividend; Company B grows 20 percent a year and sells at ten times earnings because it does not. Both companies' shares rise at a similar annual rate, and should continue to do so as long as growth is maintained.

In this model, the investor who does not need income seems better off in Stock B, because if anything does go wrong he probably has a lower distance to fall; and there is always the chance that the stock will go on a dividend-paying basis, providing a "double play" through a substantial rise in the multiple.

Furthermore, as I pointed out, a lot of stocks with generous dividends have static earnings, and therefore never go up, so after inflation the investor is really living off capital every year by the amount of inflation.

An attractive strategy for a substantial high-bracket investor who is reconciled to volatility as a price of growth is to buy growth stocks that do not pay good dividends (preferably during a period of pronounced market weakness). He can then put himself on a "salary" of, say, 5 percent of his capital, and make periodic sales to bring his cash income up to this figure.

# Taxes

The tax merit of selecting a growth stock with low dividends rather than a stock with lower growth but higher dividends is even stronger if you can invest in a really high quality issue that you may not need to sell for ten or twenty years. You have the use of the money that you would otherwise have had to pay in taxes for all that time, during which period that money may have doubled in turn. The availability of the potential tax dollars for investment over a long period may permit payment of taxes out of their own investment profits.

Finally, if one can really discover a Coca-Cola or a 3M or a Johnson & Johnson now and again, he may be able to hold it for his lifetime, so that capital gains taxes are never paid, only estate taxes.

And for that matter, by careful estate planning even estate taxes can be kept within bounds. Suppose you have three married children, each of whom has two children. You and your wife can each give $20,000 a year tax-free to all twelve of these descendants, or a total of $240,000 a year. Over a few years that will reduce the taxable estate, and the tax burden, quickly enough!

Thus, for the substantial investor the advantages of growth stocks are overwhelming from a tax standpoint as against a strategy that emphasizes dividends, on which the taxes cannot be escaped.

# Convertibles

Most investors, including professionals (particularly foreign institutions), are baffled by convertibles. If they are more secure and the yield is higher, aren't they a better buy than the common stock of the same company? But what is an acceptable premium? Is a 20 percent premium over conversion parity excessive?

The simplest rule of thumb I know is this: Divide the premium by the improvement in yield. If the yield improvement earns you back the premium in two years, excellent. If in three years, okay. If more than that, stay with the common.

Suppose, for example, that XYZ common is yielding 2 percent and the convertible is yielding 7 percent. That's a 5 percent yield advantage for the convertible. So if it's within a 10 percent premium over conversion parity, it's probably attractive.

You must, however, have your broker look up the indenture and make sure there are no booby traps, such as the possibility of the company's redeeming the debentures below what you will be paying for them. One of the most telling refutations of the "efficient market" hypothesis is that the prices that bonds sell for in the market often do not reflect their call provisions.

This is a much more manageable approach than working out the bond value of the convertible, separately putting a value on the conversion feature, and then adding the two values together to give a theoretical price for the issue. That calculation is beyond the powers of most investors.

# Magic

Every few years the sap starts rising again in the stock market, hope springs anew, and buoyant prices bring forth from their hiding places the jugglers and music makers, the Houdinis and Cagliostros, dressed in new finery but singing the old song.

> Here is a gold coin! You see it, sir? Please touch it, Countess . . . Now then, presto! Look! Where there was one, there are now two! Two gold coins . . . See! Hold one in each hand. . . .
>
> And Abracadabra and Eureka, now there are *four*! Four, where there was once but one! Here, take them, touch them! Keep them—one for you, sir . . . and one for the damsel there . . . and for you, Captain, test it with your sword!
>
> Now then, gentles and fair ladies, my pages will pass among you with silver bowls. Take your precious objects, rings, watches, jewels, and give them to my assistants. Each will be marked and you will receive a binding receipt written on a parchment card—a card from a magical Tarot pack!
>
> The silver bowls will then be placed on the stage, and in plain sight each will multiply! . . . Like the loaves and the fishes, ladies and gentlemen! . . . will multiply into two silver bowls, each containing the same jewels and valuables placed in the first one!

One knows it has to come out badly.

"We are not here to sell a parcel of boilers and vats," said Dr. Johnson, auctioning off the bankrupt brewery that had belonged to his late friend Thrale, "but the potentiality of growing rich beyond the dreams of human avarice."

In the late 1920s, when everything was booming, when all the jigs and dies and generators and railroad cars and brick walls and boilers and retorts that American industry consists of were being bid up several percent a week, month after month, year after year, the notion became popular that the same delightful effect could be achieved even more rapidly if one used mostly borrowed money. So famous old banking houses formed trusts to buy in the stock market or to take control of public utility companies, using a modest equity capital and a lot of borrowed money, or leverage (the English term is "gearing"). That way, if the whole thing doubled, their equity quadrupled.

Alas, it is always the same. When hopes are high, it means that of necessity the market is also too high, but only then is the public in a mood to risk great losses in the hope of great rewards.

The famous old banking firms' trusts were doomed, and in a few years most were underwater: The claims on equity represented by their bonds were more than the equity was worth. Some of them eventually worked their way back up to the surface, some never did.

In the 1950s, the same idea was reincarnated in another form. Diversification! A heads-up manager, it was realized, should never be content to stay in a dull or contracting area of business when there was a more promising one beckoning just across the valley. Also, if you were in a summer business, so to speak, by adding a winter business you could smooth the ups and downs.

In the 1960s arose the conglomerate, or free-form company. A sharpshooter would find backing and buy control of a company—any company at all. He would pay for it with subordinated debentures ("Chinese paper") and add its net worth to his borrowing base. From this platform he would spring at still larger prey, often through public tender solicitations.

The reasoning was that if the earnings of the acquired company more than covered the costs of the debt issued to finance it, you were picking up speed as you went along— a kind of breeder reactor.

Daring accounting techniques were used to "manufac-

ture" higher earnings for the enterprise from each new purchase, which kept the stock up. Using his high-priced stock as
a trading token, the conglomerator would buy more and
more enterprises selling at lower earnings multiples. The fact
of the acquisition would inflate the company's reported earnings even more, pushing the stock ever higher.

Perpetual motion!

There were two main soft spots in this miracle. First,
with a few famous exceptions (such as Wattles of Eltra, Little
of Textron, and, of course, Geneen of ITT) the conglomerators were not businessmen but financial manipulators—
liars with figures, you might almost say—so that their industrial creations didn't really make sense and had to be
disassembled and reconstructed by their successors, like
cleaning up after a children's party. Second, it all depended
on faith: When something happened to break the flow, it
came tumbling down on leverage, until the stock, like Pom-
peii, or indeed the old trusts, was buried under the Chinese
paper. Thus Gulf & Western went up sixfold and Litton up
tenfold before going all the way back and starting out again
on a more sober basis.

Another nifty idea was the "hedge fund." The theory
here is that if you are usually right, why not be right both on
the long side and the short side: Set up a partnership that
goes long and short on margin simultaneously. Furthermore—goes the theory—you can bear a decline in the market and still be all right because your shorts will collapse
faster than your longs.

In perhaps 1 percent of all cases this worked.

In the other 99 percent, it was merely a symptom of
boom times. What actually happened was that the public,
scenting a fast buck, and flogged on by brokers who loved
the double commissions created by use of margin and the
high turnover, shopped around between hedge funds, looking for the most amazing performance. Since they could be
formed for the price of having a lawyer draw up a standard
agreement and without SEC approval (unlike a mutual

fund), they proliferated wildly. There was no question of going short when stocks were overpriced. On the contrary, to attract the wonder seekers they manufactured performance by bidding up small companies with thin markets, or buying investment letter stock at a discount from a doubtful market price. When the end came, there were no buyers for these stocks, so the markdowns were astonishing: 90 percent, sometimes.

In 1983 options present similar dangers to the unwary.

The really colossal frauds are, alas, perpetrated by sovereign governments, since there is no one to keep them honest.

In modern times many if not most long-term bonds, particularly foreign bonds, belong in that category. The lender never gets his purchasing power back. Many, many long-term international bond issues are defaulted on one excuse or another (frequently invasion or revolution).

Even if they aren't, inflation robs the trusting investor of his capital—and, of course, he is taxed on the "income" that otherwise might repay him.

Let us consider the archetype of such issues, the British War Loan of 1917. It corresponded to our war bonds. When it was first offered, with appropriate patriotic drumbeating, it generated a vast response. So many enthusiastic buyers mobbed the subscription offices that they had to be held back by police. Some £2 billion was raised, at an interest rate of 5 percent, to be repaid between 1929 and 1947. In today's terms that would be the equivalent of perhaps $100 billion.

In the difficult year 1932 the British government offered to redeem the bonds or exchange them for new ones with an interest rate of 3.5 percent, plus a 1 percent bonus. Ninety-eight percent of all bondholders accepted the offer, which again was couched in patriotic terms.

Unfortunately, there was no definite repayment date for the new issue.

The 500,000 English families who own these bonds have seen inflation rob them of their principal year by year. They now sell at about 20 percent of the issue price—but in today's currency, which has declined sickeningly from its former value. The patriotic investor has been fleeced, in terms of his then buying power, of all but a few percent of his capital.

The most accomplished con man could scarcely hope to beat that record.

No wonder Bernard Baruch refused to lend his prestige to the sale of U.S. government war bonds in World War II. He knew that whatever the original intention, they would end up a swindle. "Put not your trust in princes," said the Psalmist, over two thousand years ago.

# Conglomerates

It seems worth going into the conglomerate phenomenon of the late 1960s at some length because it was one of the more expensive catastrophes experienced by investors in recent generations. It will be back in another form soon enough, so one should recognize its general flavor.

The conglomerate idea was based on four financial concepts and four business fallacies.

The first concept was that if you could buy a company at eight times after-tax earnings (that is, a 12.5 percent "earnings yield") you would make money doing it by issuing a like amount of 7 percent debt, which would be a deduction from income. After taxes the 7 percent debt really cost you only 3.5 percent, so you were apparently clearing 9 percent on the deal, although you had encumbered your balance sheet.

The weakness in this arrangement was that bad times come sooner or later, and the dead weight of all that debt proved a lot more reliable than the leaky balloon of puffed-up earnings when it came to the test of sinking or flying.

The second concept was that by an accounting method called pooling of interests you could further increase the apparent earnings of your company each time you merged with another.

The third concept was that since all this tended to make the acquiring company's earnings rise each time it made a new acquisition, you could show a wonderful progression of earnings as long as you kept going, just as though you were an authentic growth company, a Kellogg or an American Home Products.

The fourth concept was that these illusory rising earnings would push your stock up to a high level, so that you could exchange it on favorable terms for other companies' stock. In other words, you first get a broad public market going for Atmotronics or Lincoln Industries (formerly Lincoln Hot Air Works) at twenty times earnings and three times book value. You then go to your old competitor, whose stock is trading for ten times earnings and two times book, and offer him 50 percent over market value, payable in your stock or in your convertible debentures. If he accepts, your earnings per share will rise the next year, and your stock price should rise twenty times as much, facilitating further acquisitions.

The first business fallacy in all this was to suppose that somewhere in the world there was a manager able to run a hundred different businesses under one corporate roof—like a teacher running a class of a hundred disorderly students who all spoke different languages. The word that was coined for this virtually nonexistent talent was "free-form management."

The second business fallacy was that somehow the children in this situation would teach each other, that if within one corporate shell you had an auto parts distributorship, a chain of pizza parlors, a savings and loan association, a farm, a bicycle tire factory, and a brewery there would be an interchange of wisdom and inspiration. It will be recalled that the buzz word coined to express this grotesque fancy was "synergism." A better word would have been "chaos." It rarely worked.

Great activity was manifested in grouping the businesses acquired into catchy categories. The pizzerias, the brewery, and the auto parts company might be put under a group vice-president for "Consumer Products." The savings and loan might buy a mutual fund and become the nucleus of the "Financial Services Division." The bike tires would become the "Leisure Time Division."

If you were doing it today you would need an Environment Division—the window-washing company—and an Energy Division—the windmill.

The third fallacious proposition was in essence to think that a good hockey coach can practice medicine. Modern business calls for very specific skills and a great deal of industry background. Manipulators and wizards with figures are rarely first-class operating men.

The fourth business fallacy was that the balloon could be blown up to infinite size. In fact, of course, limits were always reached and the process came to a stop. The world was dismayed to find that Lincoln Industries was still the old Hot Air Works and a grab bag of fifty or a hundred other affairs, marked up from seven times earnings to twenty times apparent earnings and heaven knows how many times real earnings. In spite of the noble annual report, the five-star directors, and the group vice-presidents, little had happened to the actual businesses. They were still chugging away in the same brick buildings, but with new signs in front bearing the nifty corporate logo worked up by expensive Madison Avenue talent. When the euphoria wore off, the cold vision of reality, and a realization that good old Lincoln was in hock to the gills, cooled the stock fast enough.

How much of a price-earnings ratio should one give to cooking the books? That's basically what it amounts to.

# Great Little Specialty Companies

In pleasing contrast to the showy picture-making of the conglomerators and manipulators is the tough, resourceful competence and technical mastery of the real pro doing one thing exceedingly well.

To me the most reassuring investment is the company that year after year holds its dominant position in a solidly rooted, steadily growing specialty industry. Such an enterprise can be managed by businessmen, rather than the philosopher-kings required for multi-industry companies. Sales are often in the $100–$500 million range. The company has successfully made the transition from being a small private business to becoming a large, complicated one. (That's a real hurdle.) Its products are the industry standard. When you mention its name to a competitor he groans and holds his head. Ideally, he also rolls his eyes.

Two signs of this kind of company are its history and its profit margins. Federal Express, Avery Products, and Pioneer Hi-Bred are all good examples. Each is the leader in its field, was started and built up doing one thing superlatively well, and has gotten more and more secure as time has passed. Most of them have amazing balance sheets, with lots of excess cash and virtually no debt. Their fat profit margins tell you that you are in the presence of an enterprise with a high degree of uniqueness. (One must be sure that it can defend its market share; if not, high profit margins become a honey pot, attracting ever more competition.)

An astute parent might well put the funds he had set aside for his children entirely into a package of such companies. Quite a few wouldn't work out, and he should therefore prune the list every year or two, either increasing the positions in the successes or trying an occasional new one. But the survivors should be big winners, until they become so large they stagnate.

The advantage of this kind of investing is that over the very long term it is just about the most profitable safe strategy that a qualified investor can actually carry out.

There are three disadvantages. First, it requires more wisdom, professionalism, and alertness than, for instance, investing in seasoned growth stocks.

Second, the return on reinvested capital in a rapidly growing specialty company is so high that the shareholders' interest is best served by plowing profits back, instead of paying generous dividends.

Third, small companies' stock prices take a drubbing in bear markets. A 50 percent drop is not unusual. For that reason they are particularly appropriate for a child's trust portfolio, since the beneficiary won't lose sleep over the volatility (or low yield) and in the nature of things has very long-term investment objectives.

# IV.

# Beyond the Stock Market

# Investing in Land

Throughout history land has been the basic store of value.

For many investors it remains a most attractive investment medium, although I suspect that this will be less true in the future than the past. In Europe it sells for much higher prices relative to other things than it does here.

I would like to underline the distinction between raw land on the one hand and every other kind of land on the other.

It is raw land, unimproved but suitable for development, that seems to me often a desirable investment for a passive investor, particularly land near where you live, or in a developing area.

## Favorable Factors

1. Raw land is comparatively immune to greedy unions, ferocious competition, rising costs, and technological obsolescence, which strangle most industrial enterprises. The price constantly adjusts for inflation. This includes hyperinflation, which otherwise is exceedingly hard to cope with.

157

2. The value builds without significant current tax (as taxes are now levied).

In contrast, stock earnings are taxed 50 percent at the corporate level and then you pay tax on the dividends all over again, so the government gets a good three-quarters of whatever is distributed. Bond interest is worse, since inflation consumes your interest payments and the tax puts you underwater.

3. An individual investor will have a better idea of the values in land near where he lives than for almost any stock. He can probably know within 25 percent what a fair price is for it—more than he can say for Polaroid or General Motors. Land investment, too, is a competitive game, and if you buy that lot down the road you've had your eye on for years you may have a better general feeling for the value than an investor from out of the area, and also a better idea of how to sell it. Even then, you need an expert appraisal to be safe. There are too many technical features to check.

4. For both these reasons, it is easy to exercise patience, which is indispensable in all investment, with land, since you can see it, touch it, and walk over it, and you know it isn't going out of business.

When a stock drops 50 percent a lot of investors are panicked into selling. If nobody has put in a bid recently on the ten acres you're holding for your children, you don't lose sleep over it.

5. It is easier to visualize the ultimate payoff. If you have a tract a few miles outside of town, you can actually see the progress of development in that direction. If you own a long-term technology play in the stock market you never quite know if it's going to make it. Usually it doesn't, in fact.

6. You have a higher batting average in land than in stocks. Most people lose money in many of their stocks. Very few people lose money over the long term in buying and holding well-chosen raw land.

7. It is satisfying to own land, particularly if you can also use it—to live on, or for recreation.

# Unfavorable Factors

The most obvious disadvantages of raw land are that there's no income—in fact, you have to pay some taxes to hold it—and that it's not liquid. You can spend months selling a $100,000 property, whereas you can usually sell five thousand shares of a well-known stock in an hour or so.

That, of course, reduces land's attractiveness to most people; the investor can often get a better long-term percentage return on a holding with an income and ready liquidity.

But for long-term investors both disadvantages have silver linings. Income is in a way a taxable return of principal. If you really want capital to grow, it's best to leave it all quietly compounding and not chip away at it. By the same token the illiquidity of land precludes the jumping in and out that hurts so many portfolios.

Still, these two features of raw land—lack of income and illiquidity—mean that it's a poor holding in a crisis. Banks won't ordinarily lend on a nonincome-producing asset. If you get squeezed and have to sell it in a hurry, you may get a bad price because of the poor marketability.

In any country that is going to the left, real estate has the disadvantage of being conspicuous. It is easy to tax and to expropriate, because it can't get away. An example is rent control, which is a form of expropriation. Large-scale landowners—as in Eastern Europe or Cuba—were often cleaned out completely when the time came, because they hadn't gotten into the habit of moving assets from place to place.

The third disadvantage to land as an investment has become much more serious in recent years: the "drawbridge effect." Zoning boards are intensely political, and once someone has gotten used to having a field next door he may fight against having you put several houses on it. Your development prospect is my green belt.

One is only safe after one's obtained all the permissions—which may require years—and then taken some physical step toward development: "appointed to the use," as they say; by digging a hole for the foundation, running in utilities, or whatever. Until then, the permissions can be revoked, even if you've been able to get them in the first place, which must never be assumed.

On balance, nevertheless, it is hard to beat raw land, suitable, and preferably zoned, for development as an investment in an inflationary but still capitalistic environment.


## How Does One Go About It?


First, do not buy a lot in a subdivision for a speculative profit. The promoter has already skimmed off the first ten years' profits.

Other than that, my advice is simply to get started.

Take 10 percent or so of your investment assets and mentally commit it to raw-land investment. Figure out how much that works out to divided among three or four properties.

Start looking as you drive around your neighborhood. Let it be known to a broker you trust that you're a potential prospect but are in no hurry.

It's usually wise to buy through only one broker in this situation, and to let him know it. That way, he'll take the job seriously. If you have several brokers, each will try to hustle you to buy something before he loses your business to one of the others.

After you've spent four or five Saturdays walking over—and preferably photographing—a variety of properties, you'll begin to have a feel for things.

If possible you should look for a property in what is called the predevelopment stage, one that in three, four, or five years will be attractive to a developer. Three-quarters of the rise in the price of land from its agricultural value to its highest and best use occurs before its surface is touched, and much of that rise occurs in the last few years before development. The objective is therefore to buy predevelopment land at modest prices not too long before it is of development interest.

Of course, you are much safer buying land in a growing area. Even if you get the exact situation wrong or pay too much, you should be bailed out sooner or later by the growth of the region. To buy a property in a decaying area because it's cheaper now than it was before means you're betting against the trend, which is too dangerous for anyone except a professional. You can see if an area is growing by simple inspection. The reasons will usually be obvious: new businesses or a better class of home being constructed. Unless things are clearly going to change, that's the place to be.

Having identified a couple of growing areas, you now face the hard part of the job, picking the exact site and determining a fair price.

The old cliché in the real estate trade is that the three rules for making money are: (1) location; (2) location; and (3) location.

There are as many elements to consider in evaluating the location of a piece of real estate as there are in evaluating a corporate stock: dozens, of which growth is the first.

It is not just difficult, it is impossible for the nonprofessional investor to carry out such an evaluation (unless, of course, the land is right in his backyard, where he should be able to do it quite well). Dozens of factors he might not consider can be crucial, with the result that he may buy a property that looks good to him, only to find that it doesn't do much, while a place a short distance away booms.

Projected roads are important. Future zoning changes can dramatically increase the value of a property. Large developments that may be planned for the area will attract business and residential construction. The schools and power supply should be examined.

A soil survey should be obtained, covering water availability, soil stability, drainage, and "percolation" (essential to sewage absorption). The U.S. Department of Agriculture may have one available.

All these factors should be evaluated by a specialist.

The safest and cheapest way for an investor in raw land to avoid serious mistakes is to hire a real estate consultant to appraise the property he proposes to buy. The investor's broker should be able to get information that will help answer a number of the questions that the consultant will come up with. The rest the consultant can get from local government authorities and other sources.

There are professional associations, including the Society of Real Estate Appraisers and the American Society of Real Estate Counselors, from which the investor can request a list of consultants familiar with the area he is interested in.

One technique should perhaps be mentioned. Sometimes the seller is an old farmer who is retiring, or some other person who is not too concerned with the tax treatment of the cash he receives. In such a case the use of a "balloon" payment can help the deal.

If the asking price is, say, $50,000, and the broker thinks the property can in fact be bought for $40,000 cash, the buyer might offer to pay $45,000, spread over several years, with interest, but with initial payments of interest alone—perhaps $5,000 in each of the first two years. For a high-bracket investor this might mean an after-tax cost of only $3,000 for those two years. If in that time the property advanced 20 percent in value, or $10,000, the investor would have made a paper profit.

Similarly, he may be able to make an arrangement with the broker in which the broker is actually retained, so that his commission, instead of being capitalized, becomes deductible.

## Alternative Types of Real Estate Investment

As soon as one departs from raw land one leaves the world of passive investment and enters the world of business.

I could discuss the various alternative forms of investment real estate, with their pros and cons, but it shouldn't be necessary. The nonprofessional investor need only think for a minute to realize that it is walking into a buzz saw to get involved with them—particularly if he remembers that to get the deal he will have to pay more than any of the pros would. Here are some of the alternatives:

Office buildings
Apartment houses
Shopping centers
Motels
Hotels
Resorts
Industrial development land
Farms
Single-family houses
Brownstones converted into apartments
Rooming houses

To be fair, I have many friends who have bought a brownstone, kept a garden duplex, rented out the upper floors, and made good money at it. None has claimed it was a trouble-free investment, though. There are always difficulties with the roof or the heating or the lady on the third floor who turns out to have an amazing number of nocturnal visitors.

The same is true of owning and renting a house. It keeps you busy.

I also have a few acquaintances in cities other than New York who report good results with rooming houses, both in college towns and elsewhere. You can usually get a serious individual or couple to look after the place in return for a rent-free deal. This shields you from the headaches if the "concierge" is reliable.

Still and all, these three arrangements are all small businesses, involving time, trouble, and risk, rather than the passive investment that raw land can be.

As for the other types of real estate investment that I have listed, for the nonprofessional they can best be described as infernal. He is likely to lose both his peace of mind and his capital.

Least of all should the inexperienced passive investor who has made a good buy of raw land be tempted into putting up more money for garden apartments or some other improvement. Entrepreneurship is a dangerous specialty, and real estate is one of the trickiest. Investment profits are made through inactivity and sticking to what one knows best.

"Neffer develop," John Jacob Astor used to say.

A highly successful raw-land investor of my acquaintance has often been able to get reluctant elderly farmers to sell by offering them a figure today for ownership of the property to take effect after the owner dies—what used to be called a "post-obit" transaction. In another variation, I once helped a French widow of a certain age make up her mind by offering her a lifetime indexed annuity, or *rente viagère*. Although unusual, these devices can be useful.

In real estate, unlike the stock market, the more money you have the better you do. There is an automatic profit in buying a large property and cutting it up into small pieces, whereas in the stock market a large block of stock is harder to move than a small one.

On the other hand, if you ever make several sales of land the Internal Revenue Service will try to hold that you are a dealer, and any profit you make will be taxed as ordinary income, not as a capital gain. To avoid this you can buy land in a corporation and then sell the stock, or when the time comes for development, contribute your land to a corporation, in which the developer then invests, so you never do sell.

As I mentioned, Europeans give much more weight to real property as an investment than we do. In part this derives from a better understanding of the investment merits of real property, and part from a comparative lack of alternative forms of investment.

A suspicion of stocks remains quite widespread on the continent. The small investor in a large Italian company, for instance, fears (probably not without justice) that the insiders are skimming off the cream. Also, the directors, to minimize corporate tax, hide some of the profits the company makes. This makes the situation even less appetizing for the small investor, whose predisposition toward real estate is thus fortified. However, the foreigner investing here should try to get over this prejudice. He is in reality much safer as one of ten thousand shareholders of a big, well-run American growth company than he is as owner of a New York apartment house, quite aside from the innumerable headaches he avoids. And if he's patient he can buy tangible assets at a discount in the stock market.

Watch out for the cycles in the real estate market, which are even more vicious than stock market cycles. I seem to observe that while the stock market looks ahead, and thus leads the economy by months, the price of real estate seems to fluctuate more nearly in step with the economy.

Foreigners, particularly, get drawn into U.S. real estate near the end of its cycle. For several years they are beguiled by reports of ever higher prices for houses or apartments, and finally, unable to resist, take the plunge just as the economy—and real estate prices—cave in.

# Speculating in Art

*The trick is to buy the right thing at the wrong time.*
—FRANCIS H. TAYLOR, *Curator,*
*Metropolitan Museum of Art*
*(in conversation)*

Since there is no current cash return from a work of art, it is more accurate to talk about "speculating" in art than "investing" in it. The buyer hopes that others will eventually pay more for an object than he did; enough more to cover two heavy commissions, taxes, lost interest, insurance, and possibly storage.

The only good reasons to buy a work of art are that you know a lot about it and want to live with it. Buying art to make money is a vulgar business, and rarely successful for the nonprofessional.

I suggest that the standard slogans one hears about investing in art are true only for the expert. Here are some restatements for the nonexpert.

1. *First, works of art in general probably do* not *tend to increase in value.*

Quite often certain specific schools or categories advance in value for a time, but others may quietly decline or even fade out completely. Also, sometimes the advance is based on a small volume of transactions. At the beginning of a *Business Week* article some time back on exotic investments there was a table indicating that certain Greek coins had tripled in value during the year. However, this was based on a single sale!

Sometime ask a really good friend in the world of art (preferably a collector or writer on the subject, rather than a person who makes his living selling it) this question: If you took every single painting that was sold for the first time in, say, 1910 or 1940, and evaluated it at today's market prices, would the whole package be worth more or less? The vast preponderance of these works have simply vanished—they are selling as bric-a-brac or gathering dust in attics. Even so, one could give a "guesstimate" value to them. It would be low, since they would be of mediocre quality and the artists themselves would be forgotten.

Then, of course, there would be the tiny handful of interesting works by painters—probably neglected at the time—that are still of interest today: perhaps one-tenth of 1 percent of the whole kit. Would the increase in this handful offset the depreciation in the others? Highly unlikely.

One interesting example was a published analysis of the prices at which Titian had sold from his own period until recently. The value in constant dollars was about the same throughout the centuries. There had been no investment return, just an inflation hedge—and then only if you had successfully picked Titian from among other painters! Not everybody could have done that.

And a study by *The Economist* mentions that a Landseer—one of the favorite English painters of his time—sold for £2,257 in 1875; after almost fifty years, in 1928, it fetched a mere £38!

Then we have the further problem that the expression "increase in value" presumably means increase in relation to other things. I suspect that the average work of art steadily declines in constant-dollar terms from the date it is first sold, but a fairer approach in a discussion of investment would be to ask: How does it make out in relation to the least interesting investments in securities? If you reckoned a total return of 6 percent compounded on a portfolio of securities, a dollar in 1923 would have become over thirty dollars by this time, before taxes.

I doubt if anyone would claim that all works of art that changed hands in 1923 are worth *on average* over thirty times as much as they were then.

2. *"Selection" will not solve the problem.* (Here again, I am talking about the nonexpert.)

Somebody was clever enough to anticipate the importance that Manet would have later on and to buy him cheap. Yes, somebody was—but is that somebody going to be you or me or the General Motors executive who goes around to the Marlborough Gallery to put $20,000 into a picture that is going to "go up"? Hardly.

Those who make money in art do it through highly skilled selection, but only professionals are likely to have that skill.

The retail buyer has to buy what is on sale, and the gallery business is tough enough so that the gallery can only afford to keep on its walls what is going to move fairly easily. For most of his life Manet was not sold in the fashionable galleries. The wealthy collector of Manet's day accumulated works by painters whose names have now been forgotten, and whose value is negligible. Look at the French Prix de Rome winners between 1870 and 1900. Not one of their names would be known today to the nonprofessional, and I doubt if one could find more than a handful of people who would hang one of their works over the fireplace.* Of course, if you went out *now,* after seventy-five or a hundred years, and picked up these efforts for a fraction of what they sold for originally (adjusting for the change in the value of the franc), you might easily do well. I do not know where you would find them. The first owner, however, would have no return at all on his capital.

One should also remember that art is a commodity. If something sells, then hundreds of imitators, who want to eat too, will pour out thousands of works in the same genre until the demand is satiated. Later revivals of this style are unlikely to be as widespread as the first one, so it might be many years before the supply can be absorbed. When the people who bought paintings by Bernard Buffet, say, because they were "going up" found instead that they were going down, they took a close look at them and decided they were not that beautiful after all. Result: a vast overhanging supply. Thousands of offices and hotel rooms now have works by neo-Buffets. It will take years for it all to go away, by which time he may possibly become an interesting investment again.

Of course, the great hope is to find an artist who needs money, and whose work you can buy cheaply, but who is so

---

*Here is the list (no prize was awarded in 1888 or 1897, although Renoir, Degas, Cézanne, Matisse, Monet, and Toulouse-Lautrec were available):

| | | |
|---|---|---|
| 1870—Jacques Lematte | 1880—Victor Blavette | 1891—Alexandre Lavalley |
| 1871—Edouard Toudouze | 1881—Louis Fournier | 1892—Georges Lavergne |
| 1872—Joseph Ferrier | 1882—Gustave Popelin | 1893—Maurice Mitrecey |
| 1873—Aimé Morot | 1883—André Baschet | 1894—Jules Leroux |
| 1874—Albert Besnard | 1884—Henri Pinta | 1895—Antoine Larée |
| 1875—Léon Comerre | 1885—Alexis Axilatte | 1896—Charles Moulin |
| 1876—Joseph Wencker | 1886—Charles Lebayle | 1898—Amédée Gibert |
| 1877—Théobald Chartran | 1887—Henri Dauger | 1899—Louis Roger |
| 1878—Francis Schommer | 1889—Laurent This | 1900—Fernand Sabatté |
| 1879—Alfred Bramtot | 1890—André Devambez | |

"special" that although he is of real merit he is very hard to imitate . . . a Van Gogh, for instance, or a Cézanne. But how likely is this to happen? Van Gogh and Cézanne sold virtually nothing during their lifetimes. Are we to suppose that the GM executive who wants to invest in a work of art that is going to "go up" will outsmart all the other such buyers and stumble on a Van Gogh or a Cézanne?

The gallery he deals with is presumably selling works from its inventory. The gallery may well have bought works of lesser-known painters at modest prices, but then it booms up the painters and foists the work on the GM executive for the most the traffic will bear. (The Franklin Mint performs a similar operation upon persons of more modest means, but using mass production techniques.)

The art market is heavily manipulated. (Some of the amazing prices you read of in auctions are created by the owner selling to himself—what is called "painting the tape" in Wall Street, where it is illegal.) The retail buyer gets a far worse break than he does at Las Vegas. It is more like his chances in one of those games in carnivals, and has little to do with prudent investment.

3. *You cannot expect to discover bargains.*

If you read books on investing in art or antiques, they usually emphasize bargain-hunting. The author is poking around a provincial antique store when suddenly he perceives a broken-down armchair which, thanks to his keen eye, he recognizes as a Louis XIII original, and not, as the dealer supposes, a nineteenth-century imitation. Feigning indifference, he asks the price ($300) and carries off his gem. Restored, it sells for $4,500.

Or at the preview of a forthcoming auction, peering at a murky canvas with his flashlight and loupe, he discerns under the varnish what may be a signature. He bids the piece in for $200, rushes home with it, gets to work with his bottles and swabs, and presently uncovers the name of that rare master, Klaus von Obergurgl. The Cinderella of the last auction fetches $12,000 at the next one.

Here again, though, one is not talking about an investment. This activity represents a major commitment of study and time. It is really a business, like prospecting for minerals. Furthermore, these books virtually never describe major coups. The best you can hope for is a series of small gains, plus the thrill of discovery, which, to be sure, is pretty good fun.

Still, investment is making capital work for profit, and this type of art buying is clearly in another category—perhaps a hobby, perhaps a part-time business.

4. *One should* not *necessarily look for the best.*

Dealers usually tell you that the "prime" object in its class is the one to collect.

I am not sure this is true. I can see why the dealer would take this position, since he lives on movement and likes starting a new collector on minor pieces which are then upgraded to first-class ones as his eye and pocketbook improve.

Nevertheless, a study of auction records seems to me to indicate that, if a period or school comes into favor, a "package" of secondary works may well have a bigger percentage gain than the most prominent representatives.

On the other hand, if interest falls off generally, there seems to be a better chance of selling a high-priced "prime" piece than a cheaper one. And, of course, a work should be honestly made and have artistic integrity.

5. *Do not be surprised to encounter a vast amount of chicanery, "hype," and conflict of interest.*

The art market resembles Wall Street in the nineteenth century. There is scarcely an uglier passage in the history of commerce than some of the transactions of that cat's cradle of Liechtenstein companies called the Marlborough Gallery.

# Some Principles of Successful Art Investment

1. *What has once been in fashion will again be in fashion.*

The few cases I know of persons who have done very well investing in art have followed the same pattern, which seems to reflect this principle.

Often the thing collected expresses the history and feelings of people in a certain time who are of perennial interest. Sometimes these feelings are freshly expressed by a small group of innovators who break away from a convention that has congealed, become sterile, and return to a more direct and personal vision. (Later they are followed by the trendy operators who chase the vogues of the moment, trying to stay on the crest of the commercial wave. These second-rate followers degrade the fresh vision into a dull formula all over again.)

One friend of mine, Cary Welch, became fond of Moghul miniatures in the 1950s, when few collectors were interested in them, and now has a famous and valuable collection. Another was entranced by early American folk painting at a time when good examples cost ten or fifteen dollars. Another, Nikita Lobanov, excited by the Diaghilev phenomenon, bought important ballet set and costume designs from the widows and ex-mistresses of the artists who worked for Diaghilev. A Boston friend responded to the harsh glamour of the clipper-ship era and formed a collection of ship paintings at a time when they could be had for a hundred dollars each. An English friend, Sir Leon Bagrit, bought Renaissance bronzes in the 1930s, when they were out of vogue, eventually developing a notable collection, and another London friend did the same with medieval coins. Still another, now dead, used his feeling for Oriental carpets to acquire works at modest prices that can no longer be found.

The common thread here is that in each case there is a profound authenticity about the objects, and a real interest in them on the part of the collector. In most cases the buyers became known authorities in their fields—since there were scarcely any other authorities. Several in due course began buying directly from the owners, since at the time the dealers did not find the category sufficiently interesting to carry.

I once developed a theory that W.P.A. art had to be as far out of vogue as it could get and started making inquiries. I found a huge cache in a warehouse on Staten Island, owned by a plumbing contractor who used the canvases to wrap pipes. He would sell the works in hundred-pound lots; you paid a premium if you insisted on selecting what you got.

2. *Crafts that become recognized as art.*

It may be that the safest things to collect for profit are pleasing objects on the borderline between carftsmanship and art that are made honestly and carefully, express the feelings of the people of a particular era, and have artistic merit, but that are not yet fully recognized as art. Examples would include American quilts and primitive folk paintings, or (at one time) the "floating world" prints, some of which the Japanese used as wrapping paper. My Japanese housekeeper received from her brother at a time when they had little value a set of Hokusai's "Thirty-six Views of Mt. Fuji." She gave some away in the 1960s when they were selling for $40 or so. Recently she found they were going for $1,000 each. Currier and Ives prints have had a similar revaluation in the last generation or two. So have scrimshaw and glass paperweights. A Mexican associate of mine, Antonio Haas, used to send his friends the appealing little crude votive oil paintings on tin sheets that peasants left in churches, which cost about thirty-five cents at the time. Now they sell for $100, and he has none himself. My own collection of "clipper cards"—in essence, advertising flyers—were originally distributed gratis by the shipowners.

If an object has these qualities and sells for much less than the present value of the time it took to make it, one should not go too far wrong in buying it, particularly if one enjoys contemplating it anyway. Such objects are presumably not yet carried by art dealers, reposing instead in thrift shops, junk stores, and flea markets.* The class of object in question is regarded as plentiful enough to be cast off with-

---

*Barron's* (February 1971) commented: "So-called 'antiques of tomorrow,' items less than 50 years old, are also popular with collectors who figure that for a few hundred dollars they can't go wrong. That assumption frequently turns out to be correct. An early Victorian marble-top table inlaid with mother-of-pearl which sold for $325 last year is valued today at $800–1,000. A ruby- and clear-cut glass decanter dated from the 1930s, purchased in 1968 for $50, now brings $250. Finely enameled 1930 com-out thought or stuck in the attic. *Saturday Evening Post* covers by Norman Rockwell cost five cents at the time and now sell for up to $100.

3. *"Bad taste."*

Another possibility is works that, while carefully made and expressive of their own *Zeitgeist,* we now find to be in doubtful taste. By the 1960s Hudson River School painters of the "stag at eve" type had gone out of style in an era of Plexiglas, chrome, and geometric prints. Then, in the late 1970s, they advanced spectacularly. Similarly, my thirty years of Prix de Rome winners, along with religious art, have probably hit bottom.

An example from my own enthusiasms is the nineteenth-century French *animalier* sculptors: the two Baryes, Mène, Rosa and Isidore Bonheur, and the rest. I'm fond of the better ones, and suspect that almost anybody would if he just kept a representative work on his desk where he could look at it by itself. Unfortunately, one usually sees them as part of the cluttered Victorian decor that we now find antipathetic. The elder Barye can almost be said to have been the reviver of animal sculpture after the great Renaissance bronze tradition died out. The school became very popular in Europe, and the works brought excellent prices about a hundred years ago. By our own time, however, they had fallen into eclipse. In World War II numbers of *animalier* bronzes were melted down for their metal content, and one dealer specializing in them has told me that many of the sellers had been using them as doorstops. From $50 to $75 for a good piece in the 1950s, they have now mounted to perhaps $1,000—$2,000, with the best examples fetching $3,000 (which has stimulated a good deal of forgery). At that, they still only cost a fraction as much as contemporary works of comparable merit.

---

pacts which could be picked up two years ago for $10, now are priced at $50 and $75."

The trouble with this approach is that the substantial investor is unlikely to have either the time or space (even if he has the inclination and skill) to acquire a large inventory of low-grade objects.

It was pleasant to read some time ago of the fall and rise of Sir Lawrence Alma-Tadema, a super-fashionable Royal Academy painter of the turn of the century. At his peak he sold his works for around $30,000. His buyers liked the large, operatic tableaux he rendered, although the feeling is gushy and unconvincing. Nothing less appropriate to the age of Jackson Pollock could be imagined, and after World War II they drifted down to "junk" prices—a few hundred dollars in some cases, with most of the buying coming from a single dealer-collector.

By the mid-1960s, though, they had recovered to the low thousands, and at a London sale in 1973 they averaged $15,000. So if you bought in 1900 and held until then you still had something, although perhaps less than the insurance and storage costs you would have incurred.

When Chancellor Hutchins of the University of Chicago abolished football, he was asked if he himself ever exercised. He is said to have replied that he sometimes felt the urge, but lay down until it passed off.

Perhaps the best advice one can give to a investor who is burning to acquire something by a contemporary artist at the height of his popularity is to wait a while . . . fifty years or so.

4. *Repurchasing history.*

Another principle that works well is collecting prime examples of the art of countries that are destined to thrive economically. For instance, after World War II, during the period of our world preeminence, there was a boom in American furniture and painting. Then the prosperous Japanese bid up the Oriental pieces, followed by a boom in Islamic art as the oil-rich Middle Easterners bought back their national treasures.

# Special Hazards

1. *The art market is very costly to operate in and provides uncertain liquidity.*

For any specific object there may well be no satisfactory market when you want to sell it. If you buy it during a period when it is in vogue, you may have to wait until the wheel comes around again. And even then, a "round trip" at an auction gallery costs around 40 percent, and at a dealer's at best 50 percent and often more. Add the sales tax and you can reckon that a complete transaction costs over 50 percent. That is a severe handicap to overcome. (A round trip in ATT, by contrast, costs about 1 percent, plus tax.)

Unlike the Stock Exchange, which is a comparatively "efficient market," the art market is full of anomalies and distortions. Sellers are out of touch, and buyers are ill-informed and impulsive. That means that the expert can make money year in, year out, buying in one place and selling in another.

And who is he making this money from? The nonexpert.

2. *The big game in art.*

The enthusiast who contemplates investment in art should be aware that a business exists of popularizing rediscovered styles, much like the couture houses' business of pushing successive vogues to beguile rich women into spending more for dresses.

At all times a few pros, sometimes allied to influential dealers, are quietly accumulating works by some forgotten artist or school from out-of-the-way auctions, obscure private collections, and individuals who have neglected pieces in their attics.

At the moment of purchase such a professional buyer knows pretty well how he proposes to sell out, perhaps three years later, to the rich but uninformed retail trade.

When he has a collection of items accumulated at bargain prices he has one of his tame dealers (or of course he may be a dealer-collector himself) start displaying the works and accustoming people to seeing them again. After a while perhaps a second friendly dealer joins in.

Then he arranges a fashionable benefit exhibition, with elegant patrons, press coverage, and champagne in a former mansion now owned by a women's college, say. A handsome illustrated catalogue is gotten up, quite possibly paid for by the tax-deductible ticket sales, and gets into the hands of several thousand potential buyers.

Our pro and his dealer friends start swapping a few works back and forth at amazing prices in the auction galleries.

Friendly writers for chi-chi magazines are inspired to start beating the drums.

A prominent outsider, an amateur who enjoys such things, may be induced to offer a collection of these works for sale, works that were actually accumulated by the pro and his colleagues but that the amateur will sponsor as his own for a share of the proceeds. He enjoys the publicity, the excitement, and the reputation for connoisseurship that he gains. The pro gains a fresh and glamorous provenance.

There is a gala evening at one of the auction houses, and our pro sells a part of his stock (reconfigurated as the collection of the amateur who is fronting the coup) for many times what he paid for the whole. He gives a few works to smaller museums at the new inflated prices for a handsome offsetting tax deduction.

He may previously have made some fictive sales to controlled European sources, who now offer the works to foreign buyers. These profits are not necessarily disclosed to the U.S. tax authorities.

Thus the merchandise is flogged up and palmed off, just as it was by the Wall Street "pools" in the bad old days before the S.E.C.

So remember that the exciting rediscovered style that suddenly blooms in the windows of several dealers on Madison Avenue and that you then are so tempted to buy may result from as scientifically managed a promotion and selling plan as anything Procter & Gamble or B.B.D.O. put out.

It is saddening to visit the apartments of respectable doctors and garment manufacturers who, like Indians trading furs for beads, tinsel, and mirrors, have given over the fruits of years of work for masses of weird, arty junk that hangs on their walls (and ceilings), stands in the middle of their living room floors, and indeed sits in their chairs; junk that their grandchildren will get no more for than we did for our grandparents' religiously polished leather-bound sets of Longfellow and Ruskin.

Duveen, of course, was the Napoleon of the Big Game in art. His customers filled the National Gallery, the Frick, and the rest with paintings whose prices often have in real terms never been seen again, and perhaps never will. Adjusted for inflation and interest, many—possibly most—"Duveens" are now only worth a fraction of what he got for them.

It took Duveen himself to hold his system together. When Duveen passed, his price structure, like Napoleon's principalities, crumbled.

3. *Forgery.*

Almost everything in art can be, and is, forged. There are whole forgery factories in Italy and other countries, including, it is rumored, the Soviet Union. Inevitably, organized crime has entered the forgery business. So never buy an important piece without an unqualified certificate of authenticity from an impeccable authority.

# Commodity Speculation

The commodities market was intended for farmers or manufacturers who want to fix their crop prices or material costs ahead of time. But today over 90 percent of the market is speculators betting against each other—and leaving several billion dollars a year with the brokers. It has become a vast casino whose function is to fleece the outsiders.

It's no place for the investor, but gamblers are drawn to it irresistibly, like dogs to a dogfight. To be long soybeans, to see them up the limit in the first hour of trading and know that all over the country armies of traders are trembling with excitement over whether to cover their short position or go short some more . . . that's living! (If you're a gambler.)

Unfortunately, almost nobody makes money over a long period in commodities except the brokers.

It is a broker's dream—which is one reason it's not one for the client. An active account can quite easily pay commissions in a year equal to half or indeed all its value, thanks to the leverage involved.

Here is the arithmetic: The commission plus the spread between bid and asked might cost .25 percent. Depending on circumstances, you can get ten or twenty times your capital in credit (margin). Each transaction with full margin thus costs you ten or twenty times .25 percent, or 4 percent say, of the equity in your account. Twenty trades a year isn't unusual, so in a year you can have paid 80 percent of your account. Not bad!

Not investment either, though.

The pendulum of prices tends to swing back and forth between historic limits. As the price of a commodity moves toward those limits, the logical wager is that it will stop and then reverse—that is, you should bet that the trend will not continue forever. Unfortunately, almost every investor has finite means, so when occasionally the trend goes farther than expected, he will be squeezed more and more painfully and eventually have to sell out, very possibly just before the turn comes.

A further problem is that the largest single elements in the market are usually the producers and the consumers, who have much more money and better information than the small speculator. If the price of wheat soars, the farmer who has it in the barn can afford to sell and sell and sell on the exchange without losing sleep, because he knows he can deliver if he isn't able to buy the contracts back more cheaply later on. The poor speculator who is being squeezed on the short side has no such insurance policy. Is it more Russian buying? A drought in western Canada? After a while he can't stand it anymore. He gives up and covers.

Similarly, if cocoa is driven through the floor in a wave of selling, the terrified speculator may dump his position because he doesn't know what's happening. The chocolate manufacturer can just add to his inventory. He's glad to, in fact, if the price is right.

You commonly hear that you should "cut your losses and let your profits run." That is certainly the only way not to risk being wiped out. On the other hand, the random jiggles of a commodity (or a stock) may easily—indeed, probably will—cause you to sell every good position for a loss at some point if you follow that rule. An army can't have a doctrine of beating a retreat whenever it encounters any resistance.

One of the largest firms in the business of managing commodity accounts is ContiCommodity, a subsidiary of Continental Grain. ContiCommodity takes full-page newspaper ads offering "basic training" for commodity traders and conducts "seminars" all over the country to attract new plungers. ContiCommodity ran three commodities mutual funds. *All three* lost their stake and had to be closed down completely.

There are no simple formulas. You need to *know* more and have more strength than the speculators on the other side.

To sum up, in commodity speculation you haven't got your money in something that's intrinsically building, but rather in a gambling game where you can never get an edge, where other players whom you can't see are in a stronger position than you are, and where the record proves that if you keep on long enough the house will almost surely take all your money.

# Options

A stock option is a right to buy or sell a stock at an agreed price for a certain period of time. You pay a premium for that right.

A call gives you the right to buy one hundred shares.

A put gives you the right to sell one hundred shares.

There are many variations and combinations of these two basic forms. A straddle, which is by far the most common, is a put plus a call: You can both buy one hundred shares and sell one hundred shares.

The striking price is the figure at which the option is to be exercised. Sometimes it is the market price at the time the option is written, sometimes above or below.

Most options expire unexercised.

Most option buyers want to buy calls. They think a stock is going up and want the leverage that an option provides. If you have a burning conviction that a stock will rise within six months, you can make from seven to ten times as much if you buy calls than if you buy the stock itself.

Institutions often sell options hoping to improve their yield. I do not think that they really do. Aside from anything else, they get into a habit of fidgeting—selling their potential great winners for small gains—that is adverse to quality investing.

European banks love selling options because they are compensated on the turnover of the account—they add on a brokerage commission—and so the high turnover generated by an option-selling program is very satisfactory. (Also, their accounts do not ordinarily pay capital gains taxes.) It is both amusing and depressing to hear them give every other possible justification for this activity.

Five publicly owned mutual funds sold with a commission were launched in 1977 to trade in options in order to

**Table 4. Option Fund Performance**

| Starting Date | Fund | Original Issue Price[1] | Net Asset Value[2] | Cash Distributions | Adjusted Net Asset Value[3] | Total Return[4] |
|---|---|---|---|---|---|---|
| 4/77 | Colonial Option Income | $12.50 | $ 9.67 | $6.36 | $16.03 | 28.2% |
| 6/77 | Federated Option Income | 15.00 | 12.43 | 5.45 | 17.88 | 19.2 |
| 6/77 | Kemper Option Income | 15.00 | 12.56 | 7.31 | 19.87 | 32.5 |
| 10/77 | Oppenheimer Option Income | 25.00 | 23.22 | 9.91 | 33.13 | 32.5 |
| 6/77 | Putnam Option Income | 15.00 | 12.62 | 7.36 | 19.98 | 33.2 |
| | Average total return | | | | | 29.1% |
| | Average annual return | | | | | 6.5 |

[1]Includes 8.5 percent load charge.
[2]As of 12/31/81.
[3]Net asset value plus cash distributions equal adjusted net asset value.
[4]On original issue price over 4½ years.

181

generate income. They did worse than any other income investment.

The professors are in doubt as to whether option-buying or option-selling is the more advantageous strategy. They can't both be, and my guess is that in fact neither is usually profitable (except for the broker). I have seen dozens of analyses, some extremely elaborate, showing that one or another strategy produced steady gains, but have never seen one that I found mathematically rigorous. None that I have tried has worked for long. It seems about as likely as a definitive winning chess opening.

# Investing Internationally

In the absence of good reasons to the contrary, it makes no more sense to invest in only one country than in only one state or one city or indeed one company. The insurance principle—spreading the risk—has many advantages and few disadvantages.

Sooner or later investments in almost any country become more or less worthless, at least temporarily. (In America, British holdings got very short shrift after the Revolution, and of course both Confederate bonds and Confederate property lost most of their value about a century ago.) It is hard to name a country where, even in this century, investments have not become of very doubtful value at some time or other. In about half the world they are that right now.

If you want to have all your investments in a single country, then logically it should be in a place where you do *not* live. That way, if you have to leave you are not wiped out financially as well.

It is curious to find two great antagonists giving reciprocal advice to someone they loved: Napoleon instructed his mother to put her money in London, while the Duke of Wellington, worried later about instability in England, wrote to his perennial companion Mrs. Arbuthnot, "I recommend you to provide Means of Subsistence for yourself in another country."

In addition to this line of reasoning, there are three others of comparable importance.

The first is that political stability is not enough. Stability is sometimes bought at the price of such concessions to labor and such high taxes—in general, the welfare-state syndrome—that little is left for capital. Economic stagnation often results. Some of the Scandinavian countries and Italy are obvious examples. Neither the economy nor individual companies in it are likely to prosper under such circumstances, and the realistic investor is well advised to move on to greener fields before too long. The United States is showing signs of this condition. The mass of stocks have not been interesting for a number of years. More and more companies report steadily shrinking profit margins. Municipal taxes are becoming astronomical as relief rolls swell and bureaucracy proliferates.

Two positive factors sometimes lead one to look abroad for investment. First, in some industries the foreign markets are growing faster and are less competitive. More of their development is still ahead of them. The most interesting part of many a U.S. company is its international operations. If you spun off the foreign operations of such a company and incorporated it in, say, Brussels, there would be no reason to look askance at it just because it was no longer legally U.S.-based.

Finally, and most important of all, it is very important to back the best horse, whatever its passport. The world is so competitive now that the weak company is likely to go under altogether. It is little consolation to the shareholder of a U.S. company reeling under Japanese competition to reflect that he is backing the home team. Many of the most attractive (and indeed largest) companies are foreign. Try to find an American-made transistor radio, sewing machine, tape recorder, fine camera or watch, or pair of binoculars! And indeed there are industries where the United States has simply retired from the field, unable to compete, such as oil tankers, motorcycles, and, of all things, baseball mitts (which now come only from Japan).

If your search for the best long-term bet in a given industry happens to lead you abroad, you should not be deterred because of that. If the country is a good one, it may be a positive advantage. The largest pharmaceuticals company is Hoffmann–LaRoche and the largest food company is Nestlé. The shareholders of each have deliberately made it impossible for control to move out of Switzerland, feeling that things thus become safer. The big Swiss banks have similar provisions. These are not governmental measures, but the shareholders acting to protect their interests. Maybe they are right! Heineken may be the world's most successful brewery. Is it a disadvantage that it is Dutch-based? It is not necessarily bad for Sony to be in Japan, or for Lloyd's to be in London.

On the other hand, by far the largest part of the world's independent high-growth specialty companies are in fact located in America. Abroad, most such enterprises are buried inside conglomerates.

The chief problem in investing abroad is that one can usually know much less about foreign companies than about U.S. companies—perhaps a third as much, to take a very rough figure, unless the company seeks listing on the New York Stock Exchange.

One reason is that to minimize taxes, foreign public corporations (like individuals) often minimize their real earnings. This discourages the public from buying the stock. The professional investor, nevertheless, can often get a great deal more information than is publicly available, through friendship with directors, bankers' indiscretions, and the like. This in turn can give him a special advantage that is unlikely in the United States. By the same token, the outsider is at a corresponding disadvantage compared to local specialists who have better information than he does.

# Japan

Assuming it can solve its energy problem and avoids returning to hyper-nationalism, Japan seems to be a favored country for general industrial investment. (For financial, service, resources, and "mass market" consumer companies, the United States remains tops.)

The essential reasons are two: (1) the Japanese workers, who are extraordinarily hard-working, disciplined, and dedicated; and (2) the integration of industry and government into the complex enviously called by others Japan, Inc.

In certain specific industries Japan also has a unique advantage of layout: Essentially the whole place is a large industrial park surrounded by water. Ocean freight is by far the cheapest form of transportation, particularly as vessels become even more immense and highly automated. For steel-based industries, for instance, this means that you can take the iron ore from the bulk carrier by conveyor and dump it straight into the blast furnace; the ingots can then go next door to the mill, and then next door again to the automobile plant, whence they move directly onto the freighter and off abroad. In the United States the material would have to do a lot of expensive overland traveling, with much higher handling costs, before setting off on its journey to the coastal port for export.

Small wonder that for years the Japanese have been able to take U.S. iron ore and sell it back to us as steel at highly competitive prices.

Finally, if anyone is going to make money as the Pacific economies expand, it will be the Japanese. The area has in fact become the Co-Prosperity Sphere that they only dreamed of before World War II.

Japan has been almost too successful with its industrialization and export drive. It is encountering severe resistance in many countries, political as well as economic. It must turn inward and take care of its own people. This should mean a long period of activity for its consumer companies, some of which are also prodigiously successful exporters and manufacturers abroad.

Anyway, there seems an excellent case for having a stake in Japan, as long as it remains politically sound and assuming it solves its energy problem, just as long as one does not overpay for the stocks.

A problem that is sometimes raised in connection with Japan is that of the periodic revaluations of the yen, which penalize the export earnings of Japanese companies. This may, however, be a necessary price of success, rather than a disadvantage.

Devaluations are usually not like a broken leg, which is set, bound in a cast, and put to rights; rather, devaluations may be more like heart attacks: a manifestation of chronic trouble.

One should favor investments in prospering countries, just as one does in prospering companies.

# The United States

What about the United States? The United States certainly is not as attractive a place to invest as it used to be:

- Americans used to be the world's most resourceful and energetic entrepreneurs, with the government, like a fond grandparent, cheering from the sidelines, so to speak.

    In recent years it has been more like a tunneling exhibition in a prison. The government, an omnipotent warden, riot gun at the ready, observes every movement with suspicion. Furthermore, government at one level or another eventually gets a good two-thirds of any money that is made, in federal, state, and municipal taxes on business, the same all over again in personal income taxes on dividends, estate taxes, plus sales taxes, property taxes, and many others.

Particularly on the two coasts, the dry rot of social decadence is spreading, as indicated by the collapse of the family, the proliferation of crime, and declining literacy and productivity.

- At one time there was a continuing stream of immigrants who were looking only for a chance to work hard for modest wages; they were often brought over for specific jobs, in fact.

    Now machines have taken over most of those jobs, and there are few unskilled jobs available in America. The descendants of the earlier arrivals, far from eager for hard work, proliferate in the bread-and-circus atmosphere of the great cities.

- The huge continental American market, within which industries like steel, cars, consumer products, aircraft, and computers could develop on a vast scale and thus with an efficiency impossible in Europe, will henceforth be less of an advantage, particularly if the Japanese continue to exclude us from their market while penetrating ours; thus the situation may be reversed.

Now let us consider some positive aspects of the U.S. situation:

- For reasons too complicated to discuss here, agriculture and socialism don't mix. That leaves America by default as the world's premier large agricultural country.
- American businessmen work together more easily and effectively than those of any other country. They also enjoy the game, work very hard, and will give their organization priority over their family, like officers in the armed services. This seems to make America a natural home for very large undertakings: computer companies, space exploration, global banks, international oil companies, or whatever.

    (This dedication to the job, coupled with corporate

nomadism, also weakens the family and thus erodes society from within. The chairman's granddaughter, complete with fatherless baby, sells leather belts and sandals on a sidewalk in Cambridge.)

- For a while, at least, the research effort of American corporations should assure their dominance of a number of industries where research is a key factor, such as computers—both hardware and software—office equipment, pharmaceuticals, aircraft, certain kinds of machine tools and heavy equipment, and the like.

- Eventually our coal, natural gas, and perhaps shale oil could make us self-sufficient in energy. At that point we and the Soviet Union will be the only autarkies among the industrialized countries. We also have a relatively ample water supply.

- Our mass-market companies are the wonder of the world. Concepts like shopping centers, motels, supermarkets, drug and discount chains, car rental agencies, "Levitt" developments, mobile homes, soft-drink companies, and so on, were pioneered and perfected in the huge American market and are now almost impossible to catch.

- Compared to what one finds in most countries, the dialogue between business and the unions here is muscular but realistic, like negotiations between business partners. (In Europe there is hysterical noncommunication and mutual sabotage.) This presumably comes about because of the professionalism, realism, and resulting success of the American unions, which as a consequence are among the more conservative elements in our society. Business and the unions can thus make common cause against the government, which in other countries tends to become uncontrollable.

Finally, the Russian bear is out of the cage and on a rampage around most of the world. The United States looks from abroad as the great safe haven of capital, and as a result investment will continue to pour in, particularly the reinvestment of OPEC's billions.

Taking it all together, one tends to conclude that the American market will for some time remain the prime theater of all portfolio investment, since if things are not ideal, at least they are fairly reliable by human standards. You can see how it all hangs together, and how big a stake almost everybody has in keeping it that way.

# Venture Capital

For most readers of this book, venture capital proposals— invitations to back inventions or new businesses—should be rejected out of hand.

Why? Because in the average venture deal the investors only get about half the business in exchange for almost all the money. The other half, often in the form of cheap stock, goes to the earliest "seed money" backers, the promoters, the salesmen of the deal, and to coax key executives over from their existing jobs.

Even then, at best one new company in ten succeeds, and probably a more realistic ratio is one in a hundred.

Also, the ordinary investor never gets a chance at the most interesting deals. They are offered first to specialized investment groups with which the entrepreneur seeks a continuing relationship, or else to established companies in the same industrial field as the new venture that can understand the deal quickly and bring management depth and marketing clout to the business.

With a little patience, one can invest much more safely. After a first-class market washout, which you can count on every four years or so, you can buy excellent companies, fully established, soundly financed, with seasoned management in place, for just the cash in the bank; with all the patents, the equipment, the buildings, and the goodwill for nothing. From time to time one can even buy good companies for *half* the cash in the bank.

Of course, sometimes you can invest in a new company with tax money, which improves the risk-reward ratio somewhat, although one should never make an investment primarily because of tax considerations.

I might say that having been involved in at least a hundred ventures, I have learned the hard way always to insist on certain qualities of management:

First, if the insiders are not unswervingly dedicated to the interest of the shareholders, as distinct from the maximization of their own position, don't look at the deal. They have a thousand ways to help themselves to your money, particularly abroad.

Second, the key people must have a track record as *money-makers,* not just thinkers or administrators.

Most venture capital deals originate with an inventor and a device (or sometimes a process). One of the worst things an investor can do is get enmeshed in the actual business, to become "hypnotized by the widget," as I call it. Rational judgment fades. The investor becomes committed to the project before he realizes it.

Rather than fuss personally with the widget, an interested prospective investor should commission a report by an impartial specialist, which will set forth the following:

1.  What the widget really can do
2.  What other similar widgets can do, and can be expected to do in the future
3.  The market
4.  The qualifications of management
5.  How realistic the company's business plan is, taking account of the foregoing

I would say that nine-tenths of the bad venture investments I have known about could have been avoided by obtaining and understanding the answers to these questions.

Obviously, if the outside expert is either not impartial or not an expert in that particular matter, then the report is useless.

The type of venture proposition that the unsophisticated investor is most likely to encounter involves an appealing gadget or process, but where the prospective management lacks demonstrated skills and a track record of profit for investors.

As Philip Fisher, a great West Coast investor in high-technology companies, once said to me, "The first thing to look for in a high-technology company is *business* ability."

# For the Adventurous Few: How to Get Rich

The first step is to stop thinking the way people do who don't get rich.

Almost none of my "successful" friends in the East are getting rich: They either started out that way or else just have good jobs, as law partners, bankers, company vice-presidents (plus a few presidents), or whatever.

These friends of mine become respectable, but they don't get *rich*, not the way people did in the old days or still do out West or in places like Mexico, Brazil, Spain, the Middle East, or Taiwan, with palaces in town, yachts, ranches here and there, and collections they eventually give to museums. My friends in New York, Boston, and Washington have a dismal commute to work every day, stay in the office late, pay huge taxes, work around the house on weekends, and divorce their wives, when with a little more money, they could maintain a jolly girl in a penthouse full of antiques on a live-and-let-live basis like real big shots . . . everybody would be happier.

It is all just as the Cassandras in Newport and the Union Club prophesied when Roosevelt got in.

It needn't be, however. You can still get rich, although, as I say, you have to change your thinking.

All these successful but non-rich friends of mine have modest, conventional points of view. They went to the right schools and colleges, they joined the right law firms, brokerage houses, or banks; they appear in the right clubs; they have deliberately turned themselves into professionals or corporate functionaries. After federal, state, and city income taxes, capital gains taxes, real estate and inheritance taxes, and the salary ceilings imposed by the threshold of pain of the clients of the law firms or the shareholders of the banks or corporations, they can't possibly do well. Furthermore, the few dollars they can snatch from all these shark-infested waters aren't worth much. The law partner who has to live in New York will also send his three children to private schools: $12,000 each, counting the extras, which in a top tax bracket means he has to earn about $90,000 before taxes just for tuition. Let's not talk about house repairs or medical bills.

The worst of it is that the lawyer or brokerage house vice-president knows that he isn't needed. Other countries get along splendidly with almost no lawyers. A lawyer in Paris, for instance, is quite an exotic figure, and the Japanese resist the arrival of American law firms, saying they want less lawyering and more conscience. (Per capita, Japan has a twentieth of the lawyers—and crime—of America.)

The New York lawyers are like the clerics who made Europe run for centuries: highly trained, often dedicated, and given wide responsibilities because they renounce great personal advantage. Professionals, in a word, not tycoons. New York and Boston are the Vatican of such people, the trust officers, auditors, and investment counselors in their modest habits of charcoal gray.

So step number one is to abandon the entire Eastern respectable point of view, which prizes a safe seat in the shadow of the throne more than the magnificent reality. You have to think like an Elizabethan, an adventurer; like the American of a century ago, not his clerkish descendant of today. You must think as a builder, a conquerer.

Second, you must ask yourself: Where am I needed enough so that I can really get paid for it if I'm able to stand some risk and discomfort?

The answer is, in the developing countries with idle resources—specifically, the ones that have sufficiently overcome their political hangups to be able to welcome capital and entrepreneurship for what it's worth to them, not what envious professors think should suffice in another kind of world.

Much of the world's surface is lying fallow, useless to its population, for lack of entrepreneurs. If you are clever and energetic enough to make the grade in a good law firm, you probably have multiples of what it takes to play a role in building up a developing country. Never fear, the countries themselves know the score—they have investment codes, tax rates, and labor unions, not to speak of anti-free-enterprise intellectuals; but the needs and opportunities are still so great that a trained and able man can reasonably expect to build an interest in something really valuable during his career.

In such places it is taken for granted that one works hard, takes risks, creates something, and is well rewarded for it, now an almost lost idea in the respectable Eastern Seaboard circles, where "new money" is mentioned in whispers.

Young friends of mine have developed a minerals empire in British Columbia; created the principal agricultural-equipment distribution company in Central America; organized the Hong Kong television station; started a bottling company in Thailand; developed a large petrochemical venture in the south of Spain; organized a major investment bank in Madrid; put together a fertilizer complex in Korea; organized vineyards in Australia. I can cite dozens of such cases. Most of these people live magnificently, with swarms of servants who are delighted to have the work. It's expected:

They're merchant princes. That also gives them a chance to exercise a benevolent influence if they're so inclined: To give the public the Morgan Library or the Frick Museum, the founders first had to make the money.

Mind you, the way the world is going I'm not sure that my friends' grandchildren will see much of what they've earned. The governments are likely to pick most of it up along the way. That, however, may well be a good thing for the grandchildren. My father's opinion was that if you loved your children you should not leave them so much that they wouldn't have to do something themselves . . . just the equivalent of a family farm or a professional practice: a place to work, or a little nest egg. The rest should be up to them.

Let me describe the actual process. In the first place, you will have a much easier time if you know something valuable before you set off. A good grasp of investment banking (more precisely, the "deal business") would suffice, or a degree in engineering plus a few years operating in a manufacturing company, or field and money-raising experience in oil or hard-rock geology, or a thorough knowledge of some aspect of finance, such as consumer credit or leasing, or of a consumer business, such as bottling or mail order sales. You must have a business sense and entrepreneurial flair. Ask a seasoned friend how he sizes you up. You also need six months' or a year's eating money, preferably borrowed from older family members.

After you arrive in Vancouver or Caracas or São Paolo or Lisbon or Sydney or Denver or Singapore (one hopes that the place has been chosen rationally, a high growth rate being indispensable), ask around about the young Americans who are doing interesting things. Visit them. Call on a couple of banks and lawyers (preferably with letters of introduction from your own) and take soundings. Everybody will give you lunch. Write it all down. Then visit the local development bank and whatever the ministry of development is called, and then the people who run the local and the U.S. Chambers of Commerce.

If you push right along following up leads, within a couple of months you will have found three or four projects in search of an entrepreneur, including, with luck, one or two where your expertise is applicable. There will be no fast-food franchise, for instance; or a group will want to put up a chemical plant or open a mine and doesn't know which is the correct foreign know-how partner; or the local beer tastes terrible and the development bank would be glad to put money into a joint venture with local investors and a European beer company, but they don't know who to go to; or a hotel site is available but Intercontinental has said no. Who should be next? If an investment bank is operating in the area, the manager can tell you of a dozen such projects that look good but which he is too busy to do more than lend to when they mature. (Make sure the manager is a money-maker himself, though. Usually they aren't.)

In a month you will have five telephone calls waiting for you each time you get back to your hotel, and after three months you can decide to work on two or three of these projects for a piece of the action and expenses—but no salary.

If you are always honest, energetic, and careful, then even if the first project doesn't score, you will get a reputation for being serious, and after a while the solid groups will seek you out with something really worthwhile.

The obvious function for the technically competent young American in this situation is writing the feasibility study in English, using a variety of assumptions and with the figures really worked out, and then helping raise the foreign capital.

When you have got the study in adequate form, go home and ask the uncle who grub-staked you who the foreign corporate know-how and financial partner should be. He won't know, but one of his cronies in a management consulting firm will give you introductions to three or four.

Present the deal to the most likely company last. The first presentations will reveal so many shortcomings in your feasibility study that you will be partially discredited. By the last one or two you should have thought of almost everything.

It's easier to put this sort of thing together than you'd think. Have yourself cut in for a free 5 percent interest and a part-time job as assistant managing director.

After two or three years and a couple of small deals ($1 million or so) you can try for the brass ring of a $5-million hotel or bottling company or a $10-million manufacturing plant. If you do it from scratch, you can cut yourself in for some free stock, and you'll be on your way.

Why can't all this be done in the States? It can, but the competition is much tougher. Any number of large corporations are constantly sifting through stacks of self-generated expansion possibilities. There are hundreds of competent deal makers in even provincial centers, and the real G.N.P. growth in sectors where individual entrepreneurs can function is more limited.

In the United States you haven't got the comfortable margin for error that you have in the developing country, where you have more opportunities, less competing talent, and a chance to look up the answers in the back of the book, so to speak, by bringing in foreign know-how.

Of course, we do have internal frontiers. A lot of entrepreneurs prospered in Silicon Valley, and it's probably not too late to get in on the Western energy play; if you are hungry enough and have the right background, you can start a successful new service business in any rapidly growing area.

Anyway, it only takes one 10 percent free slice (or even your third of the free slice) of a $10-million project and you are off to the races. If the enterprise succeeds and after five or ten years is worth three or four times as much, you've made it. The chances may be better than you think, although by no means certain: I have other Elizabethan friends who went to the wrong countries or who weren't all that able and who *haven't* become tycoons, or even successful. But even they seem to me to exude a sense of a life more fully experienced than most of my country-club professional friends.

I am not talking about putting money into foreign ventures without going there. It will be lost. I am talking about going and staying, of committing your working life to a place that needs your energy, talent, and knowledge of a more advanced economy and will reward it. I can't guarantee that this prescription will make you rich, but it probably won't happen any other way.

And when your former classmate turns up—now a postdoctoral student in neo-Hegelian dialectics—and asks you about the contrast between your elegant existence and that of the poorer citizens, don't bother to tell him about the hundreds of people you created jobs for or the thousands who eat because you made the desert bloom. Just seize him by the seat of his pants and collar and propel him into your (heated) swimming pool.

Learned Hand put it better, as usual: ". . . in establishing a business, or in excavating an ancient city, or in rearing a family, or in writing a play, or in observing an epidemic, or in splitting up an atom, or in learning the nature of space, or even in divining the structure of this giddy universe, in all chosen jobs the craftsman must be at work, and the craftsman, as Stevenson says, gets his hire as he goes. . . . If it be selfishness to work on the job one likes, because one likes it and for no other end, let us accept the odium."

# V.

# Personal Finance

# Insurance

Insurance, like a parachute, is an encumbrance that you need for emergencies, but should avoid when you can get along without it. The policies are designed to enrich the underwriters, not the policyholders.

Let's start with the kinds one *does* need.

First comes *third-party liability,* or "umbrella" coverage. In our wildly litigious society you must be prepared for large damage suits, often frivolous. A rule of thumb is that your third-party coverage should equal several times your net worth, and $1 or $2 million in any event. It's not expensive. The company's attorneys defend your case in court for you, which improves your peace of mind.

Second, in my opinion, comes *disability* coverage, which is often neglected. Typically this amounts to 60 percent of salary, tax-free, for life in case of accident and to age sixty-five in case of illness. An inflation-adjusted policy has recently become available. Purely in financial terms, disability often represents a graver catastrophe for a family than the death of one of its members. If a spouse dies, life insurance or trust capital may become available, and the surviving spouse may remarry. If a spouse is disabled, there's no life insurance, the trusts don't fall in, the surviving spouse almost never remarries, and a full-time couple may be needed to care for the disabled person.

The policy should cover either recurrent or partial disability. To save money, one may prefer a long "elimination period" or interval before coverage starts—the deductible, as it were. They run from one month to three years. For a six-month elimination period, you might pay 30 percent less than for one month.

Since a "catastrophic illness" can cost $100,000, *major medical* coverage is important. High deductibles and partial self-insurance are fine, but make sure the policy benefits are not "scheduled"—limited to so many dollars a day, or whatever. Hospitalization used to cost five dollars a day in New York! A Blue Cross–Blue Shield base policy really amounts to lowering your major medical deductible, since the most it can save you is likely to be less than $10,000, and is thus not necessarily appropriate for a person of means.

This leads us to other types of superfluous insurance. In general, it's anything you can afford to pay yourself, starting with the first few hundred dollars of damage to a rented car. I've saved a lot of money by always checking "no" on the rental form. Similar is *collision* coverage on your own car, except perhaps for the first couple of years of a new Rolls or Mercedes. It only pays, after your tax salvage, if you have frequent crashes that are *your fault.* (No-fault refers to personal injury.) But if you make repeated claims your coverage may be cancelled anyway. And remember that after a total loss, you don't get your purchase price back, just the value of a similar used car.

Another doubtful category is *theft* coverage on standard household objects that one can afford to replace: TV sets, stereos, ordinary flatware, and so forth. The net result of such insurance over a lifetime will just be to increase their cost. As to jewelry and rare coins and stamps, again it doesn't ordinarily pay to insure them; they belong in a safe-deposit box. For guns, furs, and the like, buy a secondhand safe and put it in the cellar: Burglars hate cellars, because they're trapped if the police appear. Fine arts coverage, on the contrary, is quite cheap.

Older persons should note that the I.R.S. routinely asks for back insurance policies, where higher valuations may appear than an executor would want to argue for.

For *homeowner's* coverage, here are some suggestions: (1) Keep the deductibles as high as possible. (2) Photograph everything or have it reappraised occasionally. Keep the shots in your office, not at home. (3) Make sure the coverage on the structure is for at least 80 percent of *replacement* value (not cost or market) or you may not get a partial loss reimbursed in full. An "inflation guard" amendment is helpful, but you must still review the coverage periodically. (4) Don't insure against small losses. After several such claims the company may well throw you out or bump you into a higher risk category. It won't mind paying off on the target event, but hates a series of small claims that roughly offset the premium payments. (5) Decide whether you want to insure the value of your furniture as is ("cash value") or the cost of replacing it new ("replacement value"). (6) Read the policy carefully. It may lapse if you leave the house unattended for some time or contain other surprises.

As to *life insurance*, the risk one does need to insure against is untimely death. A young man with a family should carry enough coverage to pay off the mortgage and see his children through college. But as he rises in the world, and his pension rights and invested savings build up, he needs less and less. So most breadwinners should consider $200,000, say, of term coverage, to age fifty-five or so. One may also want term life to fund a partnership buyout or to provide cash for an illiquid estate. "Renewable" term avoids the need for subsequent health examinations. If it's correctly done, a business can deduct the premiums on $50,000 of group life for an executive without his having to pay tax on them.

Other than such term coverage, a person of means usually needs less life insurance than he may think. Remember

### Table 5. Types of Homeowners' Insurance Policies

| *Basic (HO-1)* | *Broad (HO-2)* |
| --- | --- |
| 1. Fire and lightning | Costs 15–20 percent more than Basic. |
| 2. Loss of property taken out of endangered premises | Risks 1–12, plus: |
| 3. Wind and hail | 13. Falling objects (e.g., branches) |
| 4. Explosion (not sonic booms or electric wiring) | 14. Weight of snow and ice (including to plants) |
| 5. Riots | 15. Building collapse |
| 6. Aircraft | 16. Damage to hot water system |
| 7. Vehicles (not damage to fences, etc., if driven by occupant) | 17. Water or steam damage from appliances |
| 8. Smoke | 18. Frozen pipes or domestic appliances |
| 9. Vandalism | 19. Electric shock |
| 10. Theft | |
| 11. Broken windows | |
| 12. Third-party liability[1] | |

[1]Specified amount of property damage, bodily injury, and medical payments, except that caused by a contractor or employee, or insured's business or vehicles.

| Broad and Extended (HO-3) | Comprehensive (HO-5) |
|---|---|
| Costs 25 percent more than Basic. | Costs 65–70 percent more than Basic. |
| Risks 1–19, plus: | All risks *except* |
| 20. Damage to pavements, terraces, septic tanks, and fences | 1. Flood |
| | 2. Tidal waves |
| | 3. Earthquakes |
| | 4. Nuclear radiation |
| | and others specified in policy |

| Tenants (HO-4) | Condominium (HO-6) |
|---|---|
| Like Broad, but *contents* of building only. Also used for cooperative apartments | Like Tenants (HO-4) but adapted to condominiums |

the theory of insurance: It's a wager whose odds favor the house. And over any long period the benefits stand to be decimated by inflation.

*Whole life* (also called ordinary, permanent, straight, level premium, or cash value) is the wager on untimely death combined with an investment ("endowment") component, so that if the insured doesn't die he still gets a cash value eventually. It's almost always a bad deal *for the person of substantial means who saves systematically.* The buildup of value on the investment side of whole life is far less than you can obtain elsewhere with no greater risk. If it were offered separately as a mutual fund, you'd probably reject it.

Life insurance on children is usually silly.

# Estate Planning

This is a subject of cardinal importance and amazing complexity.

Every person of means must have an estate plan or, regardless of how clever an investor he is, he risks dissipating his life's savings and frustrating his intentions.

There is no shortcut. Do-it-yourself techniques are often disastrous. (That is why I will not make many specific suggestions.)

Go ahead and smoke in bed, drive with worn-out tires, or climb without a rope. You *may* be all right. But don't try to skimp on a good trusts-and-estates lawyer or you will get your family into a mess.

Find a good one, call him up, and go to see him. He should be a man you trust completely, with enough personal stature so that, like a doctor, he can recommend somewhat unwelcome courses in the expectation that you will follow them. For instance, every person of wealth should have a regular program of giving to his children, and yet often nobody around him dares suggest it.

Where should you find this paragon? Ideally, you know him already, at least by reputation. If not, a safe way is to try the law firm of a trust company other than the one you deal with. It is usual for one or two directors of a trust company to be from its law firm. If you go to one of them, he will bring in a younger trusts-and-estates man, who will look after you. The junior will know that his eminent chief is aware of you, and will be careful.

To save time, do as much thinking as you can in advance of your visit. Make an inventory of the main items of property you own and the persons and causes you want it to go to, with extensive comments. Otherwise the learned counselor must do this task for you through the question-and-answer method, at much greater expense.

Also, do a schedule of your expected earnings, including stock options, deferred compensation, pensions, and the like, and any insurance you may have. A few back tax returns and summaries of your annual expenditures would be helpful.

In other words, try to arrive with as much as possible already done, so that the lawyer can set to work efficiently.

You may want to ask him to send you a standard legal handbook on trusts and estates so that you can both use the same language. I like one called *You and Your Will,* by Paul Ashley, published by McGraw-Hill.

I find that a good way to rewrite one's will is to review that book, or one like it, considering the various possibilities, and then to write a rambling memorandum in longhand on several pages of paper that sets forth one's views of things and states in general terms what one hopes to achieve.

For instance, a useful observation in such a memorandum might be, "My son Harry is interested in art but not in business, and while he is reliable in family matters and should be consulted, he would not be a good person to designate as trustee. In fact, it might be wise to keep capital out of his hands until he is about forty-five, except for specific needs, such as to buy a house.

"My daughter Susan has extravagant taste and seems to attract men of an unreliable sort. It would be better for her in the long run if she—and thus her admirers—had no prospect of getting control of large amounts of capital. That way, if anybody marries her it will be for herself, rather than in the hope of separating her from a substantial part of her fortune.

"George, although young, is completely practical and solid, knows when to seek advice, and will become an even better trustee as he grows older and gains experience."

Remember that wills can be changed easily, and, indeed, should be changed every time some significant family circumstance changes. So these dispositions need not be considered set in concrete.

This memorandum would be a completely confidential document, intended only for the lawyer's eyes. But it will enable him to construct a tailor-made instrument. If one fails to set things up this way, then all too probably one will get a boiler-plate will, off the shelf, which will not quite correspond to the situation of one's particular family.

I like to receive a copy of a client's will, whether in draft or in final version, and do a diagram of its provisions and make comments. Because of the continuing nature of his involvement in a family's affairs, an investment adviser should have a good feeling for the economic considerations; and since one sees these problems worked out in many different client families, one can often be helpful by making suggestions based on the family's particular circumstances.

Remember that a will is not set in concrete. Your circumstances and views will evolve and the laws likewise, so your will or trust(s) should be modified periodically.

Always have your lawyer do a simple *diagram* of your estate plan. It makes things much easier to understand.

Ask the firm in question how, when the law changes, it reviews its wills and trusts. Some of the most efficient firms put the significant provisions in a computer so that when there are new developments the machine can regurgitate the instruments that require attention.

There is one idea which I touched on earlier that you should mention to your lawyer. Quite often trusts have a bank as trustee. These days banks and trust companies are bought, sold, or merged quite freely. Some of them end up in the hands of Texas oil men, foreign conglomerators, or other un-fiduciary personalities. They also grow so large they become more like industrial companies. I think a trust instrument should provide that a committee of the adult beneficiaries, or some designated individual, should be able to remove the corporate trustee and replace it with another. This also enables you to take action if you slip into the hands of a dullard within the trust company.

Elderly persons sometimes like to place their property in a living, or revocable, trust, which becomes a testamentary trust upon death. During the lifetime of the settlor he can observe how the trustees work together, whether the investment adviser is serious, and in general whether he is happy with the way his intentions are being fulfilled.

A standby revocable trust can be designed to enable some trusted persons to take over if an elderly person becomes unable to look after business matters. This arrangement should be used much more widely than it is.

There is another class of professional called a personal financial planner. He acts as your chief financial officer, doing as much or as little as you like, including advising you on tax shelters, the insurance you should carry, and similar matters. Some large banks have such services, and there are independent firms as well. Corporations sometimes offer the use of such a service as a fringe benefit to their more important officers.

Some orderly individuals have annual meetings with their lawyer, investment adviser, tax accountant, and, if appropriate, their financial planner. It is an excellent idea.

# Property Transfers

Here are some ingenious methods used, where circumstances permit it, to transfer substantial amounts of property to a younger generation with little tax.

1. Outright sale
   a. *In return for an interest-free note*
      One possibility is to sell the property to one's children and take payment in the form of an interest-free demand note. Each year one can demand payment of a principal amount equal to the after-tax income from the property. This technique freezes the value of the property in one's estate and reduces it over time through payments on the note. The payments are not taxable when paid, but one must recognize the entire capital gain at the time of sale.
   b. *In return for an interest-bearing note*
      One can defer the capital gains tax on the sale by taking back interest-bearing notes with a fixed payment schedule. One is liable for capital gains tax as the notes are paid. The disadvantage is that it is tax-inefficient for the children to make high taxable-interest payments if they are in a lower tax bracket than the parent generation.

      In a sense one is freezing the value of the property in one's estate at today's value plus interest, rather than at today's value.
2. Sale of a remainder interest
   Instead of selling the property outright, one can sell one's children a remainder interest in it. The property is valued at current market value discounted at 6 percent to the seller's estimated year of death based on I.R.S. actuarial tables.

This has two advantages over an outright sale. First, the value of the present transfer is far less, perhaps no more than one-third of present market, and thus the capital gain is correspondingly less than in an outright sale. Second, during one's lifetime one keeps control and use of the property, including the income. Any appreciation after the sale date will accrue to the children and will not be included in one's estate. One can receive either interest-free or interest-bearing notes.

One loses some flexibility after such a sale, at least in theory. If one later wanted to sell or substantially alter the property, one would need the children's agreement. Also, the children could resell their remainder interest without the consent of the parent.

3. Sale in return for an annuity

   Another possibility can be to buy a joint-and-survivor or lifetime annuity from one's children in exchange for the property. This freezes the value of the property in one's estate and provides an income for life.

   The amount of the annuity should be determined from the annuity tables found in the I.R.S. regulations, to avoid an I.R.S. challenge that the payment rate is too low and that one has, therefore, made a gift of part of the value of the property. If the annuity payments total more than the after-tax income received by one's children from the property, they must make up the difference.

   An annuity is taxed partly as interest income (using an imputed 6 percent rate) and partly as principal. If the property value used in the calculation is above one's tax basis, the principal portion of the annuity is considered partly return of capital and partly capital gain, in the same proportion as the original tax basis bears to the appreciation.

   Thus, the annuity is treated for tax purposes very much like an installment sale, with the difference that one continues to receive payments for life (and thus should not run short of cash), but at death there is no residual value in one's estate.

4. Creation of a family partnership

Under this arrangement one can avoid realizing capital gains while transferring future appreciation to one's children and providing oneself an income during one's lifetime.

One forms a limited partnership with the children as general partners and their parent(s) as limited partners. The parent(s) acquire the limited partnership interest for the market value of the property in a tax-free exchange.

The limited partnership interest can be designed so that one receives all the income from the partnership up to the value that the property had when one contributed it, and thereafter a smaller share. The general partners (the children) would receive the rest.

Upon sale of the assets, or upon liquidation of the partnership, one might receive an amount equal to the value of the property when contributed, plus some interest factor, less all sums paid out previously; the children would get the rest. The distribution provisions can be designed to suit one's needs, but the original value of one's limited partnership interest should be equal to that of the property, so that the children's interests have no value at first. In this way one avoids gift tax.

Although the children will have management control as general partners, one's consent can be required in order to sell the assets of the partnership, liquidate it or change one's interest in it.

5. Creation of a family corporation

A variation of the family partnership, this involves exchanging one's property interest for preferred stock in a family corporation in which the children are the common stockholders.

It works like the partnership, but is usually less tax-efficient. Earnings paid out are taxed twice: once at the corporate level and a second time as dividend income at one's own level.

Since these are complicated matters, with both the law, the Internal Revenue Service's positions, and specific case decisions subject to change, one must be guided by tax counsel in analyzing the appropriate tactic for one's particular circumstances.

# Income-Splitting Through Clifford Trusts

A Clifford trust is an irrevocable *inter vivos* reversionary trust whose income is payable to someone other than the grantor or his spouse. It amounts to "parking" the corpus in a trust for a lower-bracket person. The corpus reverts to the grantor or his estate no less than ten years after the trust is funded, or on the death of the income beneficiary, or at some other specified event that, when the trust is funded, cannot reasonably be expected to occur within ten years.

A Clifford trust permits a grantor to reduce tax by diverting income from the grantor to a lower-bracket beneficiary, such as a child, elderly parent, or retired employee, without permanently giving up the property.

In general, the grantor should not be the trustee. When the I.R.S. attacks a Clifford trust, it is most typically because the settlor had not fully shed all control over it. Particularly, only an independent trustee can accumulate income or allocate it between beneficiaries and after-borns, or lend the trust's money back to the grantor. A grantor may under some circumstances borrow the original capital back from the trust against a personal note, so long as the original gift to the trust was made in good faith; the interest paid to the trust is deductible by the grantor and taxable to the beneficiary.

A money fund makes a neat holding for a Clifford trust, since there is a place for high-income liquid reserves in a family's financial picture, and they can advantageously be placed in a low-tax "pocket."

1. Gift tax

   Settlement of the trust represents a gift to the beneficiary of the income produced during the trust's term. The value of the gift is the present worth of this income interest. The Treasury has published a table for use in determining present worth which assumes a rate of return on the trust assets of 6 percent. If the trust generates more than 6 percent, the gift tax does not rise. Until things change—which they may well—this constitutes a tax planning opportunity.

   To take maximum advantage of the annual exclusions available to the grantor and spouse, a Clifford trust can be funded with a series of annual gifts, so long as the term of the trust extends at least ten years beyond the date of the last gift.

   The annual exclusion is $10,000 per donee per year, or $20,000 for married taxpayers. The following table shows the effect of a five-year program to "park" about $200,000 in a fourteen-year Clifford trust, never transferring a present value of over $20,000 a year, so as to avoid giving rise to gift taxes.

   It will be noted that an income of about $5,000 for ten years can be transferred each year in this way, using a recoverable corpus of approximately $45,000.

2. Estate tax

   Income earned on the corpus during the term of the trust, and income on that income, is excluded from the grantor's estate. The grantor's reversionary interest

| Year of Program | Remaining Years of Trust | Annual Capital Added to Trust | Times the I.R.S. Valuation Factor of | Present Taxable Value of Gift | Cumulative Capital in Trust | Cumulative Income Assuming 12% Yield Before Compounding |
|---|---|---|---|---|---|---|
| 1 | 14 | $35,861 | .557699 | $20,000 | $ 35,861 | $ 4,303 |
| 2 | 13 | 37,653 | .531161 | 20,000 | 73,514 | 8,822 |
| 3 | 12 | 39,758 | .503031 | 20,000 | 113,272 | 13,593 |
| 4 | 11 | 42,264 | .473212 | 20,000 | 155,536 | 18,665 |
| 5 | 10 | 45,289 | .441605 | 20,000 | 200,825 | 24,099 |
| 6–14 | — | — | — | — | 200,825 | 216,891 |
| | | | | | | $286,373 |

215

in the trust corpus is included, and computed as the present value of the right to receive the corpus upon termination of the trust, based on the same Treasury tables used to value the income interest.

3. Income tax

A Clifford trust is usually drafted as a simple trust, which means it is required to distribute all its income currently. The income will be taxed to the trust beneficiary as long as the grantor receives no direct or indirect benefit from it. Although the trust files a tax return, no tax is owed. Capital gains and losses are taxable to the grantor, so it is usually desirable to hold assets that have high yields and high cost bases.

# Crown Loans

In considering a Clifford trust one should compare it with a "Crown" loan—an interest-free demand loan between family members. The interest-free loan approach is much simpler. A parent lends a child (for example) $50,000 without interest, and the child keeps the $6,000 a year it earns if the funds are invested at, say, 12 percent, thus transferring that income from the parent's bracket to the child's. (One should be careful not to let the demand loan run on for too many years, or collection becomes unenforceable under the statute of limitations. If the claim is abandoned, a gift, subject to gift tax, has been made to the borrower.) The I.R.S. dislikes the Crown loan procedure, claiming that the "forgiven" interest constitutes a gift, but has lost almost all the cases it has brought in tax court. The I.R.S. may also claim that there should be a tax payable on imputed interest. Someday the I.R.S. could prevail, or the law may change, so this technique might no longer be as useful.

It could be that by that time, when one might want to switch from a Crown loan to a Clifford trust, the Clifford trust advantage might be reduced. For instance, the 6 percent discount on future revenues for calculating the value for gift tax purposes could be raised to a realistic level. Or the $20,000 annual joint gift tax exclusion might go back toward its former level of $6,000. Thus, the present advantage may not last forever, and if appropriate, should probably be taken advantage of.

# Powers of Attorney

One should usually designate some trusted person one's attorney-in-fact (that is, give him a power of attorney) to act on one's behalf when one is away or otherwise unable to act. A case can be made for giving preference to a non-family member.

At the time of signing a power of attorney, one may wish to add a limitation as to date, such as "Valid until January 1, 1985." Otherwise the arrangement may be hard to extinguish.

Some states permit a "durable" power of attorney that is valid even in the event of the grantor's incompetency.

One's attorney-in-fact should not be a trustee of any trust of which one is creator or beneficiary. The appointment could be set aside on the grounds of conflict of interest.

One should consider, in naming one's spouse as attorney-in fact, that in the event of marital discord there could be problems before the power can be revoked.

If the attorney-in-fact commits imprudent or improper acts, he, not the grantor, is liable unless there is a special "indemnification" clause in the instrument. He may well request such an indemnification against any liability he may incur.

Powers of attorney should be noted or copies filed in a central place and reviewed occasionally, so that they can be revoked or changed when they become inappropriate.

# Custody

For many reasons I think it is preferable for a substantial investor to confide the custody of his securities to a qualified bank, rather than use a stockbroker or a safe-deposit box.

1. The bank and the broker incur similar costs in providing similar services to the investor. However, the billing system is different. The bank charges a custody fee, while the broker increases his commission.

The custody fee, though, is tax deductible to the investor; the broker's commission is not. So on an after-tax basis, an investor is likely to pay more for custody to a broker than to a bank.

2. Banks are safer than brokers. Since the custody function of a bank is sealed off from the lending function, in the unlikely event that a bank should get into financial difficulties the investor's securities are never at risk. If, on the contrary, a brokerage house fails (a more frequent occurrence than a bank failure), the customer's securities may become mingled with the broker's general assets. Even if that is not so, it can take a long time to sort things out. Should this period fall when it would be to the investor's interest to buy or sell, he may suffer grave inconvenience.

3. If a broker has custody of an investor's securities, he expects to do all the stock exchange business of the account. That, however, is not in the customer's interest. When my firm is buying or selling a stock where the transactions must be conducted with care, we begin with a particular broker

and give him instructions on how to handle the orders. He will execute orders depending on strength or weakness. From time to time we will withdraw the order entirely.

An investment counsel firm should not instruct both its principal broker and a number of clients' brokers to buy or sell the same stock at the same time. The specialist who makes the market on the floor of the exchange will think that there is more interest than is actually the case.

So in this situation, one first executes the transactions of those clients who are not tied to a particular broker.

4. An investment adviser may not like any one broker to know everything he is doing. There is nothing to stop him from disseminating a report of the transactions within his own circle. Indeed, it is likely to happen.

5. In using a safe-deposit box for custody, one saves a few hundred dollars a year after tax, but loses the bank's record-keeping services, their alertness to the need for timely tendering of stock in a takeover situation, and many other advantages, quite aside from the inconvenience of the arrangement.

# Residence and Tax

Many foreign countries have almost confiscatory taxes on investment income or estates, and others will have them in the future.

Some other countries, on the contrary, have lower taxes than here.

An American proposing to reside—and thus potentially become taxable—abroad needs to face his or her new tax situation as early as possible, and make sure the appearance of things conforms to the status he wishes to achieve. One should get all this straight *before* making the move. Sometimes a single ill-considered step makes the desired solution almost impossible to achieve.

The general principles in almost all jurisdictions are that:

1. You become a local resident for tax purposes after a certain time and/or when it becomes apparent you intend to stay. A woman tends to acquire her husband's residence for tax purposes and should therefore be particularly careful if that is not desired.
2. Some types of money transfers are not (or only lightly) taxed. These include transfers identifiable as "capital" rather than "income" in most countries. Annuity payments from abroad are treated differently in different jurisdictions, but are in general lightly taxed.

If one recognizes the problem early enough one can usually do a lot about it, both by not fully taking root in the new country while maintaining one's links with the old (should that be the objective), and by selecting the funds to be brought into the new country so that they are not subject to heavy taxation there.

A somewhat similar situation exists as between different states of the U.S.

Residence and Character of Remittances are discussed in the two following sections, and the U.S. situation in the last one.

# Residence

During the time an American living in a foreign country is still not considered to be a local resident for tax purposes, his U.S. income is usually not taxed, except to the extent that it is brought into the country. Where U.S. tax rates on investment income are lower than those in the foreign jurisdiction, it pays to try to avoid getting caught up in local taxation. The rules vary in each country, but the general one is that when the foreigner looks as though he has decided to stay, and severs his connections with his country of origin, then he becomes a local resident for tax purposes. All his income worldwide may become subject to local income taxes and his property worldwide may become subject to local estate or wealth taxes.

Any U.S.-situs trust of which he is trustee may become subject to British tax, for example, once his residence there is established; a counter to this is to have a majority of non-U.K. trustees.

Thus, it is usually better for an American not to own a residence in his own name in a higher-tax foreign jurisdiction. To have one creates a presumption of residence, and in some countries also attracts a wealth tax. Rather, if the American is, for instance, the beneficiary of a trust in the U.S., the trust can own the residence. (This is ceasing to be true in France.)

Ideally, it should do so through an offshore holding company, so that local capital gains, transfer, and estate taxes can be avoided by transferring the holding company rather than the residence itself to a subsequent owner when the time comes. (Real estate transfers in Europe are in general much more heavily taxed than in the U.S.)

To postpone the moment of local residence and thus taxability, one should diminish the appearance of permanent local residence and continue appropriate links with one's homeland. Some of these are:

1. Maintaining an interest in a house or apartment in the home country, preferably with one's name on the door, and getting as much mail there as possible
2. Taking vacations at home
3. Going home to vote

4. Having one's name in the home telephone book
5. Maintaining home charge accounts and club memberships, with bills going to the home address
6. Owning a plot at home designated for one's burial
7. Having an essentially temporary residence permit or visa
8. Giving the home address to local authorities and using it
   in contracts and wills

Conversely, one should to the extent possible *avoid* these
ties as to the foreign country in order *not* to create a presumption of residence there. Ideally, one does not have a
place of one's own to live in, but stays in a hotel or with
friends.

Some jurisdictions use a count of the number of days'
residence in a certain number of previous years as an indicator.

For advice from British counsel on this subject, see Appendix III, page 249.

The Inland Revenue usually accepts that foreigners who
are living in England while their children are being educated
there and do not take root permanently in other ways do not
thereby become domiciled for tax purposes.

There is another side to this question. Sometimes one
may prefer to establish that one *is* resident abroad and *not* in
the U.S. For a discussion by U.S. counsel on this subject, see
Appendix III, page 247.

# Character of Remittances

Insuring that the character of the funds brought into the
host country is such as to minimize taxation also requires
careful planning. One can sometimes arrange distributions
abroad from a U.S. trust so that they are considered "capital"
rather than "income" and thus not necessarily subject to local
taxation. The articles of the trust should permit that flexibility; that is, they should leave as much discretion as possible
with the trustees. Also, the capital should be transferred at

irregular intervals into a specially designated "capital account" in the other country.

Another approach is to borrow money from a bank in the foreign country where one lives, guaranteed by one's U.S. assets.

My firm has solved this problem for U.S. clients living abroad by selling anticipated U.S. income to a U.S. investor in return for a capital amount. This need not have a U.S. tax effect. The proceeds can often be brought into a foreign country without tax there. It must, of course, be a *bona fide* sale.

# State Domicile in the U.S.

If a United States resident lives in more than one state, both may well attempt to collect tax in full from his estate.

Even if the estate succeeds in convincing the courts that one state and not the other was the principal domicile, the legal cost of establishing that point may be high, and during the period of litigation the estate may not be able to make distributions.

It is therefore important to decide definitely which state one wishes to have as one's domicile.

This involves income and estate tax and other elements.

Having made the decision, one should go about establishing the indicia of residence in that state in exactly the same way one does as between different countries: (1) Try to concentrate one's time and principal activities there; (2) get one's driver's license there and relinquish any others; (3) vote there; (4) make sure that all billings go to that address; (5) make sure that it is the address of record in all documents relating to government agencies; (6) be active there, such as by joining parent-teachers associations, civic groups, clubs, and the like.

Finally, one should make a declaration of domicile, attach it to one's personal papers, and circulate copies to one's lawyer, accountant, and other professional advisers.

These questions are far from simple, and require the assistance of specialized legal counsel as early in the process as possible.

# Tax Shelters

My view of this subject is sufficiently different from what one usually hears that I should probably state my credentials. I have been involved in almost all the activities that give rise to tax shelters, including several years in oil investments, agriculture—domestic and foreign—on a large scale, mining, real estate, cattle, "start-ups," and others. A number of these enterprises are international. Many worked out, some were "dry holes." I have been asked to lecture on tax shelters by the American Management Association and similar groups.

The advice on tax shelters in general that I give to such audiences is, briefly, forget it. Pay the tax.

Particularly, there is not likely to be happiness in a tax-shelter program that is sold through a prospectus. If a program is, by some miracle, going to be economically rewarding to the investor it will probably be (1) odd and hard to understand, and (2) offered privately.

## Tax Shelter and Tax Deferral

Here is an important distinction. As I use the terms, a tax *shelter* is a program that takes taxable income and turns it into capital, so that it may never be taxed. Tax *deferral* means taking income that would ordinarily be taxable this year and bumping it over to next year or later years.

The pattern of deduction now and income later flows from the nature of what is being invested in. For instance, oil-drilling programs can be carried out in one year, and tend to produce income (if ever) quite promptly. Tree-crop agriculture normally shows losses of five years plus another year for each bout of bad weather, and with luck can pay off well thereafter. Mining-exploration programs should take three years (one for a broad sweep, one to focus on a few prospects, and the last to block out one or two sites); income is not likely for a good five years after that. These are all tax *shelters* if successful, as is backing an inventor. In all these cases you can sell the assets you've created.

If you back a play successfully, you get a tax deduction at the outset, but will have taxable income later on if the show is a hit. So that's a deferral.

There are also artificial tax *deferrals*, intended to push a capital gain back a year. The I.R.S. dislikes this maneuver, and one should never do it for a series of capital gains, as the problem piles up and gets worse and worse.

If you are sixty years old and a successful professional, you will probably be paying a lot of tax. It would in theory be good business for you to take, say, $10,000 a year off your top bracket between now and retirement, and put it in a deferral program that will, if all goes well, give it back to you with interest thereafter, in your then lower bracket.

## Fresh Versus Obsolete Incentives

When first created, most tax incentives correspond to a valid national economic objective. Sometimes the purpose is fulfilled, but as with most government programs, a pressure group of the recipients and the bureaucracy concerned has been built up and the program has acquired a life of its own. Thus, there are tax benefits for people who breed racehorses that were doubtless useful in the age of cavalry but may be less needed now, and likewise for producers of Broadway plays, probably not an urgent federal interest. One would think this might create interesting opportunities. Unfortunately, I do not actually know of any obsolete incentives that are worth pursuing. For every dollar that goes into Broadway or racehorse breeding, the value of what the investors have at the end of the year is probably about twenty cents. It seems that the idea of a tax break stimulates people's gambling instinct, and lures in more money than the merits of the situation justify.

# Schizophrenia

Another problem with tax incentives is that the government is of two minds about them. With the right lobe of its brain it wants to get a job done—finding more gold, let's say—and feels that a tax incentive for the investor is the neatest way to make things happen. On the other hand, as soon as some optimist responds to the carrot and inches forward, the left lobe starts shrieking, "Tax dodger! Loophole snatcher! Profiteer!" and tightens up the tax net with "recaptures" and disallowances so that he won't get his carrot after all.*

That seems most unfair. If I am hypnotized by the recruiting sergeant's blarney and sign up for a three-year hitch in the army, he shouldn't then call me a fascist cannibal, and if I am induced to drop good money into a program that Congress has just set up, it does not mean I am guilty of antisocial behavior.

It does to the Internal Revenue Service, though. Congress knows what it wants and legislates the incentives, but

---

*I cannot leave this subject without commenting on the unwisdom and unfairness of taxing a "capital gain" that has been manufactured by the government's own inflation.

If I bought a cast-iron anchor for $10 in 1935 and sell it now for $40, its intrinsic value has not increased and I haven't gained anything. I can't buy as much now with the $40 as with the original $10. Why should the government tax the $30 as "profit"? Also, of course, if your salary is augmented to offset inflation, that puts you in a higher tax bracket every year even if your buying power is unchanged or indeed diminished.

the I.R.S.'s job is to collect taxes, and it views every taxpayer as an adversary.

# The Payoff . . . Or Lack of It

In the 1930s and 1940s and even into the early 1950s, the public at large didn't really understand the economics of drilling for oil, so there wasn't much money available for the drilling that needed to be done. Furthermore, there was much more oil awaiting discovery. You could build a fortune by bold and skillful drilling. And by the 1950s, the maximum tax bracket had gotten up to 92 percent. In other words, the interest of drilling as against paying the tax was at its highest. For a while the investor developed fifty to seventy-five cents of value per dollar he put in, but on an after-tax basis had risked only twenty-five cents of his own money, say. The government would have gotten the rest anyway.

Then things became quite different. The top Federal bracket was reduced to 50 percent (a most sensible move—although in some areas state and city taxes get it up to 65 percent pretty fast), and the oil is more and more costly to find.

Furthermore, the principle of tax drilling is universally understood. There are literally hundreds of drilling programs, many involving tens of millions of dollars. There is, in fact, more drilling money than can be well spent. And, of course, the good deals never find their way east.

So the risk-reward balance has tipped against the investor. I would guess that recently all private oil-drilling investors as a class were not much better off than the backers of Broadway plays. Until the OPEC rise in oil prices, they probably developed twenty cents or so of value for every dollar they put into the ground, and if they are salaried executives or professionals, they are probably using fifty-cent dollars—very poor odds indeed! Oil drilling appeals to an investor's gambling instinct, not his prudence.

Of course, higher oil prices improved the odds again for a while.

Oil is the best known of the tax shelters, and therefore tends to give the worst odds. The more exotic the program and the longer the payout (that is, the longer it takes to recover your cash), the more likely the odds are to be acceptable. In mining, for instance, it takes forever to get your money back—often ten years or so—and there are relatively few programs available. I think that a minerals exploration program run by a gifted and honest miser may well be an acceptable risk, particularly if you absolutely refuse to develop with your own money whatever orebody may be found. Turn it over to a mining company for the best deal you can get.

Finally, some tax shelters are so intrinsically attractive they attract too much money, forcing the return down below zero. I have mentioned racehorses and Broadway plays; one thinks also of California vineyards. I find it hard to believe that there isn't far too much money going into them.

So in general, for almost all the familiar tax-shelter areas, if it's possible to understand one easily and if it has real intrinsic charm, then there probably isn't an attractive return.

# Sponsorship

The sponsorship (as distinct from the operating management) of a tax-shelter program is of cardinal importance to the investor. The sponsor should be of high integrity, should have a solid record of success in whatever business the tax shelter is about, and should have ample personal means. Most tax-shelter programs are failures; virtually all are failures when the sponsorship does not meet these three tests.

Integrity is important because the day-to-day operations of a tax shelter are not regulated the way the Stock Exchange is, and the opportunities to cut corners to the disadvantage of the investor are many. Furthermore, limited partnerships do not have annual meetings like corporations, where the stockholders can put management on the griddle. The limited partners do not ordinarily even meet each other, and class-action suits are much rarer than in corporations.

The sponsor's personal wealth becomes important if a tax shelter doesn't work out right away. Money is raised from investors to cover the loss phase of an operation. The money doesn't go to buy hardware, since then it wouldn't be deductible. So at some point the investors' money has been spent, the loss incurred, and the question becomes what to do. The asset in question may not be of sufficient value to support the financing needed for that construction. If the sponsor is financially strong, he can guarantee a loan in return for his share of the profits. If he isn't, he may have to "turn" the project to another company on a fire-sale basis.

The importance of a record of success seems obvious, and yet most projects are sponsored by individuals or organizations with no background (or even with a record of failure) in the type of project involved. I suppose that is because most tax-shelter sponsors are essentially salesmen working with other people's money and getting a commission regardless of success, so they are willing to go into projects that one would not take on with one's own money.

It is hard for the investor to evaluate the track record of the sponsoring organization. Years ago when I was active in buying oil and gas properties here for a European group, we examined over a dozen completed drilling programs of various organizations with a view to possible acquisition. In only one instance did we find that what the investor owned was worth the money he had put it. Naturally, this was not the word he got from the sponsor, who would distract his gaze from the vulnerable subject of present worth with the red cloth of future revenues. Your $20,000 should eventually return you $30,000, the participant is told. He is not told that he could sell that possible $30,000 equity for only $10,000 right now, given the time and uncertainties involved.

It should be obvious why it is so important that the sponsor get his compensation only *after* the investor has recovered his capital.

## What's Left?

The general rules on tax deals, then, are the following:

1. If it's attractive and easy to understand, probably it's not economically interesting.

2. If it's offered by a prospectus and sold by a sales force, almost certainly it's not interesting. The costs, notably legal and printing, are high; together with the salesman's commission, they come right off the top. Add to that the promoter's free cut and the comfortable management fees, and the deal is significantly diluted. A good investment banker's name on the prospectus is no assurance of either quality or fairness.

3. If you've never heard of anything like it, if the organizers are unquestionably able and honest, if of the operating management you can use the word "superb," if everybody seems to be working for very little, and if nobody on the inside gets a nickel until the investors are paid out, then maybe there's hope. But not much!

# Tax Havens and Foreign Trusts

People who have made their own money, younger investors, Europeans, and families with giant fortunes are usually interested in any proper device for preserving capital, including foreign trusts. Older investors with some inherited wealth rarely like the idea.

# Tax Havens

Some countries are, as it were, the "resorts" of international finance. They go to all reasonable lengths to make themselves attractive to foreign corporate visitors. For the corporation or trust that has no particular national ties, the selection of a base in one of these countries offers many advantages. Almost all of them distinguish between profits earned inside and outside the country. The preferential tax rates apply to those earned abroad. Some of the more popular countries for offshore base corporations, as they are called, are Holland (including Curaçao), Switzerland, Panama, Liechtenstein, the Channel Islands, Nassau, Bermuda, and (mostly for shipping companies) Liberia.

There is nothing odd or improper about setting up a corporate base in such places. The largest U.S. and foreign banks have offices there to help one do it. It does not save taxes in the countries where the corporation actually operates, but only at the international headquarters level. It may even end up not saving significant taxes but rather providing a more convenient place to operate the international division from, particularly if the parent company is located in a country with currency control.

On the individual level, most well-off Europeans keep some undeclared money in Switzerland or in a private Panamanian corporation, for instance. One can condemn this practice, but after centuries of foreign occupations, revolutions, and expropriations, and the risk of communism today, it is understandable. One has the right to own property, and that includes the right to bury it in the ground (or Switzerland) if it is likely to be stolen. It would not be surprising if governmental unrealism eventually produced similar effects in the United States, as happened when Prohibition made technical criminals of ordinarily law-abiding people.

For the individual American investor, the offshore corporation offers little advantage, since with a few exceptions our tax law looks right through the corporate structure of an

American-owned offshore investment company. It is not treated much differently from a domestic one, and is less convenient to operate.

# Foreign Trusts

The individual would ordinarily not be concerned with offshore corporations, but with personal trusts. In the right cases one can, through such trusts, still legally take steps to shield some assets for quite a long time from the risks of expropriation, prohibitively high taxation, or currency control.

You have to pay a price, but it can be worth it, notably if there's a *bona fide* foreign settlor.

There are three main purposes to foreign trusts. The first is to protect against a political upheaval. When the Nazis took over Germany and then overran Europe, they appropriated the bank accounts of people they didn't like. The same happened in the Spanish Civil War, the Soviet occupation of Eastern Europe, and the Cuban revolution. To protect against this, if you see it coming, you can either get the money out silently and then hide it, or else openly put it in a foreign trust. When the secret police demand that you hand over your foreign assets, you can give them the facts on the foreign trust and the address of the trustee. He, however, will refuse to yield them the money. He will argue that you are not a free agent and that his duty is to hold on to the assets (which is correct, under trust law).

Another reason for a foreign trust is to avoid currency control. In most countries today you have to apply for foreign exchange to buy a home abroad or even to go for a trip. To preserve freedom of movement, some funds in a foreign trust can be helpful.

Still another reason is taxes. Once the settlor has paid the initial tax, which may be high, on the movement of the funds into the foreign trust, there should be no further significant taxes for two generations. The tax savings change constantly as the laws change, but remain considerable. You do have to watch out for the "throwback" tax when the trust is wound up.

In all these cases I am talking about a trust set up in a country that still has low taxes and a free currency. Otherwise, there would be no improvement.

The trust is a common-law concept, so the possible locations are pretty well restricted to the British Commonwealth countries and Liberia. The favorites, at the moment, are Bermuda and Nassau for Americans, and the Channel Islands (perhaps too much so) for the British. Grand Cayman (which is near Jamaica) is beginning to be used as a backup situs, in case something goes wrong with the original location.

Nassau has by far the best supply of competent trust companies, a number of which are well run and owned by first-class international banks. Two problems are potential political instability and Nassau's reputation as a hot-money haven. The existence of legalized gambling is a serious problem as well. Gambling attracts gangsters and fosters an atmosphere of corruption that is inconsistent with a tradition of fiduciary management.

Bermuda is convenient to New York and has excellent telephone communications. While its political situation is tolerable now, one can foresee trouble in the future. Bermuda exercises some selection before permitting new companies to incorporate. It has two established trust companies. The Bank of Bermuda is by far the larger but is technically spotty, owing to the difficulty of recruiting staff.

Unlike Nassau and Bermuda, which are independent, Grand Cayman is a crown colony, though it may well become independent eventually. Its population is so small (10,000) that its eventual political evolution is unpredictable. Furthermore, if you had to sue the trustee, you might not get much satisfaction. It is an hour's flight (over Cuba) from Miami. Since all foreign trusts should be set up with a provision that the situs can be shifted, and will automatically shift if there is trouble, I see no point in setting up a trust in Cayman now simply because Nassau or Bermuda may deteriorate. Cayman may not be satisfactory either by then. It might be appropriate as the backup situs (what the English call the funk hole) in the event of an automatic shift, but you would have to worry about it all the time. Also, unsavory elements are reputed to have appeared.

Nassau and Bermuda are reasonably interesting places to visit. Cayman is not, on the whole, having ceased to be quaint without becoming cosmopolitan. The principal sight is a turtle ranch.

The Channel Islands, notably Jersey and Guernsey, are possible locations for offshore trusts if nothing too complicated is required. Convenient from London or Paris, pleasant to visit, having a hardworking and serious population, they resemble Switzerland in the last century. Many excellent English banks have branches there.

Probably the best offshore situs is none of these, however, but England. The U.K. "offshore corporation" is essentially tax-free, and the technical facilities in England—banking, legal, and the rest—are superb. There is an excellent discussion of the U.K. as a tax haven in a pamphlet published by the Economist Intelligence Unit, entitled "The UK as a Tax Haven."

In these matters it is essential that the arrangement have substance. The trustee should be respectable and authentic, significant fees should be paid, reputable independent counsel should approve the transaction, and so on. The I.R.S. is quick to smell a rat, and nothing that has a rubber-stamp flavor should be contemplated.

One should obviously go to the proposed trust location and talk at length with the chosen trustee and with local counsel. For this and other reasons, an American should probably not consider the more remote locations.

If the trustee is compensated by an extra commission on the purchase and sale of securities, one should invest the trust funds in either a no-load open-end fund or a closed-end fund. That way there need be little turnover. It also gives the trust company fewer chances to make mistakes.

As a further safety measure, the physical securities should always be in custody in a different country from the trust situs (and ideally in the trust's own name, not the trust company's nominee name). That way, if one morning an interventor with a detachment of soldiers takes over the trustee bank they will not find your certificates in the vault, and the automatic successor trustee will have little trouble establishing his control of assets.

If you wish to have the portfolio supervised in New York, a U.S. investment adviser can be engaged.

There are other possible choices for the trust situs. An experienced international lawyer can easily tell you their advantages and disadvantages. (A lawyer not experienced in this field will charge you more, since he'll have to research the problem, and then may not get it right.)

Communications and technical skill are important. If it takes weeks of confusing Telexes to reconcile your quarterly appraisal, you will wish you were dealing with someone else. This is all too frequent, I might say. Also, the probity and substance of the trustee are essential. If your trustee is in reality two or three promoters in a little office, you can expect grave trouble sooner or later, including raised eyebrows from the I.R.S.

A trust situs that may become attractive in the future is Liechtenstein, which has passed legislation that permits the common-law type of trust. On the other hand, the independent role and accountability of the trustee, which have been defined by centuries of tradition and statute in common law, are novel concepts there. I am not aware that the I.R.S. has accepted the reality of a Liechtenstein trust. It seems prudent to wait until there is some case law and the matter can be considered settled.

Always in considering the best situs for an offshore operation, one must ask, "For whom?" The English should be careful of the Channel Islands, which are too accessible to their Treasury; Americans should avoid Nassau, which is tainted by the Mafia, and so on.

I find that Europeans are happiest if the alternative situs is in the western hemisphere, since they are usually worried about war or political upheavals in Europe which would presumably not affect Bermuda, say. By the same token, the U.S. beneficiary of a Bermuda trust might feel more confident if it were specified that in case of trouble there the situs shifted to Europe, such as to a major international bank in the Channel Islands.

# Envoi: Preserving Capital

At the end of this book I want to echo the beginning: The alpha and omega of investment is preservation of capital in real terms—to generate a secure income that keeps up with inflation and taxes. It is a very respectable objective, rarely attained. Let the reader approach portfolio investment in that spirit, and perhaps he will do much better.

If he tries for miracles, he will probably do worse.

However, unrelenting forces oppose him. He will need all his wisdom and skill to succeed.

# Appendixes

# Appendix I
# Proving the Pudding

Can one really identify major market moves as they unfold in the manner suggested in this book? Yes, quite often. At the risk of sounding like an "I-told-you-so," I quote some extracts from articles I published at different times. The point is that these principles *do* work, if you have the courage to apply them.

## End of an Era*

The stock market peaked in 1966, but for twenty years up to that time everybody who since the war had said that stocks in general were good because of their growth and that bonds were bad because of inflation has been proved right, and the traditionalists more and more discredited.

Actually, I am skeptical of the "growth" and "inflation" arguments when used near bull-market peaks. To a considerable extent the market is essentially a bandwagon, where people join the crowd because they see the crowd growing. You have to use the "growth" argument to justify a prolonged up-movement in stocks, but in fact, the Dow stocks only grow at a limited rate.

There must come a time when the inflationary tendency in the economy is fully reflected in the prevailing interest rates, and the multiples that most stocks sell at fairly reflect growth prospects.

* Written November 1972. Reprinted by permission from the *Christian Science Monitor*. Dow Jones Average 1020.

Is it possible that we have reached that point, at least for the present? The secular trend of both Dow Jones earnings and prices has been roughly flat since 1966. Over the long term they may find it hard to resume their old growth rate, because of the rising expectations of labor, the pressure of domestic and foreign competition, market saturation, and governmental controls. In the early 1960s, for example, the whole Dow Jones Utility Average sold for over twenty times earnings. Will that happen again soon? U.S. Steel's mean price-earnings ratio in 1961 was 27, and its operating profit margin 10.7 percent. Now both—and also the price of the stock—have been cut by more than half. No growth there! Meanwhile, the bonds of the company become progressively more interesting, since it does have to raise money, and if the stock is unappetizing, then it has to make its bonds attractive.

In the early 1950s, when the great modern bull market began, "growth" was fairly priced because people did not understand it. Bargains really were available. There were only a handful of "growth" funds. (The one run by my then firm grew 500 percent in ten years, invested only in top-quality equities.) Now there are about 170 "growth" funds, and no bargains. In fact, in the last five years the "growth" funds actually appreciated on average only about 9 percent, while the "income" funds (very few in number) appreciated on average 28 percent.

A long-term factor overlooked by many investors is the prospect of eventually saturating even the foreign markets. Many U.S. companies with good growth rates have become "commodity" companies domestically and are making their real gains abroad, particularly in Europe. The European and Japanese companies are not idle, however, and in due course many foreign markets will become as competitive as the domestic one. What then? There will be even less overall growth. Stocks may therefore become less attractive than ever, and investors may turn more to bonds, which will have to be priced at a level that reflects inflationary expectations.

In other words, investors, disillusioned with the mass of stocks, will switch out of them into bonds, forcing stock prices down and bond (or preferred) prices up.

How far can this process go? Very far indeed. . . .

# Growth Stocks—
# a Rare Opportunity*

A few years ago nobody would have believed it. Some of the best companies in the world are once again selling for one-digit price-earnings ratios, almost as though people were going to stop eating, smoking, and reading newspapers all at once, tomorrow. (In addition, of course, a lot of smaller companies that have been lost sight of by the institutions are selling at giveaway prices.) The April rally did no more than make a tiny dent in this undervaluation.

Thanks to the "smokestack" craze, the indexing fad, and today's preoccupation with yield, the most interesting stocks—those with earnings growing fast enough to offset inflation—are selling at an irrationally low premium over the run-of-the-mill industrials, very many of which should, alas, be considered as wasting assets.

In contrast, consider the newspaper chains, the pharmaceuticals, the specialty electronics companies; Capital Cities, Philip Morris, Schlumberger, and their ilk. They are generating torrents of cash; they have no depreciation problems; and both their earnings and their dividends (in some cases generous) are growing much faster than inflation.

As long-term investments these companies are in a different league from the standard cyclicals with profit-margin problems, labor problems, Japanese problems, ecology problems and low unit-growth to boot.

But you wouldn't know it from the prices of these superior stocks! Harte-Hanks Communications is 11 times 1978 earnings, Philip Morris 9 times, and Schlumberger 12 times, as compared with a nominal 8-plus for the Dow Jones Industrial Average, which, taking account of replacement-cost depreciation, should really be a much higher figure: perhaps 10 times? 12 times? 15 times?

An example of the current cheapness of growth stocks is the T. Rowe Price New Horizons Fund, which is invested in higher-growth stocks. Over the last fifteen years the average price-earnings ratio of its holdings has fluctuated from a high of 40 in 1961 and 1967 to a low of 10 in 1974. Today it's barely over 10. Similarly, the New Horizons price-earnings ratio was twice that of the Standard & Poor's 500 in 1961, 1967–68, and 1972. Last year it got down to the all-time low: a lower price-earnings ratio than the Standard & Poor's! And today the ratio is only fractionally more than the Standard & Poor's.

Even after the sharp April rally, stocks like these remain as underpriced today as they were flagrantly *over*priced in 1968–72.

* Reprinted by permission from *Forbes* magazine, May 15, 1978. Dow Jones Average 840.

# How to Sell:
# The Tao Theory*

An experienced investor—by which I mean one who has lived through, let's say, at least three complete cycles of about four years each—often gets so he can feel in his bones where one is in the sequence. Is not the message clear enough when we learn that one new technology company after another zooms in price right after going public for the first time? The owners of a business don't sell their stock to the public for love, or to enable it to share in the benefits of the free-enterprise system: They do it to make money. If they and their underwriters think that a full price for a business that they know intimately is 10, and the public jumps in and runs it up at once to 20, can we not be fairly confident that Mr. Market has gotten out on the right side of his bed and is in a buying mood that we would be wise to take advantage of?

As one begins to see and hear the speculative pot bubbling, one should start getting increasingly cautious and analytical about what's going on.

The blowoff rarely comes in exactly the same form as the time before. One time the froth is in the "—onics" stocks, another time the hedge funds, another time the conglomerates. Today, the public is infatuated with options as a route to quick wealth, like the leveraged trusts of the 1920s. Even more extraordinary is the vast excitement surrounding commodities. On a good day the dollar volume in soybeans alone equals that of the whole New York Stock Exchange! All those frantic commodity speculators are going to retire impoverished and bitter from that crazy casino. Commissions take 50 percent to 100 percent of their equity in a single year. They can't fight that. And their disillusionment will take a lot of other values down with it.

I'm fond of climbing, and I know well that there are no bold guides who are also old guides. Sooner or later the long-shot avalanche or sudden storm will occur, and if you're out of position, you're cooked. What happens if any of the many factors that could cause the present bull-market blowoff to end suddenly occurred and you were loaded up with start-ups and concept stocks? Your portfolio could experience a grave impairment not only of market prices but of real values, as both the market and business decline.

So relax, try to develop an accurate perception of the value of your holdings, and if Mr. Market is desperate to buy them, then observe the Golden Rule and let him have a few.

* Reprinted by permission from *Forbes* magazine, January 19, 1981. Dow Jones Average 980.

That's what I call the Tao of investing; giving way intelligently, just as in judo.

# Sound the Charge!*

At the Battle of Waterloo, Wellington sees the Old Guard waver and start to fall back from its attack. *"La Garde recule"* comes the horrified cry from the French ranks. "Oh, well," mutters the Duke, "in for a penny, in for a pound." He waves his hat, the whole British line advances with a roar, he clears the field and wins the day.

The stock market, too, consists of opposing forces. The bulls have won in the American market, and the investor might as well profit. It should have a good long run before it's over.

This has been a classic bear market bottom.

First, American market cycles last four years. The reason for this remarkably persistent pattern is rooted in American politics. Let's begin at the top. Markets, like hospital patients, fear uncertainty. The market tends to be jittery as the election approaches. Then the incumbent administration injects a strong dose of monetary stimulation. The economy, and employment, and confidence—and inflation—pick up.

Then one candidate wins. His first task is to reassure his opponents, now that he's not just a partisan leader but a chief of state. To govern, he must win over a substantial number of the opposing party in Congress for his measures, which means building some popular support on the other side. So if the incoming president is a Democrat, he will proclaim his support for incentives to industry and for sound money, and may appoint a Republican as secretary of the treasury. If he's a Republican, he'll announce higher employment as a cardinal objective, and perhaps appoint a Democrat secretary of labor. The whole electorate feels better. This period of optimism typically falls in January of the inaugural year. The economy, the money supply, and the stock market are buoyant.

Then the new president, seized of his powers, gets down to work. First, taking advantage of the "honeymoon" he can expect from Congress during his first months, he introduces some of the measures on which he based his campaign: higher taxes on the rich, if it's a government of the left; rearmament, if the Russians are on a rampage. The other side calculates the cost, and is upset. At about the same time the monetary authorities proceed strongly to disintoxicate the economy from the excesses of the election

* Written September 1982. Reprinted by permission from *Investors Chronicle*, London. Dow Jones Average 910.

period. The inflationary syndrome must be broken. This is done early in the presidential term, so that it will be forgotten by the next election, when the mixture can be repeated as before. The stock market, which is extremely conscious of the competing tug of high interest rates, collapses.

As it falls, explanations proliferate. (Predictions usually follow prices, not vice versa, both as to specific stocks and as to the market as a whole.)

Despair—and falling prices—feed on themselves until the impulse is finally spent. The routed army will flee, but it won't flee all the way to China. Somewhere, things stabilize. Then the ever-present buying power of insurance companies and pension funds starts to find no resistance, and prices move up, surprisingly briskly. Since markets decline much faster than they rise, this usually happens in the post-inaugural year.

There are three distinct "bottom" phases through which the market passes in rapid succession: (1) All Is Lost. When the market, panicked, is making what are in facts its final lows, nobody believes they will hold. (2) It's Too Early To Buy. Prices advance for several months because of a disappearance of selling, but the public can't believe it. (3) It's Too Late To Buy. After the market has moved up 15 or 20 percent, and some stocks—or even the averages as a whole—are making new highs, investors, like Columbus's sailors, are gripped by the terror of the unknown. That's where we seem to be today.

But it's a non sequitur: In a bull market the whole market may go up 50 percent, and many stocks will double. That it should start out is a necessary precondition to getting there!

At a good bottom there is usually a bear story. So today and its fears of international financial collapse are, as I say, typical. Cash hoards—which could send prices soaring if invested—are massive. And stocks are cheap by plenty of objective measures.

First, the whole market is selling for little over half its own replacement value. Second, private buyers, usually large enterprises, are paying premiums of up to 100 percent over market prices when they take over listed companies.

Bonds should do well, but stocks should do much better. Bonds don't double. And bonds present a real danger in a basically inflationary era. Nobody can say that inflation is beaten for good. Indeed, the best escape from the mountain of debt that crushes the world may be to inflate it out of existence. It can never be paid, or perhaps even serviced, and repudiation would be worse. So it may have to be inflated away, and what has to happen, however unlikely it may seem, somehow does happen.

So my answer to the question of what to buy remains high-growth inflation-proof equities.

In Europe, and among some American institutions, the "cry" is the large-capitalization enterprises: Kodak, Johnson & Johnson, IBM, and so forth. All right, but these famous old names won't do as well as smaller, higher-growth speciality businesses that are not so well known. I would much rather have a package of three or five speciality electronic companies than one U.S. General Electric. GE is a conglomerate of over a hundred smaller divisions, but a less exciting collection—and more expensively priced—than a package one can assemble for oneself in the market.

And don't get worried by the setbacks.

# Appendix II
# Train's Law

## "Price Controls Increase Prices"

The idea has been obvious to experienced men at least since Babylonian times but is often forgotten, perhaps because it has lacked a neat formulation. Populist politicians sometimes run for office *against* it. If they succeed, the voters pay.

Train's Law,* then, is:

## Price Controls Increase Prices

The reason is that price controls inhibit production, and a plentiful supply is what brings prices down.

The result of price controls is that the producer cuts back, the supply diminishes, and the black market becomes the real market. Black market prices are higher than the pre-controls prices were.

If the government actually succeeds in enforcing the controls and in stamping out the noncontrolled "parallel" (or black) market,

---

* I am told that every book with pretensions to intellectual respectability must promulgate a "law" these days.

which is extremely difficult, then the results are worse, since if the producer can no longer get a reasonable price for his output he tends to go out of business, whereupon the government takes over. City Hall is a much less efficient producer, for reasons everyone knows. It costs about twice as much for the government to do most things as for private enterprise.

So the corollary is this:

*Price controls bring on government ownership, which increases prices even more.*

(It also seems to be at least partly true that price *supports* tend to *lower* prices, by building up excess capacity and possibly a stockpile that overhangs the market. Not the same day, of course, but rapidly.)

"Oh, what a web of lies we weave / When first we practice to deceive." You control the price of one product, and then you must control the raw materials that go into it. Then you have to freeze labor prices, and the prices of things laborers consume. Soon you have a huge paper fishnet tangling up the whole economic process, and an immensely expensive bureaucracy to try to enforce it— unsuccessfully.

A horrible example arose in the late 1970s: the U.S. Government's coping with rising oil use by holding down oil prices, instead of letting rising prices both increase production and inhibit demand, as was done later—much too late.

# The "Zapato Único" Syndrome

In South America, where politics runs wild like jungle flora, we can see the fatal scenario being enacted in one place or another anytime we care to look:

- The revolutionary government ("right" or "left," it makes little difference) announces a substantial wage increase for all workers.
- Prices start going up, reflecting but also offsetting the wage increase, so after some months the government denounces the producers and freezes prices.
- The producer begins selling shoes (for example) as first quality that formerly passed for second quality. The consumer is glad to have them at any price.
- After a few more months the government catches on to this dastardly deception, jails a few producers, and imposes strict quality standards.
- These prove unenforceable. The distinctions between first quality, second quality, and other qualities become blurred.

- The government excoriates the producer and rules that henceforth there will only be one quality of shoe produced (the "*zapato único*"), one quality of bread, and so on.
- The producer abandons the plant to the government and flees, but is caught at the border, brought back, and jailed for suspected economic sabotage.
- A government interventor comes in as manager, raises wages all around, and carefully observes the price ceilings. The plant loses money even faster.
- The government denounces the former producer as a bloodsucker and sends him a bill for the plant's monthly losses. It takes over his home and other property in lieu of cash.
- Misery ensues. The government cannot subsidize plants beyond a certain point or inflation goes wild. The former owner is bust. Outside investment has dried up. There is no working capital. Production collapses.

# Appendix III
# Residency
# Requirements

## Advice on Residence from U.S. Legal Counsel

The term "residence" and the term "domicile" are used with different meanings under the U.S. income and estate tax laws. Residence under the U.S. income tax laws refers to presence for a prescribed period of time, while domicile for U.S. estate tax purposes has a broader meaning which connotes the permanent place of abode to which the person intends to return. Thus a person may be deemed a resident of the U.S. for U.S. income taxes although he is deemed domiciled outside the U.S. A person acquires a domicile in a place by living there, for even a brief period of time, with no present, definite intention to abandon it. Residence without the requisite intention to remain indefinitely does not constitute domicile.

Under U.S. and other common law concepts, a person is deemed to continue his old domicile until he has effectively acquired a new one. The fact of actual residence and the intention of the person determine what domicile he has acquired, but his intention will be determined by his acts and conduct and not by his private or personal feelings.

It is vital to avoid any possibility that the U.S. might conclude that his U.S. domicile has continued because no new one has been acquired.

In this regard, it is recommended that an unequivocal record be made which establishes the fact of residence and the intention to make that residence his domicile. The residence requirement is established by moving into a new home. The intention requirement is more complex, but an essential element of this requirement is that the home be permanent or be for a substantial period. Documentation at the present time should be made by obtaining (1) executed copies of the lease or other documents establishing the establishment of a new home; (2) statements from persons such as the local police chief or similar officials, secretaries, accountants, doctors, ministers, and friends indicating the individual's established intention of remaining at the home residence; (3) a list of organizations and persons regularly addressing correspondence to the new address (including brokers, banks, professional advisers); (4) type of passport or visa used indicating that permission therein granted is of indefinite duration or easily renewable as a matter of course; (5) description of any local activities that such person engages in, such as charitable institutions, which illustrate the establishment of roots in the local community; and (6) club memberships, subscriptions, automobile registration, driver's license, hunting and fishing licenses. In addition to the foregoing (a) the District Director of Internal Revenue of the person's former district as well as state tax authorities should be notified of the change shortly after making the change; (b) the post office, board of elections, and state motor vehicle department should be notified shortly after the change; (c) local authorities such as immigration officials should be advised of present, not former, address; (d) if pets are owned, a local veterinarian should be used; and (e) all documents executed by the person where an address is required, such as wills or contracts, should refer to the new address.

If one who is now considered by the U.S. to be a nonresident does not severely alter his periods of residence in or visitation to the U.S., his status as a nonresident should continue. He should never spend more than six months in the U.S. in any year. He should not

1. Own a residence in the U.S.
2. Use a U.S. address for insurance, periodicals, charge accounts, clubs, hotel registrations, and the like, and particularly not passports, wills, U.S. tax returns, or any other government reports.

# Advice on Residence from British Legal Counsel

The Inland Revenue has made the following statement with respect to domicile:

> Broadly speaking a person is domiciled in the country in which he has his permanent home. Domicile is distinct from nationality or residence. A person may be resident in more than one country, but at any given time he can be domiciled in one only. A person acquires what is known as his domicile of origin at birth: this is normally the domicile of his father and therefore not necessarily the country where he himself was born. A person retains this domicile until he acquires a different domicile—a domicile of choice or of dependency.
>
> To acquire a domicile of choice a person must sever his ties with the country of his domicile of origin and settle in another country with the clear intention of making his permanent home there. Long residence in another country is not enough in itself to prove that a person has acquired a domicile of choice there unless it can be regarded as indicating intention; there has to be evidence that he firmly intends to live there permanently.

As is indicated in the Inland Revenue's statement, a combination of residence in a country and intention to reside there indefinitely is necessary to establish a new domicile of choice.

In determining whether one has acquired a domicile here any circumstance which could be evidence of intention to reside permanently or indefinitely here must be considered. Included in such considerations are the motive for taking up residence in the country; where business interests are located; and the ownership of property. Generally a person's tastes, habits, conducts, actions, ambitions, health, hopes, and projects must be considered in determining domicile.

# Appendix IV
# Selected Subscription
# Services

*Cycli-Graphs*
Securities Research Company
208 Newbury Street
Boston, MA 02116

> My preferred graphic presentation of stock movements, earn-
> ings, dividends, and trends.

*Dow Theory Letters*
P.O. Box 1759
La Jolla, CA 92038

> Wise and experienced.

*Executive Wealth Advisory*
Research Institute Executive Information Center, Inc.
589 Fifth Avenue
New York, NY 10017

> Excellent on personal finance techniques—trusts, taxes, etc.

*The Johnson Survey*
John S. Herold, Inc.
Greenwich, CT 06830

> Formerly *America's Fastest Growing Companies:* a valuable compi-
> lation.

*The Professional Tape Reader*
RADCAP, Inc.
P.O. Box 2407
Hollywood, FL 33022

> The overall market analysis is excellent.

*Value Line Investment Survey*
Arnold Bernhard & Co., Inc.
711 Third Avenue
New York, NY 10017

Indispensable.

*Vickers Associates, Inc.*
226 New York Avenue
Huntington, NY 11743

Offers several services that report what investment managers
and mutual funds are doing.

# Appendix V
# Selected General Investment
# Magazines

*Business Week*
Overwhelmingly detailed: perhaps more useful for businessmen than investors.

*The Economist*
The business section is excellent, particularly for international
developments.

*Financial World*
Specializes in investment ideas.

*Forbes*
Lively, topical, voluminous.

*Fortune*
Invaluable for background.

*Investors Chronicle* (London)
The most useful periodical on the U.K. market.

*Money*
Well done, although elementary.

# Glossary

*Account Executive: See* Broker.

*Accumulate:* Wall Street expression for buying on a large scale over time, typically by an institution. "Accumulation" of a stock is said to occur if a number of institutions are gradually adding to their holdings.

*Advance-Decline Ratio:* This ratio is a useful barometer of the underlying condition of the market. Toward the end of a long upward sweep, speculative interest is concentrated on the small number of stocks that are still struggling forward while, masked by the activity of those few, the rest of the market fades. As the Dow Jones approaches its peak, the number of stocks going up becomes less and less. If each day you plot a graph of the number of stocks that advanced minus the number of stocks that declined, that line will normally turn down months before the Dow does.

*Agency:* An agency of the U.S. Government.

*Air Pocket:* Said when there is virtually no support for a stock, so it falls sharply on little volume in the face of selling.

*American Stock Exchange (or Amex):* Successor to the old Curb Exchange, which was conducted on the street. Smaller and less widely held companies than those listed on the New York Stock Exchange are traded on the Amex or over the counter.

*Asking Price:* A specialist on the floor of a stock exchange always indicates a "spread" for a stock, e.g., 25–25¼. If you want to

253

sell he offers to buy at his bid price; if you want to buy he sells to you at his asking price.

*Back Office:* Equivalent to the kitchen of a restaurant: the part of a brokerage house in which the mechanical functions are carried out, and which the customer does not see.

*Banker's Acceptance:* A participation in a bank's short-term commercial loan.

*Bear:* Investors who thought a stock was going down have long been called bears. The expression derives from a centuries-old proverb advising you not to sell a bearskin before you caught the bear. So stock sold *short* was said to be a "bearskin."

*Bear Trap:* When a stock declines, attracting heavy selling, and then surges.

*Beta:* An unreliable measure of the volatility of a stock as compared to the general averages. A beta of 1.0 would mean that a stock moves hand in hand with the general market. But betas can be computed in different ways, and change anyway.

*Bid: See* Asking Price.

*Big Board:* The New York Stock Exchange.

*Bigger-Fool Theory:* A risky investment technique, but effective when practiced by a master speculator. It consists of applying to the investing public the type of calculation made by a skillful politician. Just as the truth is often unpalatable to the electorate and unsound policies are often popular for a while, so too the reaction of the public to a plausible story about a company is sometimes easier to foresee than how the business itself is going to make out. One of the most successful investors I know made a killing in King Resources—in and out at the right time—even though he agreed with me (who had been in oil investment for some years) that the thing had to be a Ponzi Scheme. "They'll eat it up, John," he would say. "They'll love it." Briefly, the bigger-fool-theory investor knows he is not buying a solid value, but thinks he can foresee a desire by less informed investors—the "bigger fools"—to take it off his hands when the time comes.

*Block:* A large stock transaction, e.g., five or ten thousand shares or more.

*Blue Chip:* A large, stable, well known, widely held, seasoned company with a strong financial position, usually paying a comfortable dividend.

*Bond:* A corporate I.O.U., typically bearing interest at a fixed rate for a definite term of years, and often supported by specific collateral.

*The Book:* A specialist's order book for a stock, in which he records offers to buy below, and offers to sell above, the current market price. A look at "the book" can be helpful in evaluating a stock's market position.

*Book Value:* The book value of a company is based on its financial statement, not on the appraised value of its assets. One takes the balance sheet assets of a company and deducts all debt and other obligations. Since assets often increase in real value because of inflation, whereas for balance sheet purposes they are depreciated, the book value of a good company may well be lower than its real value. For a company with obsolete equipment, both may be meaningless. "Hard book" means that all doubtful assets have been written down.

*Bottom:* In a major market decline, the point at which enough buyers are available to absorb all selling is called a bottom, particularly if it has been tested, and has held, several times.

*Breakout:* Movement of a stock above the highest price previously recorded.

*Broker:* A stock exchange firm's employee who deals with a customer; also called a registered representative, account executive, or customer's man. Alternatively, a floor broker. Also, sometimes, the firm itself.

*Bull:* A market optimist.

*C.D.: See* Certificate of Deposit.

*Call:* A right to buy a stock for a specific period of time at a predetermined price, for which one pays a premium.

*Cats and Dogs:* This refers to third-grade stocks, unseasoned issues. Sometimes they go up very fast and sometimes they go down very fast. Since their future prospects are unknowable, they are not suitable for conservative long-term investors.

*C.B.O.E.:* Chicago Board of Option Exchange.

*Certificate of Deposit:* An unsecured evidence of indebtedness of a bank, which may be sold to others, usually with a face value of $100,000 and bearing interest below the prime rate.

*Chartist:* A variety of technician who bases his forecasting on the formations traced by stock prices.

*Churn:* Trade an account excessively to generate high commissions.

*Closed-End Fund:* An investment company with a fixed equity capitalization, which does not sell or redeem its own shares.

*Commercial Paper:* Evidence of short-term unsecured corporate indebtedness.

*Contrarian:* A practitioner of a valid stock market approach popularized by Humphrey Neill under the name of "contrary opinion theory." In almost any market situation, one is safest acting against the prevailing opinion of the moment.

*Convertible:* A bond or preferred stock that offers the investor the right to convert his holding into common stock in exchange for a lower interest rate than he would otherwise receive.

*Correction:* A minor movement against the major trend of the stock market. *See* Secondary Reaction.

*Cover:* To close out a short position.

*Curb:* American Stock Exchange.

*Customer's Man: See* Broker.

*Cyclicals:* Some industries are perennially subject to the vagaries of the business cycle: mining, steel, construction, automobiles, chemicals, machine tools, and the like. It is impossible to get away from the cyclical effect in business, just as there is always alternation between good and bad weather, so the cyclical type of company has an irregular earnings pattern, and usually an irregular stock price pattern too.

*Dead Horse Fallacy:* Sometimes a company's situation changes drastically for the worse, and the share price drops accordingly. It is tempting to refer to brokers' write-ups of the year before and say, "If Equitable Equine was supposed to be a good buy at 60, it *has* to be a good buy at 20." The name of the fallacy refers to horse racing. If the $5,000 plater in a claiming race expires right on the track, it would still not make sense to buy him for a "bargain" $1,000.

*Discount Broker:* A stock exchange firm offering a stripped-down service at a cut-rate price. Sometimes preferable to a full-service broker, if one does not wish to be bombarded with purchase and sale suggestions.

*Discretionary Account:* One that a broker, investment adviser, or bank can manage without consulting the customer, usually under a limited or trading power of attorney.

*Distribution:* When stocks are passing from a few large investors, typically institutional, into the hands of many smaller ones; usually amidst much public excitement and unreasonably high prices.

*Diversification:* Most investors find it wise to own interests in at least ten different companies, and quite often in twenty or more. The Benjamin Graham technique of investment calls for even greater diversification, often into several dozen stocks.

*Dividend:* That part of a company's earnings that is distributed to the shareholders.

*D.J.I.:* The Dow Jones Industrial Average.

*Dow Jones Industrial Average (also called the Dow, the Industrials, and the D.J.I.):* An index of stock market prices based on thirty large, representative companies. There are also Dow Jones Utility and Transportation Averages.

*Dow Theory:* Briefly, the view that market currents tend to move in major and minor trends. A major trend in the D.J.I. should be "confirmed" by the Transportation average, on the reasoning that improved business must be reflected in higher carloadings, and thus better railroad profits.

*Down Tick:* A stock trade at a lower price than the last previous transaction.

*Efficient Market Theory:* The fallacious belief that whatever can be known about a stock is at all times reflected in its price, and that it therefore does little good to study the facts.

*Equities:* Equities is another name for shares. The capitalization of a company consists of "equity"—or ownership—represented by common or preferred shares (stock), and debt, represented by bonds, notes, and the like. (In England, "corporation stock" means municipal bonds, incidentally.)

*Eurodollars:* Dollar claims reloaned in Europe without passing through the U.S. banking system.

*Exercising Price:* The price at which the owner of an option has the right to buy or sell the underlying stock. (Also, the striking price.)

*Face Value:* The amount that a note or bond promises to pay its holder. Not the same as its market value, which is usually expressed as a percent of face value.

*Favorite Fifty:* A list compiled regularly of the fifty largest holdings of institutional investors.

*The Floor:* The trading area of a stock exchange, where the representative of the buyer meets the representative of the seller to complete a transaction.

*Floor Broker:* A broker on the floor of the exchange, who actually trades with other brokers, as distinct from a broker who deals with a customer. A "two-dollar broker" acts on the floor for a number of different firms.

*Free Wheeling:* When a stock is making new highs, after having successfully penetrated a resistance area, then one says it is "free wheeling." Everybody who owns it has it at a profit. It is believed that the stock can then rise more easily.

*Fund:* An investment company.

*Fundamentalist:* One who believes that the best investment results are obtained by studying the facts about a company and its industry and the economy in general, as distinct from studying cycles in investment psychology, or divining the future of the market by stock patterns.

*Gap:* If a stock trades at 20 at the close on Tuesday and begins trading on Wednesday morning at 21, a one-point gap has opened.

*Glamour Stock:* A stock that is exciting public interest at the moment.

*Go-Go:* Said of funds or managers who trade overactively in a booming market.

*Good Buying:* Said when a stock is being accumulated by strong, informed buyers.

*Gunslinger:* A go-go money manager.

*Head and Shoulders (top or bottom):* The formation said to exist when a stock has rebounded three times from a resistance level.

*Hedge Fund:* An investing partnership intended to invest either on the long side or on the short side of the market, or both at once. The theory is that it will be on the long side when the market is going up and on the short side when it is going down. Another theory is that if the manager has no opinion on the overall market he can be long the stocks he likes and short the stocks he dislikes, and so make money in both directions. In practice, however, almost no manager exists who can perform this stunt, and even if he does exist, he is not the one that the public will confide its money to (nor will he accept that money) at the times when hedge funds and such vehicles are popular. As a result, hedge funds as a class lose much more money than they make. Their popularity is, in fact, a bull-market indicator.

*Hedging:* Typically, going short a stock to balance a long position.

*Hot Issue:* A newly issued stock that is in strong demand; often it will go to a premium over its original issue price.

*Indenture:* The text of a bond.

*Index:* Any of a number of stock market averages, including the Dow Jones Industrial Average, the Standard & Poor's 500, the Over-the-Counter Average, the Wilshire 5000, the Indicator Digest Average, the *New York Times* Average, the New York Stock Exchange Index, or whatever. There are also indices for the major foreign exchanges and for a number of commodities, and, more recently, for categories of art.

*Indexing:* A popular but feeble theory among institutional portfolio managers that since their portfolios rarely beat the averages, usually because they buy when stocks are strong and sell when they are weak, matters can be improved by investing to follow the performance of the averages themselves. What would in fact achieve this affect is owning a diversified portfolio and doing nothing; that, however, would obviate the functions of the portfolio managers in question. Instead, therefore, they devise computerized systems of building portfolios whose performance will closely follow whichever average they index to. Since the composition and weighting of the major averages change regularly, this creates movement, expense, and a function for the portfolio manager. It thus slightly impairs performance, and begs the question of whether certain types of stock, e.g., high income or low income, may not be more suitable for the investor in question.

*In the Money:* Said of an option when the underlying stock is selling for more than the exercising price.

*Institution:* A bank, investment company, investment adviser, insurance company, or other large pool of investment buying power.

*Institutional Broker:* A broker who deals with institutions.

*Investment Company (also called a mutual fund):* A company registered under the Investment Company Act of 1930, which provides that in the proper circumstances a company whose only activity is investing need not pay corporate tax. Such companies are very closely supervised by the Securities and Exchange Commission.

If an investment company continuously offers its stock to the public and also redeems it from shareholders who wish to sell, it is said to be open-ended.

If it has a fixed capitalization, it is said to be closed-ended.

*Kicker: See* Warrant. Typically, an equity bonus to "sweeten" a bond deal.

*Letter Stock (or Investment Letter Stock):* In the latter days of a bull market, "sophisticated" buyers, including hedge funds and even institutions, are willing to buy stock directly from a company without the benefit of a prospectus or a public issue. They get a discount from the quoted market—often from 20 to 40 percent. The S.E.C. requires that the buyer give the seller a letter stating that unregistered stock is being bought for investment, and also requires that it be held for a considerable period of time, usually about two years, to indicate *bona fides*. Unfortunately, the situation of the company can change drastically during the period, and the buyer is stuck with his stock. Since the time when such stock can be sold is usually the euphoric period of a market rise, a large outpouring of letter stock tends to be part of the market-top syndrome. When the end comes, the discount on unregistered stock broadens and the "sophisticated" owner takes a drubbing.

*Leverage:* Leverage (in England, "gearing") is of two sorts: financial leverage and sales leverage. Financial leverage exists if a company is capitalized half in stock and half in bonds, for instance. A 10 percent increase in profits will produce roughly a 20 percent increase in earnings per share, since there are only half as many shares as there would be if the company's capital was entirely in common stock; and by the same token, if earnings decline, then earnings per share will decline more.

Sales leverage occurs when a company is operating near the break-even point, so that a small increase in sales produces a proportionately larger increase in profits.

*Line:* The old-time operators spoke of being long a "line" of steel or motors, or whatever.

*Liquidity:* The extent to which a stock trades widely in the market, and can thus be purchased or sold without excessively influencing the price. Also, a company's net asset position, particularly in cash or cash equivalents.

*Listing:* A stock or bond's admission to trading rights on the New York or another stock exchange, based on its record of size, profitability, degree of public ownership, etc.

*Load:* The commission applied to the sale of a mutual fund, typically about 8 percent.

*Long:* To be long a stock simply means that you own it.

*Long Term:* Either that period of time which qualifies a holding for this category of tax treatment (currently one year) or else a considerable period of time, e.g., "In the long term we'll all be dead" (Keynes).

*Margin:* The percentage of the purchase price that an investor must produce in cash to hold the stock at a brokerage house. From time to time it is either raised to discourage speculation or lowered to encourage public participation in the stock market.

*Margin Call:* When a stock or commodity declines to the point where it is about to fall below the required margin, it "touches off" a call by the margin clerk, meaning that the broker demands additional collateral from the investor, failing which his stock or commodity position is sold in the market.

*Mark to Market:* To value a stock or bond at its current market price, as distinct from its cost or face value.

*Market Analysis:* Great tides flow in the market, and an unemotional investor can improve his odds by taking them into account. In the euphoric times when almost every new issue goes to a premium, when the cats and dogs are twenty times earnings, when everybody you meet is bullish, the veteran sells out and goes to Europe. In the midst of gloom, when sound values are being jettisoned because they are "going lower," when many companies sell in the market for less than their cash in the bank, and when the subscription services are bearish, then he reappears with his bushel basket and sweeps in the bargains.

Of course, euphoria can progress to a manic condition and gloom degenerate into despair. Nevertheless, it is helpful to know what the patient's current status is, as measured by odd-lot short sales, mutual fund cash, brokers' credit balances, net advances, and the like. They can be studied in figures or shown in graphic form. Such graphs are like the graphs produced by a lie detector (heartbeat, breathing, sweating, and so forth). They have nothing to do with the astrology of "double tops," "penants," and "rounding bottoms" that the so-called chartists play with.

*Market Order:* An order to buy or sell without limitation as to price.

*May Day:* May 1, 1975, when by S.E.C. order the New York Stock Exchange abandoned the old fixed commission schedule.

*Modern Portfolio Theory (or M.P.T.):* An obsolete approach to managing large institutional portfolios, based on deciding which way the market should go, what degree of volatility and other characteristics are acceptable, and then, using computers, choosing stocks with those characteristics.

*Money Manager: See* Portfolio Manager.

*Multiple:* Short for price-earnings multiple.

*Mutual Fund: See* Investment Company.

*Naked Option:* Usually, a call that is sold when one does not own the underlying stock.

*N.A.S.D.:* National Association of Securities Dealers. (*See* Over the Counter.)

*Nifty Fifty: See* Favorite Fifty.

*No-Load:* A fund sold without a commission.

*Noah's Ark Fallacy:* Short for Noah's Ark Shipbuilding and Dry Dock Company. The hack analyst claims that the N.A.S.&D.D. has to be a bargain at three times antediluvian year's earnings, even though the good days were intrinsically a one-time situation. I devised this expression in exasperation at the uranium analysts of the 1950s. The U.S. Government had ordered uranium from Canada to accumulate its nuclear stockpile. Once the A.E.C. had its supply it had it, however, and there was no other important buyer in sight for decades. Nevertheless, some analysts insisted on analyzing the Canadian uranium mines (e.g., using Hoskold's Formula) as though they were copper properties, which would go on producing year after year indefinitely. Folly! It seems to me that the high multiples of some beer-brewing stocks are a manifestation of the Noah's Ark fallacy. Their sales growth has often been based on absorbing smaller breweries, a one-time situation.

*Odd Lot:* A transaction of less than a hundred shares (except for a very few high-priced stocks, for which the number is lower). A trade of less than a round lot pay a higher commission.

*Offshore Trust:* A personal trust may be either domestic or foreign (offshore). If foreign, its situs would normally be in a country that does not have significant taxes on such trusts.

*Oligopoly:* A monopoly exists if there is only one supplier for a given commodity or service. In an oligopoly, there are only a very few suppliers.

*Open End: See* Investment Company.

*Opening:* The price at which a stock first trades on a given day (also called the opening price).

*Option:* The right to buy or sell a stock or commodity at a specific price for a specific period of time, for which one pays a premium.

*Out of the Money:* Used when an option on a stock or commodity has not become profitable.

*Over the Counter:* A market of stocks in smaller companies that are traded electronically between members of the National Association of Securities Dealers.

*Par:* Of a bond, the face value, typically expressed as a percent, e.g., 98 or 102. Of a stock, 100 (rare).

*P/Es: See* Price-Earnings Multiple.

*Ponzi Scheme:* A fraud in which a fantastic return on investment is promised, and for a while delivered by using later subscribers' investments to pay the promised returns to the earlier investors. The original Mr. Ponzi said he had discovered a wrinkle in the use of international postal reply coupons that enabled him to deliver a very high return on funds confided to him. At the height of the excitement he had bags and bags full of money piled up on the floors of his collecting offices. In due course, of course, it all collapsed.

Pyramid clubs are Ponzi Schemes: At some point they have to fall apart. So is the "Dare to Be Great" type of franchise business in which subscribers pay substantial sums for the right to enlist many more subscribers. King Resources promised investors in its drilling syndicates a much higher return than the industry had historically been able to deliver, because the drilling investor could exchange his stock for that of King Resources itself, which was supposed to stay up because it was selling so many drilling participations—and so on. Eventually something happens to break the flow and the whole monstrous structure crashes to earth; like Humpty Dumpty, it is unable to get going again.

The market itself during the blowoff phase of a bull market becomes a bigger fool or Ponzi Scheme. People forget that all those jigs and dies and milling machines and brick buildings cannot be revalued by 30 percent a year forever.

*Pool:* A group of investors, who, particularly before the existence of the Securities and Exchange Commission, banded together to buy a stock (or sell it short) to attract public interest, and then sell out to (or buy back from) the public during that interest.

*Portfolio:* The generic term used of securities, like a *library* of books.

*Portfolio Manager:* The individual in an investment advisory institution who supervises an investor's portfolio, as distinct from a broker, who sells specific securities.

*Preferred Stock:* A class of stock with priority rights, both as to dividends and in liquidation, over the common stock of the same company. To avoid double taxation, corporations pay a much lower tax on dividends from their investments in other corporations (where it has already been taxed) than on business earnings. Preferred stock is usually priced at the level that makes it attractive to a corporation, taking account of this tax exemption. As a result, preferred stock is rarely a tax-efficient holding for taxpaying individuals.

*Premium:* The payment for an option.

*Price-Earnings Multiple (also P/E):* The number of times its own earnings that a stock is selling for in the market; e.g., if a company earns $3 a share and the stock sells for 30, the multiple is 10.

*Prime:* The prime means the prime rate: the interest charged by banks to top-rated credits. (Some customers get an even more favorable rate, however.) Prime commercial paper is issued by this class of borrower.

*Put:* An option to sell a stock at a given price for a specified time, for which one pays a premium; the opposite of a call.

*Rate of Return:* The internal or discount rate of return of an investment is that interest rate which applied to future earnings reduces them to the present market price.

*Registered Representative: See* Broker.

*Resistance Area:* There may be something to this idea. If the chart shows that over a period of time a great many shares of a stock changed hands in a particular price range, and if the stock is now selling for much less, then it may be hard for the stock to repenetrate that range. You quite often hear people say, "I bought Profits Galore, Inc., at 30 two years ago, and here it is at 10. I'm going to hold on until it gets back to 30, and then I'll drop it like a shot." I suspect that the fellow wants to punish the stock for its temerity after first getting it to confess, like an inquisitor or the judge in a communist show trial.

 Anyway, it seems plausible that vast numbers of disgusted stockholders waiting to sell might constitute an impediment to a stock's advance. (If so, this is an exception to my suspicion of technical analysis of stocks.) When a stock is approaching a resistance area, some people therefore wait until it gets through before buying.

*Retail Broker:* A broker who deals with the public.

*Reverse Split: See* Split.

*Round Lot:* Generally one hundred shares. *See* Odd Lot.

*S.E.C.:* The Securities and Exchange Commission, which regulates all transactions in securities.

*Secondary (Issue):* A major stock or bond offering by an existing owner, rather than by the original issuer.

*Secondary Reaction:* A movement against the main trend of the market.

*Short Interest:* The total of all open short sales, which is tabulated and published for each stock. A very high short interest constitutes support for a stock, since eventually all the shorts will have to be bought back: "covered."

*Short Sale:* If one does not own a stock but sells it anyway, expecting to buy it back for less, one is said to sell short.

*Short Squeeze:* If the short interest is so high that the amount of trading in a stock does not permit the shorts to cover their positions, then their own buying will force the price up, making it harder than ever for them to cover. The short sellers are then said to be squeezed.

*Short Term:* For tax purposes, less than one year. Otherwise, up to a few months.

*Sideways:* A stock is said to be moving sideways if its price changes little from day to day. The Wall Street community does not find this expression peculiar.

*Specialist:* A floor broker who in return for the right to keep the "book" on a company's stock undertakes to maintain an or-

derly market at all times by buying or selling if no other investor is willing to do so.

*Speculator:* One who buys an asset because he expects it to rise,
rather than because he finds that the foreseeable stream of
earnings, dividends, or interest is attractively priced.

*Split:* When a stock reaches a high price, often the management of
the company will split it two for one, three for two, or whatever, to create a smaller price per share and make a larger
number of shares available for trading. Sometimes the dividend is raised at the same time.

   A split is considered to be good news, but in fact has no
effect on the intrinsic value of the stock.

   In a "reverse split," a low-priced stock is consolidated to
increase the price per share. On the Canadian exchanges such
stocks are thereafter called "Consolidated" Gold Bug (or whatever).

*Split Funds:* Invented in England, and then imported here, these
are mutual funds that have two classes of stock, income shares
and capital shares. All the income of both classes is assigned to
the income shares, and all the capital gains (if any) are assigned
to the capital shares. If split funds can be created without
limitation, the capital shares must necessarily go to a discount
from net asset value, since new funds can be formed until the
supply exceeds the demand.

   At breakup, the income shareholders get their original
cost back, and what is left over goes to the capital shares. Unfortunately, the net asset value per share may decline over 50
percent, and the capital shares can thus be wiped out, as has in
fact happened. Split-fund capital shares are ultimately a
gussied-up margin account, and the income shares amount to
loan secured by a stock.

*Spread: See* Asking Price.

*Squeeze: See* Short Squeeze.

*Stock:* A share in the ownership of a company.

*Stop-Loss Order:* An order left with the specialist to sell a holding
when it falls to a specific price.

*Straddle:* An option to buy and a separate one to sell a certain
number of shares of a stock at a specified price.

*Striking Price: See* Exercising Price.

*Strong Hands:* Substantial buyers, who one presumes will hold for a
considerable period. The opposite of weak hands.

*Tape:* At one time stock transactions were recorded on ticker-tape
machines. Today, the quotations are usually transmitted on an

electronic display board, but the old term persists. The "broad tape" is the news ticker.

*Tax Sale:* A sale, usually near year-end, to realize a gain or loss for tax purposes.

*Technical Analysis of Stocks:* The technical analyst tries to predict stock movement through the shapes on a stock's chart, without reference to value.

*Technician:* Practitioner of technical analysis.

*Ticker: See* Tape.

*Total Return: See* Rate of Return. Another version of this expression heard in Wall Street is unsound, namely, the dividend yield from a stock plus the rate at which that yield is growing. For instance, if a stock yields 5 percent, which yield is growing at 15 percent, then the "total return," according to this usage, would be 20 percent. On the other hand, so would a 0.1 percent yield growing at 19.9 percent, which, however, is a much less attractive situation.

*Transfer Agent:* The bank that handles the paperwork involved in buying and selling the common stock of a company.

*Turnaround:* In Wall Street parlance, a turnaround occurs when an investment banking firm or a new management group takes control of a troubled company, improves operations, and gets it back on a profitable basis. Very few investment banking firms are prepared to take on this job, one of the most constructive, but difficult, in the business.

*Two-Dollar Broker: See* Broker.

*Vestal Virgins:* An expression used in the go-go days of the 1960s, referring to the Favorite Fifty variety of institutional darling.

*Volatility:* The degree to which a stock is moved up and down by buying or selling interest.

*Warrant:* Option to buy a stock issued by the underlying company, and often given as a "kicker" when a bond is marketed.

*Weak Hands:* Speculative retail buyers of stock. *See* Strong Hands.

*Window Dressing:* Toward the end of a reporting period, mutual funds and banks will sometimes round their holdings to even thousands, or sell positions that have gone down and thus constitute an eyesore.

*Wire House:* A stock exchange firm specializing in retail brokerage.

# Index

267